Abolition Time

Abolition Time

Grammars of Law, Poetics of Justice

JESS A. GOLDBERG

UNIVERSITY OF MINNESOTA PRESS
MINNEAPOLIS
LONDON

Published by the University of Minnesota Press
111 Third Avenue South, Suite 290
Minneapolis, MN 55401-2520
http://www.upress.umn.edu

ISBN 978-1-5179-1788-3 (hc)
ISBN 978-1-5179-1789-0 (pb)

A Cataloging-in-Publication record for this book is available from the Library of Congress.

Printed in the United States of America on acid-free paper

The University of Minnesota is an equal-opportunity educator and employer.

UMP BmB 2024

Contents

Preface   vii

Introduction: Justice Is Not an Event   1

ONE Accumulation: The Excessive Present,
     the Middle Passage, and the Juridical Event   39

TWO Perforation: Inhabitation and the
     Vulnerability of the Law   81

     An Interlude on Method, or Abolition Is
     Not a Metaphor   125

THREE Witnessing: Impossible Recovery, Failed
       Recognition, and the Obligation of Risk   137

FOUR Breath: Aspiration, Ungendered Mothering,
      and Im/Possible Futures   173

      Coda: On Thinking the Impossible   207

      Acknowledgments   215
      Notes   223
      Index   257

Preface

My friend scholar and activist Erica Meiners says that liberation under oppression is unthinkable by design. So an abolition politic insists that we imagine and organize beyond the constraints of the normal. . . . Our charge is to make imagining liberation under oppression completely thinkable, to really push ourselves to think beyond the normal in order for us to be able to address the root causes of people's suffering.

—Mariame Kaba, *We Do This 'til We Free Us*

How do we who are doing work in black studies tend to, care for, comfort, and defend the dead, the dying, and those living consigned, in aftermath of legal chattel slavery, to death that is always-imminent and immanent? How might theorizing black studies in the wake—and black being in the wake—a conscious mode of inhabitation of that imminence and immanence (revealed every day in multiple quotidian ways) ground our work as we map relations between the past and present, map the ways that the past haunts the present? The existence of black studies as an object of study does not ameliorate the quotidian experiences of terror in black lives lived in an anti-black world. To do that, I argue that we must be about the work of what I am calling "wake work."

—Christina Sharpe, "Black Studies: In the Wake"

This book is an attempt at practicing abolitionist literary studies. It is an attempt to think about the study of literature, language, and textuality as a site for making liberation thinkable in the anti-Black world of the afterlife of slavery. Literary studies is, of course, not reducible only to close reading, but it is close reading that I spend the most time doing in this book. I want to ask, What would it mean to practice that highly disciplined methodology of close reading toward abolitionist goals, or as abolitionist ethics, or with abolitionist politics?

I should be clear that when I use the term *abolition*, I mean, first of all and with all seriousness, the political project of ending the prison–industrial complex and all of the interlocking (though nonsynonymous) hierarchical systems of power—racial capitalism, white supremacy, (settler) colonialism, cisheteropatriarchy, ableism—that cohere to hold together the modern World.

I also use the term *abolition* as a self-consciously transtemporal marker. That is, while I am committed to doing the historically specific work of contributing to the contemporary prison and police abolition movement as one might know it through the work of organizations like Critical Resistance or Survived and Punished or of individuals like Angela Davis or Ruth Wilson Gilmore, I am also always thinking of Joy James's clarity in stating that "prison is the modern day manifestation of the plantation."[1] As a historical project, abolition exceeds any single epoch or moment. That is why, for me, above all, it is an ethics and a politics that can be applied within specific contexts. In *Abolition Time*, I narrow that context to literary studies.

At its heart, that means that this is a book about method. It is not, however, a book about "method wars." Rather, *Abolition Time* offers an argument about a set of Black Atlantic literary texts that I see as articulating ways of understanding the world that explicitly diverge from juridical narratives of progress and precedent. These texts, I show, develop an understanding of time itself as an ethical problem that the law and its physical manifestations—prisons and police—cannot solve. This argument against the disciplining impulse of the law unfolds through the highly disciplined practice of close reading. I invite the reader to move with me through readings of a number of texts across differences in genre, geography, and historical period, not to argue that the texts themselves must necessarily be interpreted in a certain way, but to see what happens when we read for poetics of justice that exceed the juridical. How can that old reading method be invigorated in our moment of compounding crises that themselves trace to crises ongoing since at least 1492? The argument happens in the reading itself.

Because I am narrowing the context of abolitionism to the realm of literary studies in this book, readers will not find an extended, detailed defense of or argument for abolition itself. If the reader is looking for historical or social scientific analyses of prisons and police that lay out the reasons they should be abolished, I point them to *Abolition Time*'s notes, particularly, at the least, to the work of Davis, Gilmore, James, Kaba, Eric A. Stanley, Beth Richie, Dennis Childs, and Sarah Haley. Even more so, I point the reader to abolitionist organizations already doing work in their communities. So instead, as someone committed to abolitionism beyond my employment as an academic writing a book for a university press, I will proceed with the assumption that abolitionist thought is at the very least a valuable framework for interpretive analysis. As such, this book is not for the reader who is not ready to indulge that assumption. However, I welcome discussions of abolition's practical work in the contemporary world, in life as it is lived beyond the covers of this narrow book. I hope that what I offer in the Introduction and following chapters as a model of abolitionist close reading is useful even for those readers who do not themselves wear the "abolitionist" tag. Fundamentally, I argue, abolitionist thought's primary pedagogical function, which is transferable across particular iterations of the literary studies classroom, is to teach us how to think against received principles that, through disciplining thought itself, secure and reproduce the World as it is, even if in the aesthetics of new forms. Abolitionist thought teaches us ways of thinking toward other ways of knowing and ways of knowing otherwise. In Kaba's terms, abolitionist literary studies may help us "jailbreak our imaginations."

The injunctions by Kaba and Sharpe in the epigraphs to this preface—for Kaba, to "make imagining liberation under oppression completely thinkable," for Sharpe, to "tend to, care for, comfort, and defend the dead, the dying, and those living consigned, in aftermath of legal chattel slavery, to death that is always-imminent and immanent"—guide the ethics of my reading practices and humble my aspirations for my arguments in this book.[2]

Thinking in the overlap of abolitionist thought and the intellectual tradition of Black studies means thinking in the aftermath of and toward the end of the World. When I capitalize *World* in this book, I am talking about the systemic hierarchy of white supremacist colonial gendered capitalism that governs the political structure of the globe and was inaugurated as a product of Western modernity as it was produced through conquest, most especially in the aftermath of the founding of a "new world" in 1492, to draw heavily on Sylvia Wynter's framing.[3] My capitalization indexes that the World is a construct; it is contingent, and therefore, though hegemonic, it is not omnipotent. As I often repeat in teaching and writing, *there are worlds within the World.* But as Toni Morrison has told us, "slavery broke the world in half."[4] The violences of Atlantic chattel slavery and Indigenous genocide that were the conditions of possibility for Western modernity constitute an apocalypse, an ending of many worlds (small *w*) in service of creating the World (capitalized). Both abolitionism and Black studies—which are not synonymous, even as they share the characteristic of being defined not by their objects of study but by the liberatory aspirations of their analyses—aim at bringing about another apocalypse of the World itself in service of creating new worlds not bound by violent hegemonies. In my interpretive synthesis of Kaba's and Sharpe's words, the objective is to end the capital-W World such that a new one—a world in which, in the words of Gilmore's often-repeated mantra, "life is precious"—may emerge from the ashes of hegemony.

To bring about the end of the World is a tall task, to say the least. And it is a task that no individual project alone can accomplish. This is part of the reason for the narrow focus and humble ambition of *Abolition Time.* A book written by an academic published by a university press is not going to abolish anything, and so I set my sights on the smaller desire to *offer*. In this book, I want to offer something useful. That is all. I am not seeking to overturn decades of precedent in literary studies or to make a decisive intervention into debates of method or to theorize a brand-new understanding of temporality or to offer a new road map for accomplishing the total abolition of (a world that could even have) prisons. I am offering a way of reading that I hope will be useful for some people wondering how reading texts can *matter* in a world that so desperately demands change on an apocalyptic scale. I will not argue that my way of reading is the only or the best way to read; instead, I will offer that I do think it is useful, and I do think it can help us do exciting work in our literary studies classrooms to build imaginative and intellectual skills that exceed those rooms (wherever they may be situated, in or outside of institutional spaces).

And I believe that this is a task that reveals the inseparability of methods from ethics. Because as I offer this reading method, I do so in recognition of the abolitionist call to imagine liberation and the Black studies imperative to "ameliorate the quotidian experiences of terror in black lives lived in an anti-black world" that requires that we do work other than that which is recognized and sanctioned by any academic institutions of employment. Another clarification to forefront here is what I mean by *ethics*, of course. Against a common-usage understanding of ethics as a set of guidelines or rules—an understanding that cannot escape the juridical logic of law-as-rules but instead houses rules in something other than political power—I understand ethics as the messy, uncertain terrain in which we formulate questions about how to live together in ways that facilitate flourishing. Ethics, for me, pursues justice not as retribution for wrongs but as right relation—among both human and nonhuman persons, among both living creatures and living and nonliving environments, and across stretches of time and geography.

To be clear, abolition is a political project, which is to say that it has concrete systemic goals to eliminate governing structures of sociality to build new ones. Abolition is not reducible to thinly conceptualized ethics *as* rules or guidelines for interpersonal relation. Changing how we treat each other in interpersonal relationships is part of abolition, but it is insufficient. I do not want to be misunderstood as evacuating abolition of its political commitments by turning to ethics as a "safer" or less material realm of analysis. Instead, ethics in my thinking is a terrain of tremendous risk and a field of open questions that help us train our collectively produced and forever-revisable epistemologies away from the World, which is held in place by what the law tells us is possible. Rather than comprising a list of rules to follow, ethics is the making possible of asking questions that gesture toward exactly that which the existing World would tell us is impossible: living together without the threat of violence/enforcement as that which secures (an illusion of) safety.

As I invoke ethics, I should mark in this preface that I do this work as a white person fully committed to the work of Black studies. I have grown increasingly impatient over the years with the propensity of well-meaning white folks to announce their own whiteness and "acknowledge their privilege," both in academic and in organizing spaces. Such moves often wind up recentering whiteness, reifying individuation, and framing analyses along the axis of identity instead of power. On the other hand, it remains a reality that white academics continue to accrue material benefits for doing work in fields organized by epistemologies developed through intellectual traditions in which we are guests or invaders, without identifying ourselves as such. In the most extreme examples, this looks like white scholars pretending to be Black, Indigenous, Latinx, or otherwise people of color or simply never naming their own whiteness and allowing others to make assumptions.

I never write outside of my subject position and all of the ways in which it is marked as white, as Jewish, as queer, as settler, or as otherwise. I always write as an attempt at coalitional work, as an attempt to undo the forces that overdetermine my subject position. I write with the lesson I learned through my experience in antiprison activism, where fellow organizers admonished white ostensible comrades for being silent in the face of pro-prison construction arguments when uttered by Black lawmakers: the lesson that what philosopher Olúfẹ́mi O. Táíwò calls "deference politics" is not only ineffective but an abdication of the responsibility to do the work of analysis and take the risks of uncertain action.[5] I write to abolish whiteness even as I cannot simply declare away being white. As abolitionists, we must do the work of displacing whiteness toward its necessary abolition; that is, I recognize that the work is not simply in being a good white ally or even a white comrade but in relentlessly fighting against white supremacy such that in the future brought into being by abolition, whiteness as concept and positionality cannot even cohere into existence. I hope that my writing throughout the book will show by example how I do this, and I know that there will be places where I will fail to do so ethically, because ethics is always a practice of risking doing harm. I write within a structure of accountability and welcome the ongoing work required of obliterating a fundamental constituting force of my own current positionality. At the risk that I may have already too strongly recentered whiteness and recentered myself, I end this prefatory statement of my own whiteness here.

Abolition is a horizon that will not manifest because of an academic monograph. Abolition will not come primarily through the colonial institution of the Western academy, though I believe we can do some abolitionist work while using some of its resources. Abolition will not be made material by reading texts, alone. And so *Abolition Time* will not, and never claims to, bring about abolition. In fact, no one tool, and no one person, can do that. I have heard the figure of the chorus or the choir invoked numerous times by organizers discussing the importance of working together in numbers rather than in individual silos. The idea is that when singing in a group, not all the voices are singing the same exact notes—a bass and a soprano, for example, in fact cannot do so—and when someone needs to stop to take a breath, the song continues because other singers can keep going until it is their turn to breathe. I offer here, then, just one voice, a voice we might humbly rather than ambitiously call abolitionist literary studies, to sustain the song and, at its best, invite a few more singers.

Introduction

Lacking the certitude of a definitive partition between slavery and freedom, and in the absence of a
consummate breach through which freedom might
unambivalently announce itself, there is at best a tran-
sient and fleeting expression of possibility that cannot
ensconce itself as a durable temporal marker. If periodization is a barrier imposed from above that obscures
the involuntary servitude and legal subjection that
followed in the wake of slavery, then attempts to assert
absolutist distinctions between slavery and freedom
are untenable.

—Saidiya V. Hartman, *Scenes of Subjection: Terror,*
Slavery, and Self-Making in Nineteenth-Century America

All of it is now it is always now

—Toni Morrison, *Beloved*

The ghost or the zombie or the reincarnation or the specter or
the avatar of the single dead child who crawls up out of the water
and walks to 124 Bluestone Road is neither singular subject nor
composite figure, neither revived flesh nor dead corpse, neither
recoverable nor dismissible, but in her series of ontological nega-
tions she enacts an ethical force that precedes the social contract
and ruptures the grammar of the law with a clear and distinct call
for justice: it is abolition time.

Beloved the character, like *Beloved* the novel, always indexes more than a singular temporality. Not merely an intrusion of the past within the present, *Beloved's* refusal of the divide between the living and the dead is a refusal of what Saidiya Hartman identifies as "periodization [as] a barrier imposed from above" manifest as a "black feminist futurity" that Tina Campt argues is brought about as the "power to imagine beyond current fact and to envision that which is not, but must be."[1] Simultaneously past, present, and future, Beloved demands abolition after the "non-event of emancipation."[2] This demand, hauntologically conjured by a living-dead figure appearing in a novel of speculative historical fiction, in its suturing of past and present and future together through a refusal of normative grammar—"all of it is now it is always now"—coheres the strands of thought that I weave here in *Abolition Time: Grammars of Law, Poetics of Justice.*[3]

Abolition Time argues that, perhaps counterintuitively, the disciplinary method of close reading as inflected by legal humanities interdisciplinarity can be deployed as a tool of abolitionist world-building, particularly through attention to alternative understandings of time. I cite Toni Morrison's often-analyzed novel, and the ghostly figure moving through it, as my starting point because it brings to light how the axes of time, law, language, and ethics come together as the nexus driving my project here. As I explain in this Introduction, a primary force "from above" that imposes periodization, in Hartman's formulation, is the law, and, leaning into a double meaning of the word *period*, I figure that imposition of period-ization from above as a grammar of law. In this sense, the grammar of law is an ordering of time.

Extending Hartman's insight in *Scenes of Subjection*, Rinaldo Walcott offers the "long emancipation" as one name to describe this ordering of time as the "continuation of the juridical and legislative status of Black nonbeing" without "simply suggest[ing] that Black people are still enslaved."[4] Beloved, both the character and the novel, ruptures the juridical grammar of emancipation with what I identify throughout this book as poetics of justice. Where *grammars of law* refers to the ordering impulse of the law's figuration of linear periodized temporality, *poetics of justice* refers to practices of language, writing, and reading that disrupt, refuse, eschew, or deconstruct the order imposed by law's grammar. Not a simple binary, poetics of justice often mobilize or inhabit grammars of law, either intentionally or unconsciously, precisely because of language's capacity to exceed the intentions of speakers or writers.

In this complex interplay between law and justice—two terms that *are*, in my thinking, distinct, in that justice is something very much beyond the reach of law and all of its violence—we see a conflict over worlding. Grammars of law seek to set everything and everyone in the world in place to maintain an overarching structure: the capital-W World. The World is a construct brought into being by the historical, ongoing processes of slavery, colonization, and imperial expansion and held together by white supremacist racial capitalism and its attendant structures of cisheteropatriarchy, ableism, and (settler) colonialism. The "holding together" of this World characterized by hierarchical domination is epistemologically accomplished by the entrenchment of grammars of law that—and this is the crucial point—demarcate possibility itself within the World. That is, the ability to imagine how to organize society is delimited so all that is possible when we think within law's grammar is the continuation, even and especially through reform, of the existing hierarchical structure of the World. Grammars of law lock the World in place by demarcating the limits of the possible. In contrast, poetics of justice move in excess of law's grammars, even as they cannot escape the law's reach altogether, not to triumphantly defeat law itself but to make possible thinking and imagining beyond the borders of possibility demarcated by grammars of law. Poetics of justice are acts of language and aesthetic form that make possible thinking that the law would seek to render impossible. The tension between grammars of law and poetics of justice is the epistemic conflict over worlding.

To attend to poetics of justice is to follow Morrison's guidance in her essay "Unspeakable Things Unspoken: The Afro-American Presence in American Literature," that the study of literature written by authors who have been excluded from canonicity must be a rigorous study of form and technique and not mere sociology. Near the end of her foundational essay, Morrison writes:

To those who talk about how as well as what; who identify the work-
ings as well as the work; for whom the study of Afro-American
literature is neither a crash course in neighborliness and tolerance,
nor an infant to be carried, instructed, or chastised or even whipped
like a child, but the serious study of art forms that have much work
to do, and which are already legitimized by their own cultural
sources and predecessors—in or out of the canon—I owe much.[5]

I have taught "Unspeakable Things Unspoken" for years, and
this passage is consistently one of the most important to our
class discussions. At every level, from introductory general education English courses to a graduate course in theory, students
come to my classes with an already-formed but vague sense that
it is important to read works by historically marginalized authors because, somehow, doing so will teach us something about
"diversity" or injustice. What Morrison's essay does in this moment is put pressure on that *somehow*. It combats a preexisting
and often unconscious rather than maliciously intentional impulse that Christina Sharpe identifies in *Ordinary Notes*: "There
is a certain mode of reading connected to a tradition of colonial
practices in which every book by any Black writer appears as sociology. Then all of that book's explorations, its meanings, and its
ambitions lodge in a place called identity."[6] In other words, literary texts by Black authors in particular—but also, I think I can
add, at least in my teaching experience, texts by non-Black authors
of color, queer authors, and disabled authors—are often read as
gateways into "cultural competence," as reservoirs of social data
about a group of people. Moving past this thin diversity-centered
approach to expanding the canon as "a crash course in neighborliness and tolerance," Morrison's essay demands harder, more
rigorous work than mere recognition of representational diversity. She demands that we engage the work of language.

So when teaching *Beloved*—again, at any level, from the general
education classroom to the graduate seminar—it is important to
step past a common initial impulse to see the novel as worth reading primarily because it fills in some kind of representational gap,
like adding a data point to a checklist. (*Aha, now we know about*

slavery and African American history when we didn't know enough before. Now we understand something about the "Black experience," so might say non-Black readers, or *Now we understand something about the enslaved ancestors,* so might say Black readers.) Alternatively, a reading and discussion of *Beloved* explicitly focused on ethics or questions of justice might move along threads of empathy with or "relating" to the characters. For example, the very first time I taught the novel in an undergraduate general education course on neo-slave narratives, a handful of white women in the class began discussing whether they would have killed their child rather than see the child enslaved if they were in Sethe's position.

This is a common approach to reading literature that presents difficult ethical situations: imagine yourself in the world represented by the story and ask how you would act. Such an approach, however, deals exclusively with the narrative "content" of the text without explicitly attending to form or literary technique. So in that class session I waited and listened to the student discussion for a few minutes before intervening, not simply to correct the students, but to ask a question: *Does anyone in the room know what it is like to be enslaved?* (I asked this because one student asserted her authority on interpreting the novel stemmed from her knowing what it is like to be a mother.)[7] In the silence that followed, I asked a follow-up—*Since the axis of "experience" isn't helpful here, how does Sethe herself explain her decision? Before you answer, notice I didn't ask what she says to explain her actions; I asked how she explains it. How does her thinking appear and move in the text?* We then spent the last twenty minutes of class close-reading the final passage of part II of the novel, when Sethe explains herself by refusing to explain herself to Paul D, making particular note of the novel's narrative point of view as a mechanism for representing Sethe's interiority while preserving her opacity.

I return to a reading of the novel in a later section, but the point here at the start is that *Beloved*'s call for justice emerges as much from the form as from the content of its language. That is, it is *just as if not more important* that the ghost's words appear on the page with irregular spacing and without standard punctuation in the phrase with which I opened this Introduction as it is that the words' denotatively mean that everything (*all of it*) is literally (*is*) immediately present (here)/present (*now*), not only now but also now and now and now and at any iteration of now that will ever be (*always*). This irregular spacing and punctuation rupture the grammar of the law, which is a grammar of ordered, linear temporality that would render a demand to abolish slavery nonsensical in *Beloved*'s present. This manipulation of spacing and punctuation is an example of what I call throughout this book *poetics of justice*. And we can understand *justice* as much through transtemporal abolitionist thought as through deconstruction as through the Black radical tradition and a number of other intellectual histories as beyond or outside or prior to the law.[8]

In this book, I think of this realm distinct from the law in which justice might emerge as a realm of ethics. And just like how *Beloved* demands that we ask better questions than the reductive binary *Was Sethe right to kill her child?* the realm of ethics that I traverse in *Abolition Time* demands that we ask better questions that do more than simply seek new rules, as if abolition were just replacing the-law-as-bad-rule-making with ethics-as-good-rule-making. In the passage I've quoted as an epigraph, the novel punctures law's grammar with a poetics of justice that explodes periodization into a *now* that is excessively filled with every moment that has ever been and will ever be an iteration of its own *now*. There are no borders (periods are borders), temporal or spatial, in the chapter of *Beloved* narrated by Beloved the character. If, as Jacques Derrida argues, the ghost always appears to make a demand, Beloved-as-specter makes her demand in language not captured by the law, not ordered by dominant grammar.[9]

In addition to time, the narrating voice of Beloved explodes the *geographic* borders of *Beloved* in its allusion to the no-place of darkness in the hold of the slave ship. Beloved's memory of the hold emphasizes that the history recalled but never actually recovered by Morrison's novel is not merely *American* history but a history of the Black Atlantic. This shows how the geography of justice in the afterlife of slavery exceeds the juridically drawn and militarily enforced borders of the nation-state. In *Beloved*, then, language becomes a means by which the geographical and temporal ordering logics of the law's grammar are ruptured by a poetics of justice that makes clear that abolition, as distinct from the juridical logic of emancipation, is a logic of ethics.

Extrapolating from *Beloved*'s demand for a justice that law can never deliver, whenever I discuss *justice* in this book, I am referring to something not grounded in law. That is, my baseline assumption is that justice is not a legal concept but an ethical one. My engagement with the law and positioning within legal humanities is an attempt not at refiguring or reforming the law so as to have it achieve a truer justice within its terms but to read literary texts for ways of directing us away from law as an arbiter of justice.

It is on the axis of *time* that I believe such redirection most sharply pivots. Within the grammar of the law, justice is an event and a response. That is, it is something to be *done* in the aftermath of harm: someone steals my property, so they have to pay me back or serve a prison sentence after it is proven that they did the thing (theft) that caused harm. In the ordering grammar of the law, justice is sequential, and once it is served, it is over. But for abolitionists, responding in the aftermath of harm, alone, cannot approximate justice. For the abolitionist, *justice is not an event*. This is the pivot from law's time, ordered as it is by grammars of law, to abolition time—a temporality that Beloved utters as *always now*.

The highly circulated 2001 "Statement on Gender Violence and the Prison Industrial Complex" codrafted by the organizations INCITE! and Critical Resistance synthesizes twenty-one analytical and political imperatives that, when read together, argue that conceptions of justice that respond only to harm—whether from a juridical or community-based perspective—without accounting for the necessity of ongoing, everyday collective work fall short of their promise.[10] Instead, justice requires continuous self-reflexive community work to build a world in which the conditions of impetus for harm are drastically reduced. Mariame Kaba, Angela Davis, Dean Spade, Ruth Wilson Gilmore, Liat Ben-Moshe, and Eric A. Stanley, among others, articulate, with different inflection, justice as the ongoing work of making the world anew. Likewise, on-the-ground activists and organizers often incorporate tenets of socialist, anarchist, communist, feminist, antiracist, crip, and/or decolonial critique (in varieties of configurations and with varieties of emphases) into their analyses and messaging to urge members of our communities to change our thinking about justice from something that happens after a single event of harm occurs to justice as the *presence* of those conditions that sustain life. Instead of the threat of violence (incarceration, the death penalty, poverty imposed by economic extraction) being that which figures justice through punishment, abolitionists posit the presence of life sustenance (access to food, health care, and livable housing; stable climates and clean environments; racial, sexual, and gender liberation) as that which figures justice through transformative accountability and mutual aid. Altogether, an abolitionist sense of justice departs from a juridical sense of justice precisely as a refiguring of temporality from an event-bound account in the law to an opened account of the unbounded and ongoing project of ethics that cannot be reduced to law. Grammars of law keep time in order. Poetics of justice refuse order to open up abolition time.

Abolition Time, at its core, is an investigation of literary texts that temporally refigure justice from legal event to ongoing question—from the period at the end of a sentence (the jail imposes a sentence as a period) to the open uncertainty of abolition's ellipses.

ABOLITIONIST LITERARY STUDIES: IN CHORUS

Whether inside or outside the academy, abolition work is choral work. This section of the Introduction therefore outlines some clusters of scholarship that make my work possible as I outline the fields in which I position my discretely literary project. But before accounting for that section of the chorus we might recognize as the "literature review" at the beginning of an academic monograph, I should account for another important academic sphere of influence on my thinking: teaching.

Just as I opened the Introduction with accounts of how, in past courses, students and I have discussed Morrison's novel *Beloved* and essay "Unspeakable Things Unspoken," throughout *Abolition Time*, I return again and again to reflections on how texts have lived in my classrooms. I do this for multiple reasons. First, it allows me to reflect on reading trends that I notice among my students rather than invoking an abstract, generalized figure of a reader or attempting to make sweeping claims about how a text is "often" read. One of my teaching practices is to make notes of things that are said in conversations, including sometimes writing down what students say as conversation unfolds in the classroom and other times writing reflective notes at the end of a day or a week; in writing *Abolition Time*, these notes have been as invaluable to me as any of the annotated books and PDFs in my library.

I make that clear not only to put my gratitude for my students on the page but to make the point that in teaching and other forms of collective reading is where my thinking has been most strongly polished. Thus one of the underlying ambitions of *Abolition Time* is to prompt readers to think about how we talk about literary texts in classrooms and how our pedagogies can facilitate the kinds of thinking in the discomfort of uncertainty or modes of questioning that may move against rubrics of content mastery demanded by educational institutions. This is not the main focus of the book, but as a reader, thinker, and writer, my teaching is foundational to all of the analysis in these pages. Although readers will not find lesson plans or course designs here, I encourage readers of *Abolition Time* to take its modeling of close reading into collective reading spaces like classrooms or reading groups. I hope that this book can help readers bring tools to their own chorus.

While this book has been made possible by the experience of testing readings and asking questions together with students in classrooms and comrades in reading groups, I am of course also building on scholarly work in multiple fields that lay the foundation for *Abolition Time*'s core arguments. My focus on time as a framework for thinking about justice in excess of law has meant that Saidiya Hartman and Christina Sharpe have been the thinkers most influential on my work. Hartman's "afterlife of slavery" and Sharpe's "wake" have given me language with which to think toward my own theorizations of temporality.

Especially in *Scenes of Subjection: Terror, Slavery, and Self-Making in Nineteenth-Century America*, Hartman's methodological insistence on rigorous historicization simultaneous to a rejection of periodization is fundamental to the transtemporal scope and appositional reading methodology in *Abolition Time*. And in *In the Wake: On Blackness and Being*, Sharpe's activation of multiple simultaneous meanings of *wake* highlights, for me, the analytical and ethical imperative to attend simultaneously to the nonending of "the past that is not past" in the ways that slavery's afterlife continues to structure our present and to the irreducibility of Black life, and indeed ontology itself, to only an overdetermined product of the Middle Passage.[11] Taken together, I read Hartman's and Sharpe's corpuses as eschewing a binary debate between pessimism and optimism and instead as opening a space for thinking the *possibilities of impossibility* that abolitionist activists articulate in spaces beyond the academy. That is, Hartman's and Sharpe's analyses offer tools for understanding *how* futures that the dominant grammars of the present render impossible are nevertheless present as possibilities within the poetics of art, literature, performance, and daily life. In their work, both the past and the future are present in the now that they investigate.

What José Esteban Muñoz would identify as the prison house of the here and now certainly employs the force of law and the mechanisms of, in Kara Keeling's terms, "quotidian violence" to render abolition an impossibility. But Hartman's and Sharpe's analytical tools—for example, "critical fabulation" and "anagrammatical blackness"—allow us to read for the ways that literary texts imagine in excess of the violence enforcing the borders around epistemic possibility.[12] Even as their work so lucidly and vividly accounts for the nonseparation of the past from the present, Hartman and Sharpe, in different ways, open this rejection of progressive, periodized teleology toward questions about the possibilities for life lived in the space produced by immanent and imminent death, rather than toward conclusions about life's impossibility. In grammatical terms, I see their work as happening in ellipses rather than in periods, and this is the kind of thinking I seek to mobilize throughout my close readings. I synthesize these axes of their work in chapter 1 of *Abolition Time* to analyze the Middle Passage as unbounded by "event-time" in order to theorize what I call the *excessive present*, a temporality in which past,

present, and future fold into a single, dynamic *now* irreducible to
the stasis imposed by cages.

My notion of the excessive present is not simply a synonym for
"slavery's afterlife" or "the wake," not least of all because Hartman's and Sharpe's terms are not synonyms for each other. I read
Hartman's "afterlife of slavery" as a naming of the world-forming,
continuing forces of power that sustain the linked structures of
white supremacy and anti-Blackness through institutions and
norms that re-form—as in change in shape, but not in substance—
the foundational racial-sexual order of chattel slavery as logic of
global capital. And I read Sharpe's "wake" as both a naming of the
nonending of the so-called past that is the world-destroying force
of slavery and an activation of both an epistemology and an ethics
required by the conditions of that nonending in order to enact an
undestroyed world in which Black life is not lived in immanent and
imminent proximity to death. Building on these terms, the excessive present is a way of describing temporality in direct opposition
to legal conceptions of time that are necessarily periodized and
teleological. Against the notion that a law or court case can be the
"period" at the end of a historical era, the excessive present posits the persistence of the past within the present. Simultaneously,
rejecting the notion that the law's "periods" have the power to determine what is possible in the future, the excessive present also
posits the persistence of the future-in-the-present, wherein past
futures that the law supposedly forestalled persist as potentialities
and wherein futures we may think of as on a distant horizon are in
formation right now. As such, I intend for the term *excessive present* to build on Hartman's and Sharpe's insights to specifically think
time against the law. I want to shift the definition of *justice* from the
terms given by law's grammars to an openness we can find in ethics
that exceeds law. So my positing of a new term is not a departure
by way of disagreement but a synthesizing of conceptual tools to
use in a particular direction to give specific inflection to ongoing
questions in Black studies, carceral studies, queer studies, and the
legal humanities.

In mobilizing the excessive present as a conceptual fulcrum
around which to pivot the idea of justice from law to ethics, I am

working within an ongoing scholarly conversation in African Americanist literary studies. Books of literary criticism by Karla FC Holloway, Daylanne K. English, Dennis Childs, and Patrick E. Alexander are all deeply influential on the development of my own reading practices in *Abolition Time*. Holloway's *Legal Fictions: Constituting Race, Composing Literature* remains an exemplary model of law and literature scholarship rigorously grounded in both African American literary history and legal history.[13] Holloway traces how Black literature engages, intentionally or not, legal questions of property, contract, precedent, and evidence at every historical turn. Her particular engagement with the concept of *precedent* as a force of the past in the present on axes of both jurisprudence and racial construction and representation resonates with how English explicitly sees time as the terrain on which law and literature collide in her study *Each Hour Redeem: Time and Justice in African American Literature*. English clarifies that "as represented in the African American literary tradition, time and justice . . . are actually contingent and unevenly available: in other words, they are *political fiction*."[14] Taking seriously this relationship between time and justice, Childs and Alexander attend specifically to the literature of neo-slavery. Childs develops theories of hauntology through the paradigms of critical prison studies to read the "haunting future-orientation of the neo-abolitionist appeal" in letters, novels, and embodied performance by Black subjects across historical periods, and in *From Slave Ship to Supermax: Mass Incarceration, Prisoner Abuse, and the Neo-Slave Novel*, Alexander focuses on scenes wherein incarcerated and captive subjects are literally abused by their captors to show how the "social control practices that structured carceral life on slave ships and slave plantations have long, post-Emancipation afterlives."[15]

Abolition Time directly builds on the work of these four books, each of which, to different degrees and along different axes, I see as engaging in abolitionist literary studies, by continuing to mine the entanglement of time and law in Black literature with the tools of legal studies and critical prison studies. Whereas Holloway, English, Childs, and Alexander are chiefly concerned with demonstrating the continuity of carceral anti-Blackness across periods of legal and literary history, with Childs and Alexander going a step toward calling for future work to abolish the afterlives of slavery imposed by the grammar of the law, my book opens toward theorizing the future-in-the-present that exists simultaneously with the hauntological afterlife of slavery. This emphasis on enacting futurity at the very moment of the past's nonending marks *Abolition Time*'s departure from previous work in these fields precisely as it marks the book's indebtedness to this work for so thoroughly demonstrating the uninterrupted persistence of juridical anti-Blackness.

Throughout my close readings, I draw on Black feminist theory and queer studies to examine ways in which this uninterrupted persistence of juridical anti-Blackness manifests normative regimes of gender and sexuality as "grammars of law." Hortense Spillers's foundational theorization of "ungendering" and its extension by scholars including C. Riley Snorton, Sarah Clarke Kaplan, Marquis Bey, Patrice Douglass, and Sarah Haley make possible my analysis, especially in chapters 2 and 4, of how gender is not a preexisting variable but a contingent mode of being produced by and through racial-sexual terror.[16] Jennifer L. Morgan's foundational work theorizing the infamous *partus sequitur ventrem* law of slavery, and how Morgan's work is built on, not only by Kaplan, but also by Alys Eve Weinbaum and Brigitte Fielder, is of particular importance to my readings of not only gender but also reproduction as both economic and biological formation.[17] Though *Abolition Time* is not a comprehensive theory of gender, one of its persistent threads of analysis is examining how gender has not only been delimited by but also has been mobilized as a particularly insidious and violent grammar of law that seeks to narrow the horizon of liberation within the colonially imposed scope of Western binaries.

Near the end of *Black on Both Sides: A Racial History of Trans Identity*, Snorton asks, "Put differently, how does one access a language outside of and in contradistinction to the governing codes that currently determine human definition such that it gives rise to new meanings, forms of life, and genres of being?"[18] Snorton's question is thrillingly expansive in the avenues it opens up; for me,

it speaks to the difficulty of elaborating temporalities of justice
that cannot be articulated in the law's grammar of bounded events.
In addition to opening up ways of thinking gender itself within
Abolition Time's focus on theorizing within law's shadow, Snorton's
question indexes how queer and trans studies have been important fields of thought for my thinking on time and justice. Queer
temporalities as figured through Black studies help me to enact
Snorton's question as I reach toward new forms of life beyond juridical Humanity. Abolition is a kind of Black feminist futurity, as
Campt defines it. And as such a futurity, it is *also* a "future of the
past," as Keeling articulates in *Queer Times, Black Futures*.[19] That is,
on the other side of Hartman's "nonevent of emancipation" in the
nineteenth century is extrajudicial "wake work," in Sharpe's language, that "insists black being into the wake" such that, even as
freedom remains deferred, abolition emerges as unrealized possibility with the ethical force of the future perfect tense.

Abolition, as a conjuring of forms of life that eschew individuating ideologies in favor of "new genres of being," as I elaborate
in chapter 4 of *Abolition Time,* is one dimension of a utopian queer
futurity to come. It is both not yet here and also already present as
that future of the past that cannot be defined solely by emancipation's *nonevent.* Queer futurity, slavery's afterlife, and the ongoing
wake of the ship cohere in *Abolition Time* to enunciate Stanley's
sense that "the time of abolition is both yet to come and already
here."[20] Abolition time is time against the law. It is time that refuses the law's grammar of progressive, periodized teleology that
would prescribe limited terms of the possible.

Finally for me, Alexander Weheliye's *Habeas Viscus: Racializing Assemblages, Biopolitics, and Black Feminist Theories of the
Human* links the task of thinking liberatory futures to the work
of analyzing ontologies that exceed the law. Weheliye draws on
the work of Spillers and Sylvia Wynter to critique Michel Foucault's and Giorgio Agamben's theorizations of bare life, social
death, and biopolitics. In doing so, Weheliye recognizes that "the
legal conception of personhood comes with a steep price" but
moves from *habeas corpus* to *habeas viscus* to underscore that "the
flesh is nothing less than the ethereal social (afterlife) of bare

existence."²¹ In short, the law's violence both marks the bare life of racialized assemblages like the Black subject *and* is exceeded by a "fleshy surplus" through which alternative genres of the human are practiced beyond the law's force. Building on both Weheliye's theorization and Derrick Bell's sense that, within a juridical framework, racism (in the Americas, at least) is *permanent,* as well as on Mari Matsuda's guidance toward legal theorization produced "from the bottom" and thus outside the law's canonical perception, I extend "the flesh" from the realm of ontology to the realm of ethics.²² As I extrapolate in chapter 2, analogous to how *flesh* precedes *body, ethics* precedes *law* as a realm where we might find something like justice, but not in any clean, analytical sense. Instead, thinking with Derrida, Walter Benjamin, and John D. Caputo, in addition to Black feminist work on rigorously thinking *care* as an ethic, I envision *justice* as far more deconstructive and, as I explore in great but inconclusive detail in chapter 3, "messy."

The rest of this Introduction proceeds first by briefly defining some of the book's key terms, then by sketching the terms of this book's subtitle, *grammars of law* and *poetics of justice,* through an example from the U.S. Supreme Court and a return to *Beloved.* The dynamic produced by these two forces of grammar and poetics, of law and justice, gives shape to the call for abolition that is a call for a future that should have already been and thus must be. The abolitionist call is insisted into being in fleeting moments, *now,* after the world has already ended and in anticipation of its future ending. This dynamic is *Abolition Time*'s original offering, indebted to all of the work I have discussed as its epistemic conditions of possibility and opening new ground for future work in abolitionist literary studies that can, hopefully, take these methods of reading into other archives of literature, law, theory, and culture.

KEY TERMS

The core aim of *Abolition Time* is to pivot justice from law and order to abolitionist ethics through close reading. Along the way a number of key terms proliferate its pages. I want to sketch here how these terms fit together to provide an anchor point to which readers can return.

Taken together, the readings I perform in this book attempt exemplifying what we might call *abolitionist literary studies*. While the work of abolition most concretely, urgently, and immediately takes place through the praxis of intentional organizing, because abolition demands that we "change everything," as Ruth Wilson Gilmore has repeated in numerous venues over the past half-decade, there is abolition work to be done even in the colonial institutional space of the academy, even in that traditional discipline that is my academic home—literary studies. Affixing the adjective "abolitionist" to "literary studies" is not a flagging of specific content; that is, abolitionist literary studies is not the study of texts explicitly concerned with prisons and police. Rather, abolitionist literary studies names an orientation toward reading and study grounded in the search for unruliness in both content *and* form. And sometimes, the unruliness to which I attend is the unruliness of textuality itself which exceeds the intentions, politics, or even conceptual vocabularies of particular authors. This orientation toward unruliness is set in motion in this book through close reading, which I see as a *method* as distinct from *practice*. For me, method is disciplinary—it is the part of my argument grounded in academic literary studies; practice is political—it is the part of my argument that reaches beyond one discipline and beyond the academy. In *Abolition Time*, my writing is most concerned with method, while I reach toward practice at all times mostly to underscore the limits of method, which to follow my own definition by distinction means the limits of disciplinarity. Close reading as one (and only one!) method of abolitionist literary studies opens philosophical and imaginative horizons for thinking justice against the law, and then it meets its limits precisely where practice, as that which happens when the books are closed, picks up.

While *abolitionist literary studies* names an orientation toward and in an academic field, the two terms of my book's subtitle, *grammars of law* and *poetics of justice* name possible functions of language in relation to that unruliness to which my attention is always tuned. More specifically, grammars of law and poetics of justice index the force exerted on epistemology and, by extension, ethics by language's potential for shaping thought. The conceptual nexus that links these two terms, then, is *im/possibility*. On the one hand, *grammars of law* are those juridical acts of language—often but not always performative—which set in place borders around what is allowable (read: possible) and what is beyond what can be thought within the order that the law imposes (read: impossible). For example, we can think of the legal male/female gender-sex binary as a grammar of law insofar as it orders bodies into two discernable and governable categories for the state to administer. On the other hand, *poetics of justice* are those acts of language which, while not necessarily escaping the terms set by law's ordering force, spin out in other directions to make possible ways of thinking, knowing, and doing which aren't captured in the law's grammars. For example, in this Introduction's epigraph from *Beloved*, the lack of punctuation in the textual representation of Beloved's words allows her *now* to be something other than a discernable moment of injury or redress and instead to be a time that exceeds law's ordering grammar of past event, present trial, and future retribution.

In *Freedom Time: The Poetics and Politics of Black Experimental Writing*, Anthony Reed puts it this way: "The possible is a codification of the present and a calculation based on present knowledge that figures the future as a future present. To 'say the impossible' is to produce a statement that interferes with the existing forms of thinking and knowing in a given moment."[23] In the terms I set out here in *Abolition Time*, a book that seeks to echo Reed's powerful attention to formalist reading practices, *grammars of law* are ways for language to say the possible, so that even if the world is remade it is through the logic of reform, where nothing outside of the present's hegemonic terms of order is thinkable. In contrast, *poetics of justice* are attempts—however fleeting, incomplete, or compromised—at saying the impossible, at reaching beyond order toward the horizon of unruliness.

Together, these four terms—grammars of law, poetics of justice, possibility, and impossibility—form a dynamic of worlding at play throughout *Abolition Time*. As I state earlier, when I use *World* with a capital-W I am referring to the historical process of constructing a hegemonic sociopolitical World through the violences of multiple linked hierarchical structures. This is a process of *worlding* that is imposed by grammars of law. In addition to being structures of hierarchy and systems of power, those overwhelming powers that we name white supremacy, racial capitalism, cisheteropatriarchy, and (settler) colonialism are grammars which order the terms of knowledge in the World they produce and hold together. When we speak in those received grammars, the World we might imagine is still being ordered by what those grammars deem possible. When we follow poetics of justice, there is the potential for the impossible to become possible, and for the World to be decapitalized, to again be many worlds. The work of decapitalizing the World indeed must happen in practice, but the thinking that that practice puts in motion can and does happen in the methods of abolitionist literary studies, which is nothing other than the attempt to follow language from the realm of the possible to the impossible and back again.

GRAMMARS OF LAW:
PERIODIZATION, PROGRESS, EVENT

In 2013, the U.S. Supreme Court ruled in *Shelby County, Alabama v. Eric Holder, Attorney General* that section 4b of the 1965 Voting Rights Act (VRA) was unconstitutional. Writing for the opinion of the Court, Chief Justice John Roberts asserts that "history did not end in 1965" in arguing that the historical progress on the issue of voting rights for historically disenfranchised people ameliorates the continued relevance of parts of the VRA.[24] Writing for the dissent, Justice Ruth Bader Ginsberg retorts, "The Court criticizes Congress for failing to recognize that 'history did not end in 1965.' But the court ignores that 'what's past is prologue.' And '[t]hose who cannot remember the past are condemned to repeat it.'"[25] One could dig through myriad layers if they wanted to parse the technical legal disagreements between Roberts and Ginsberg, from differing readings of precedent cases to the meaning of the Fourteenth and Fifteenth Amendments to differing interpretations of what counts as relevant data to deep disagreement over the principle of equal sovereignty. But my interest is in how, despite disagreeing about how much progress has been made or how that

progress was and will continue to be achieved, Roberts and Ginsberg are arguing vehemently with each other about *time*.

The VRA was passed in 1965 to combat racist discrimination
against African Americans at the polls across the southern United
States during the era of Jim Crow segregation. Section 2 of the act
contains the general proclamation that no government body may
pass any law or enact any policy that would result in racial discrimination in voting. (The act has a strong and proper focus on
results rather than on mere *intentions,* which is one reason it had
been one of the most successful pieces of civil rights legislation
passed at the federal level in the United States.) This general proclamation applies to all government bodies in all parts of the United
States. In addition to this general principle, section 5 of the act
imposes what is called "preclearance" requirements for certain
specific states and districts. The districts covered by section 5 are
determined by the "coverage formula" in section 4b, which sets the
parameters for how the Department of Justice (DOJ) will determine
which districts need to preclear any proposed changes to voting
policies and procedures with the DOJ before enacting them. It was
this final section, the preclearance formula, that Roberts and the
Court ruled unconstitutional. However, while section 5 remains
technically untouched, the invalidity of section 4b makes section
5 unenforceable and therefore essentially ineffectual, because, as
Derrida argues, the law is meaningless without enforceability.[26]

According to Roberts, the coverage formula is unconstitutional
because in the VRA's 2006 reauthorization, it was not sufficiently
updated to reflect the realities on the ground that have been
changed for the better in history's progress from the discrimination of the past to the improved conditions of the present. "If
Congress had started from scratch in 2006," Roberts writes, invoking the boldest conditional *if* so central to the grammar of much
legal writing, "it plainly could not have enacted the present coverage formula."[27] His temporal argument is essentially that because
conditions have changed—that is, because racist discrimination in
voting has been mitigated so much, in his view, that it can no longer possibly be considered "pervasive," "flagrant," "widespread,"
or "rampant"—the coverage formula, which subjects historically

racist districts to extra levels of federal enforcement over and above their state and local sovereignty over elections, cannot continue to target districts for their sins of the past.[28] For Roberts, Jim Crow is definitively over, and so the VRA coverage formula's focus on Jim Crow districts is unfair.

I see this as a form of what Sara Ahmed calls "overing": "in assuming we are over certain kinds of critique, [those who implement the genre of argumentation that we might call 'overing'] create the impression that we are over what is being critiqued."[29] For Ahmed, overing is a rhetorical move that relegates problems to the past and therefore casts any present attempts to articulate or solve those problems as blockages or even reversals of the progress of history. In Roberts's logic of overing, we are so over the problem of racist voting discrimination that he wants to sever past and future completely: "the [Fifteenth] Amendment is not designed to punish for the past; its purpose is to ensure a better future."[30] For Roberts and his concurring colleagues (Antonin Scalia, Clarence Thomas, Samuel Alito, and Anthony Kennedy), ensuring a better future is a radically distinct venture from punishing perpetuators of past injustices.

This severing of past and future, wherein a just future is a radical departure from an unjust past, is part of what I call law's periodizing force, which is one major component of *grammars of law*. That is, the law claims for itself the ability to declare moments in time over and new moments begun, essentially designating the periodization of history into discrete moments. We can think of the ways in which certain historical moments begin or end with signal acts of law. There was slavery until 1865, and then the Thirteenth Amendment passed and there was not. There was Jim Crow until the Civil Rights Act and the VRA ended it in 1965, and then there was not. Now there is something different, something new—a *new* Jim Crow in the form of mass incarceration, for example. We can think of these moments as the law penciling in a period in a run-on sentence of history to impose a discernable meaning, thus landing us on the grammar of periodization, of imposing endings and beginnings to make sense of language.

In academia, critical theory has for the better part of five decades been taking to task the concept of linear, neatly periodized
history. It is almost taken for granted that there is not a clean break
between past and present. But in the halls of the most powerful
court of law in the United States, the chief justice writes with the
conviction that history is linear, progressive, and teleological, decades of critical theory—be it poststructuralism, deconstruction,
Black feminism, critical race theory, queer theory, or anything
else—be damned. I believe that this is not a problem merely with
Roberts, or with a particularly right-leaning court, however. While
Ginsberg and her liberal codissenters in *Shelby County v. Holder*
(Sonia Sotomayor, Elena Kagan, and Stephen Breyer) see the past
as continuing to influence the present, as Ginsberg's language in
her dissent shows, there is still a pervasive faith that the law can
do the job of getting us to the next phase, the new promised land
that will be different from before (Renisa Mawani would call this
the law's "alibi of progress"[31]). While Ginsberg recognizes that
"the court does not write on a clean slate," the core of her argument most fundamentally rests on the idea that the VRA has
successfully pulled us forward from an unjust, egregious past into
an improved, though still imperfect, present.[32] And so, it can be
the tool that continues to propel us forward, away from "second-
generation" barriers to voting to a more just future in which racial
discrimination is eliminated and Jim Crow is truly a thing of the
past. She writes, "If the statute was working, there would be less
evidence of discrimination, so opponents might argue that Congress should not be allowed to renew the statute," capturing the
absurd logic of the Court's opinion as authored by Roberts. Ginsberg continues, "In contrast, if the statute was not working, there
would be plenty of evidence of discrimination, but scant reason to
renew a failed regulatory regime."[33] This catch-22 emerges out of
a conception of history wherein the law's very responsibility is to
act as a periodizing force. If it does its job correctly, then the law
inaugurates a new era in which a problem has been solved, and so
evidence of the problem depletes. And if it fails, then the law does
not get us over a problem, and evidence of the problem persists.[34]

The question for Ginsberg is whether a law that has successfully done its job of dragging time forward from the past toward a more just future should stand or whether its very effectiveness warrants its obsolescence. In any case, Ginsberg is, like Roberts, still assuming a linear, periodized conception of time and history. She only disagrees about what should be done when the law approaches successful enactment of its periodizing force.

It is in direct opposition to the periodizing force of law that I posit what I call the *excessive present* as an account of temporality that collapses distinctions between past, present, and future. It is time against the law. My goal in articulating the excessive present is therefore less about providing a definitive, overarching theory of time in all possible contexts than it is about opening space for considering ethical and political questions outside of the ordering juridical grammar of discrete moments. More than making a theoretical intervention or positing a new, better interpretation of any particular literary text or cultural object or event, my goal throughout *Abolition Time* is always to reach for an ethics and politics that crosses temporal distance and overwhelms overing. I want it to be impossible to imply that ethical responsibility to an event has extinguished because the event is over.

I should say that I do not understand "ethics" here or throughout my project as a set of rules we might discover to provide definitive answers to the problems of violence and domination. Instead, ethics is a project of seeking justice with the knowledge that something must be done, but with the knowledge of what that something is remaining, necessarily, uncertain, "if only to avoid the arrogance of so many clean consciences."[35] Collapsing past, present, and future results not in simplified clarity, because there are fewer pieces to the time puzzle to consider, but rather in more confusion, because the ordering grammar of period(ization)s is removed, making it harder, not easier, to interpret the language of a history that hurts. To think justice in excess of the law is not posited as a task with a definite answer, where ethics is a crude list of good and bad imperatives. Rather, to think justice in excess of the law is the messy project of abolition. In the words of contemporary abolitionist Mariame Kaba, "we'll figure it out by working to get there. You don't have to know all the answers in order to be able to press for a vision."[36]

It was my work with fellow prison abolitionists on a campaign to stop a jail expansion that fully convinced me that the dissertation project that has become *Abolition Time* was not a memory studies project but about something else, a different inflection of thinking about time and history. In working with returning citizens in particular to organize opposition to jail expansion in our local community, as well as in teaching incarcerated students, I was taught that the task is not necessarily to demonstrate that the afterlife of slavery continues in, for example, criminalization and imprisonment. Both the incarcerated and those manning the mechanizations of carcerality know this. The task, again in the words of Mariame Kaba, the abolitionist writer and activist whose work first helped shape my thinking down this path, "is unleashing people's imaginations while getting concrete—so that we have to imagine while we build, always both."[37] *Abolition Time* as a book and the *excessive present* as a concept are attempts at framing a space for imaging new possibilities through the concrete work of building. If the future is not only something out there on the horizon that we cannot quite grasp but something we can touch through what we do, today, how can we imagine it differently from the past in which we still live during this present?

POETICS OF JUSTICE:
EXCESSIVE TEMPORALITY IN *BELOVED*

Toni Morrison's *Beloved* famously begins with an absence that interrupts the sequential logic of linear progression. As has been said many times, the "124" that begins the novel introduces a sequential pattern of ordered knowledge, only to undercut it with an absence in the shape of the missing numeral 3 [1, 2, 3, 4]. Some have suggested that the missing numeral indicates the missing member of the family in the house on Bluestone Road, so that when Beloved returns, she completes the sequence. But numerous absences besides Beloved can fill in the empty space of the sequential set: Halle, Paul D, Baby Suggs, and Sethe's ma'am, at least, all orbit the house as absent figures of the family living under its roof. The missing numeral thus does not simply indicate the need to fill in a pre-set gap within the ordered, linear, and sequential logic of the set but instead encodes in its absence the excess that erupts order, linearity, and sequence such that the set cannot possibly be closed.

By invoking sequential, linear progression as a possible ordering logic, *Beloved* is in its first instance a novel that moves against the grammar of the law as a periodizing force. Eschewing linear time and periodization, *Beloved* is not concerned primarily with "the past" as such; rather, as Avery Gordon puts it, the novel does the work of making legible "that shadowy basis for the production of material life."[38] The very first numeral in the novel, then, rejects a reading of *Beloved* as concerned primarily with recovering a loss because the exploded set indexes the impossibility of recovery. As Hartman writes in her essay "The Time of Slavery," "what is at stake here is more than exposing the artifice of historical barricades or the tenuousness of temporal markers like the past and the present. By seizing hold of the past, one illuminates the broken promises and violated contracts of the present."[39] *Beloved* is about the present. Which is to say, it is about *now* and *all of it is now it is always now.* Which is thus to further say that *Beloved* is about the future.

In *The Shape of the Signifier: 1967 to the End of History*, Walter Benn Michaels observes, "Despite the fact that slavery ended more than a century before *Beloved* was written, Morrison's book is an antislavery novel."[40] And he is absolutely right. *Beloved* is an antislavery novel. But rather than being perplexed by this seemingly ahistorical move, as Michaels seems in his readings of *Beloved* and Leslie Marmon Silko's *Almanac of the Dead*, I see this as a deeply insightful observation about the complex interplay of temporality and ethics in Morrison's novel—an interplay that manifests not only in the narrative's plot as ghost story but in the text's poetics as it searches for language to speak the unspeakable, to say what cannot be said but must be said, to bring about that which was not but which still must be: abolition as the negation of the anti-Blackness inherent in liberal humanism and the manifestation of justice that cannot be ordered by teleology.

Whereas Michaels sees *Beloved*'s antislavery politics as a confounding anachronism reflective of American literature's general turn to questions of identity and historicism, Stephen Best helpfully situates Morrison's novel specifically within the trajectory of African Americanist scholarship. According to Best, *Beloved* is the literary paradigm of three decades of Black studies' preoccupation with the past since the mid-1980s. He writes, "The rise of *Beloved* moved the entire field of literary studies to a central place in African American studies. . . . With Morrisonian poetics as a guide, the black Atlantic provided a way of making history for those who had lost it and as such secured the recent rehabilitation of melancholy in cultural criticism."[41] For Best, the years since the late 1980s, which saw the publication not only of Morrison's iconic novel but also, he points out, of Henry Louis Gates Jr.'s *The Signifying Monkey: A Theory of Afro-American Literary Criticism*, Houston A. Baker Jr.'s *Blues, Ideology, and Afro-American Literature: A Vernacular Theory*, Hazel V. Carby's *Reconstructing Womanhood: The Emergence of the Afro-American Woman Novelist*, Valerie Smith's *Self-Discovery and Authority in Afro-American Narrative*, and Hortense Spillers's "Mama's Baby, Papa's Maybe: An American Grammar Book," have been dominated by a mode of historiography devoted to an ethics of "recovery" and "redemption." This historiography, Best tells us, often invokes itself as an ethics predicated on losses and dispossessions in the historical archive that call out to be reconciled. Though Michaels bemoans the way this focus on loss and dispossession traps contemporary political thought within static identity politics, in a more interesting and nuanced move, Best sees it as a form of melancholia—indeed, he calls this mode of inquiry "melancholic historicism." Turning to Freud, Best argues that *Beloved* and those forms of historical analysis within its paradigm enact a "persistent identification with the lost object," which, in the case of slavery, is an unrecoverable, unknowable history.[42]

Douglas A. Jones agrees with and extends Best's reading of *Beloved* and the scholarship it has propelled:

In construing slavery as ongoing, this critical disposition [of "melancholic historicism"] understands itself as engaged in the same struggle of historiographical recovery and relation as Morrison believed *Beloved* to be part of—a struggle that strives to redeem both the past and the present (since they are one) by returning us, affectively and imaginatively, to "the site of origin and the scene of the fall," to some sort of "prelapsarian wholeness."[43]

Jones and Best are right to critique just how dominant the trend has become in Black studies to take for granted the coevality of the past and present. Unlike Best and Jones, however, who seek to revivify periodization, I want to reintroduce the past and the present to the future, making all three frames coeval together. For me, then, the point is not so much a "return" to "some sort of 'prelapsarian wholeness'" but rather to see what forms of freedom might be grasped or practiced directly in the process of falling. That is, my preoccupation in *Abolition Time* with literatures of slavery as a site for thinking abolitionist justice is not a fantasy of recovering or redeeming or intervening in a past violence by salvaging a lost object but rather a somber consideration of how these texts seek ways for forestalling future loss.

My theoretical preoccupation is practical. Against the juridical conception of justice as something that can be done in sequence after harm was done, I consider abolitionist justice as a commitment to building and maintaining right relations through the ubiquity of everyday encounter and conflict (abolitionists do not imagine a world without any conflict). To reemphasize, the title of this Introduction is "Justice Is Not an Event." That is the closest thing to a single thesis statement that *Abolition Time* has. Nothing in these pages ever assumes that there is an event of repair, or a moment of healing, or a Thing That Can Be Done that would "bring" or "do" justice. So, I am not concerned with finding or fixing lost objects, despite my propensity to think against periodization in the vein of coevality that Best and Jones critique. Justice is never *achieved*; it is only and always practiced. As a reader of literature, then, I am disposed toward lingering in the moments before a text offers an answer or offers closure, moments when the only arrival is nonarrival.

Because of this disposition, I believe that Jones's diagnosis of the motivations and desires of *Beloved*-like scholarship misses the mark somewhat, at least insofar as it must be admitted that

Beloved and the scholarship one might describe as within its paradigm are not *only*, exclusively invested in recovery, redemption, and melancholy—to say nothing yet of the fact that there is no necessary connection between an ethics of redress and a state of melancholia.

Morrison has unquestionably written and spoken about how the novel and those like it are directly attempting to fill in gaps in the historical archive—in Best's and Jones's words, to recover a lost past (her much-cited "The Site of Memory" is just one example, but one could point to numerous interviews and invited talks and addresses). Best writes that, concerning *Beloved*, "Morrison resists a view of loss as the property of an immediate circle of kin and *encourages us to claim that loss for ourselves.*"[44] I think that this is a useful reading both of *Beloved* itself and of Morrison's own descriptions of what work she sees the novel as doing. But to *claim* a loss is not the same as to *recover* or *redeem* a loss. Additionally, claiming the loss *of* absence is not the same as redressing the damage caused *by* the absence, if the absence or the loss itself is taken as the object of attachment in a model of melancholia.

In the case of *Beloved*, this seemingly minor semantic distinction is paramount. *Beloved* confronts readers with the loss of slave interiority within the historical archive in order to have readers feel the pain of what results from this loss. This absence is filled in by the novel itself, but the character Beloved exemplifies the incompleteness of the novel *Beloved*'s attempt to fill in that absence. Just as Beloved as a singularity cannot stand in for the missing figure of the sequential logic interrupted by the numeral "124," the novel *Beloved* is from its outset an impossible stand-in for an absence that exceeds recovery. This thus shifts the call to redress from a demand to recover the actual lost lives of the dead to a demand to claim redress for the continuing deaths that are both different from and continuous with those that have come before (we hear the echoes in the name Garner from Margaret to Eric). The absence in the archive is insufficiently filled by the novel, but the novel's project exceeds the capacity to fill gaps and reaches out toward the possibilities for redress of the damages that unfold in the wake of this absence. *It is not the absence itself* that is being redressed, because such a redress would be impossible, *but the damage caused by the absence*—the afterlife of slavery, the afterlife of property, the nonevent of emancipation, the wake, the weather.

At the end of the novel, after all, Beloved must be exorcised; she disappears from 124 Bluestone Road and is forgotten: "By and by all trace is gone, and what is forgotten is not only the footprints but the water too and what is down there. The rest is weather. Not the breath of the disremembered and unaccounted for, but wind in the eaves, or spring ice thawing too quickly. Just weather. Certainly no clamor for a kiss."[45] By the end of the novel, recovery has failed. The character Beloved, as the presence that is bodied into the space left open by absence, is ultimately insufficient for filling that absence. The dead cannot be recovered. For Sethe's life to be sustained, Beloved must be claimed, but then must disappear again. For life to be sustained, the dead must be claimed and at the same time allowed to rest. They are coeval with the living, but they are also beyond our reach.

Like Beloved the character, *Beloved* the novel fails to fill the absence in the historical archive. Morrison's novel does not give readers "the breath of the disremembered and unaccounted for" but does give "wind in the eaves . . . just weather." Just weather, and no more. Or just weather, as opposed to unjust weather. And/or both. This ending ambiguity culminates the text's consistent displacement of readers' sense of grounding. Each time I teach *Beloved*, from introductory courses to graduate seminars, students remark how it is difficult to keep a handle on what is happening. When I ask why and push us past general claims of difficulty to pointing out what, exactly, on the page is happening that makes it difficult to orient ourselves in the narrative's plot, we always, every time, wind up discussing verb tense, focalization, and paragraph breaks. Any reader of *Beloved* needs to pay attention to the moments when the narrative slips from a third-person view of what is happening in the present moment to a focalized look at a character's inner life migrating through time to a different moment. This is difficult because, unlike standard narrational practice of signaling such a slippage through a paragraph break and switch in verb tenses, oftentimes *Beloved* refuses these standard grammars of storytelling. Teaching the novel, in my experience, requires a lot of reading aloud, slowly, to track the tense of the plot against the tense of the verbs and to track the temporality of the scenes against the structure of the paragraphs. The novel's genre may be historical fiction, which we may be tempted to interpret linearly as a story of the past as such, but the novel's *poetics* as expressed in its grammar, form, and narrational strategies evaporate the distinction between past and present, refusing the sequential logic of healing a wound to move on. This is all to say that I believe that if we attend closely to *Beloved*'s poetics, which are poetics of justice that refuse justice as event to open far more complex, painful, and uncertain ground, then it is a mistake to read *Beloved* as a novel that recovers a lost object. Like its titular character, the novel is temporally out of joint.

Beloved is not an antislavery novel in the sense that it tries to accomplish a historical moment that occurred a century and a half ago, but it is an antislavery novel in the sense that it seeks to abolish the future straight out of the past through its present engagement with cultural memories of loss. *Beloved* is a novel happening in abolition time, a temporality that is *both after the end of the world* brought about by the four horsemen of the Apocalypse who come in Baby Suggs's yard *and before the end of the world* of "this spatiotemporal catastrophe we call modernity."[46] Like the ghost's grammar without punctuation, the novel itself—and its demand for justice—cannot be bound by closure. Against the grammars of law that impose the sentence as a bounded, discrete unit of response, Beloved the character, who is not a single character, unbounds the sentence from the ordering logic of periods.

In this reading of Morrison's canonical novel, I aim to refigure what seems to have become settled discourse on *Beloved*—namely, that the novel is an attempt at recovering a violent, lost past. This settled discourse has at times become, or at least been interpreted as, a "fixation" on the object of loss that is slavery's history. But in thinking *Beloved* as an exploration of abolitionist justice, we can see an ethics of redress emerge that unsettles the settled sense that the novel is a *backward* gaze. To state it simply, demanding redress for damages done in what is called the past is not a fixation on the object of loss; it is a fixation on the possibility for justice in what is called the future.

At first glance, the novel indeed insists on grasping a story of slavery and holding on to it even though the legal end of the object it grasps happened 122 years before its own publication. And yet, one of the most striking scenes in the novel is Denver's exchange with Baby Suggs's ghost, when she is afraid to leave the yard and go out into the (white) world beyond the borders of 124 Bluestone Road:

> "You mean I never told you nothing about Carolina? About your daddy? You don't remember nothing about how come I walk the way I do and about your mother's feet, not to speak of her back? I never told you all that? Is that why you can't walk down the steps? My Jesus my."
> But you said there was no defense.
> "There ain't."
> Then what do I do?
> "Know it, and go on out the yard. Go on."[47]

In the scene, Denver "stood on the porch of 124 ready to be swallowed up in the world beyond the edge of the porch."[48] She is faced with the task of leaving the house where she, Sethe, and Beloved are starving to death since Sethe lost her job. But as she stands on the porch, Denver is immobilized by the fear that she could bump into the atrocities of slavery because, as her mother told her, if she goes to the place where terror happened, it will happen again. She is immobilized by Baby Suggs's warning that there is no defense against white people, who are able to inflict harm and even death whenever and wherever they like. She recalls Sethe and Baby Suggs arguing, Sethe saying that some white people are not so bad and Baby Suggs insisting, "There's more of us they drowned than there is all of them ever lived from the start of time."[49] This knowledge from her grandmother paralyzes Denver, and she cannot bring herself to step out of the yard and into the world.

In this moment when Denver is fixated on the object of loss and paralyzed by the threat of its repetition, Baby Suggs's voice comes to her, "clear as anything," not to comfort her and tell the granddaughter that everything will be OK, that she is sure that Denver will be unharmed, but that it is in fact true that there is no defense against white people and the violence they will do. And yet, Baby Suggs tells her, Denver must know this—she must unequivocally know that when she goes out into the world, there is no defense, no protection from the anti-Blackness that Sharpe calls "the weather"—and yet still take her steps. Denver steps off the porch and secures employment, allowing her to sustain Sethe and herself (and Beloved) while remaining deeply aware of the continuing presence of slavery's ethos, that any white person might harm any Black person at any time. Denver does not let go of the object of loss—slavery and all it has taken away—but rather clings to it without letting it hold her in place.

Rather than a "healthy" process like mourning—because the loss of slavery is ongoing and immeasurable—or a pathological paralysis engendered by melancholia, *Beloved* refuses this binary, instead representing a kind of "Black mo'nin'" that "improvises through the opposition of mourning and melancholia [to disrupt] the temporal framework that buttresses that opposition."[50] From this interpretation of *Beloved,* we can consider how *Beloved*-inspired scholarship in Black studies broadly looks to slavery not out of a melancholic fixation or stagnation but as an attempt to find the possibilities for justice, for life, for sustenance, for resistance, for breath, in its continuously unfolding aftermath.

In *How to Read African American Literature: Post-Civil Rights Fiction and the Task of Interpretation,* Aida Levy-Hussen asks, "If certain habits of reading black historical fiction have calcified into restrictive habit—then how might we re-fresh and re-imagine our readerly task?"[51] Departing from Levy-Hussen's focus on the terms of psychoanalysis, *Abolition Time* attempts to meet her question by shifting from the pairing *time-memory* to the pairing *time-justice.* I reimagine our readerly task in the post–civil rights era as listening for the ways that literary language bends and breaks and ignores the very systems of ordering grammar that allow discernable meaning to emerge. I reimagine our readerly task as listening for how literary language can, in Kaba's words, "jailbreak our imaginations." I reimagine our readerly task as insisting on the insufficiency of reading itself even as we insist on its necessity.

In the chapter of *Beloved* the novel narrated by Beloved the character, before the ghost says the infamous line "All of it is now it is always now," they observe Sethe and say, "I am not separate from her there is no place where I stop."[52] And immediately following, "It is always now," the ghost says, "there will never be a time when I am not crouching and watching others who are crouching too I am always crouching the man on my face is dead his face is not mine," and the reader has traveled with Beloved from the scene of Sethe picking flowers to the hold of a slave ship on which Sethe's murdered daughter would have never been, if we stick to the linear sequential logic of individuation and biological life spans. It is thus here that the novel defers, again, discovery or knowability. Just as the reader has put together that the girl who Sethe, Denver, and Paul D met on their return to 124 Bluestone Road after their trip to the fair was indeed the enfleshed ghost of the daughter whom Sethe killed, this character tells the reader that it has no boundaries as it becomes an unnamed enslaved person in the hold of a ship along the Middle Passage watching, listening to, smelling, feeling, and tasting death all around her. In addition to the obvious way in which Beloved is always doubled by the historical referent of Margaret Garner's murdered child and thus never coheres into a discrete singularity, even within the strictly fictional world of the novel, Beloved the character eschews the logic of individuation that would allow her to cohere into a traditionally knowable "character" at all. Beloved is Sethe's dead and alive-again child. Beloved is Sethe. Beloved is an unnamed enslaved person on board a slave ship. Beloved is just weather. Beloved is a force, and a call. Beloved is the impossibility *and* the necessity of resurrection. Beloved is drowned and resurfaced. Beloved is past and present and future. Beloved is the afterlife of slavery, its wake, *and* the excessive present of abolition's call. *Beloved* is an antislavery novel. And *Beloved* is an abolitionist novel.

FOUR POETICS

In its endeavor to outline abolitionist literary studies, this book moves forward through four chapters, each of which focuses on a particular kind of poetics: accumulation, perforation, witnessing, and breath. Each of these four is a distinct example of a poetics of justice, and so each exemplifies the kinds of things we might notice language to be doing in moments when it pivots justice away from the ordering force of law.

Chapter 1, "Accumulation: The Excessive Present, the Middle Passage, and the Juridical Event," argues that literary texts posit an *excessive present* that ruptures the temporal enclosure of singular "events." More than a description of temporality, the excessive present is an ethical problem that demands address; that is, if past, present, and future are coeval, then ethical structures of "accountability" or "responsibility" are no longer mediated by temporal distance when asking questions about redress for harms done in the so-called past. Through readings of a poetics of accumulation in Claudia Rankine's 2014 book *Citizen: An American Lyric* and Suzan-Lori Parks's 1989 play *Imperceptible Mutabilities in the Third Kingdom*, I extrapolate what it means to "exceed the event" of the Middle Passage. I trace repetition—both as a literal repeating of words, phrases, and images and as governing logic—in both texts to map how reiteration compounds on itself. This creates a temporal structure in both texts that cannot be adequately described by the language of memory, trauma, or identity. Instead, concepts and images accumulate multiple simultaneous meanings that unmoor the very logics of individuation that are necessary for an event-bound model of justice.

The excess conjured by accumulation begins to break through the ordering logic of the law that I more fully critique in chapter 2, "Perforation: Inhabitation and the Vulnerability of the Law." Beginning at the image of Linda Brent carving holes in the wall of the garret in which she hides on her enslaver's plantation in Harriet Jacobs's 1861 *Incidents in the Life of a Slave Girl*, I trace a poetics of perforation through Jacobs's text and M. NourbeSe Philip's 2008 book of poetry *Zong!* By examining how Jacobs's narration rhetorically inhabits the grammar of *partus sequitur ventrem* and how Philip's poetry inhabits in order to slash apart the legal text *Gregson v. Gilbert*, I argue that intertextual compositions like these authors' books welcome readers into discomforting spaces of ethical inquiry where thinking in excess of the law cannot escape the law's violence but, at the same time, the law's violence cannot keep it from being itself undone. A poetics of perforation also clarifies the messiness of my conceptual mapping in the book. It would be easy for readers to place grammars of law and poetics of justice on two opposite sides of a binary, where the former is the "bad" side and the latter is the "good" side. But when we attend to the meticulous ways in which Jacobs's and Philip's texts inhabit and deploy language and logics of the law itself in their very attempts to shatter them, we see that a poetics of perforation is anything but a clean break from the violence of the law. As a particular example of a specific poetic of justice, perforation reveals the messy imbrications of these two only seemingly opposite functions of language.

Following an interlude in which I reflect on the murder of Eric Garner in 2014 and the limits of literary criticism as a piece of the abolitionist project, chapter 3, "Witnessing: Impossible Recovery, Failed Recognition, and the Obligation of Risk," analyzes Fred D'Aguiar's 1997 novel *Feeding the Ghosts* and Morrison's 2008 novel *A Mercy* while returning to Philip's *Zong!* I pay particular attention to how these texts employ strategies of reader interpolation, mix realism with (critical) fabulation, and shift narrative focalization to do more politically complex work than demanding recognition or recovery within liberalism's terms of order. A poetics of witnessing that is traceable through such patterns of language invokes the legal figure of the witness precisely as the limit of the law's capacity for justice. That is, what I find most interesting in D'Aguiar's and Morrison's novels are the moments of ethical *failure*, because it is at these moments of failed ethics in the texts' plots when each text's formal techniques make space for a figure of the witness not as legal subject but as a gateway to an ethics that exceeds the law. These books demand that the reader (both of these texts and of *Abolition Time*) continue abolition work after the moment of reading ceases. An abolitionist close reading, it turns out, conjures an afterlife of reading, itself an ethical problem of impossible obligations and uncertain risk.

Stepping into the space of ethical uncertainty opened by chapter 3's poetics of witnessing, chapter 4, "Breath: Aspiration, Ungendered Mothering, and Im/Possible Futures," analyzes two texts that highlight what Black feminist scholars might call "othermothering"—David Dabydeen's 1994 poem "Turner" and Angelina Weld Grimké's 1916 play *Rachel*. In these two texts, mothering is reimagined through characters who nurture both the living and the dead toward literally impossible futures. The result is a poetics of breath that queers time and opens the horizon toward abolition even as white supremacy would seek to foreclose such possibility. While a poetics of breath remains the most difficult poetic of justice to define, given its emergence precisely in the space of uncertainty opened up by the perforations created by the accumulating analytical pressure of the three previous chapters, I navigate this final poetic most clearly through the language of gender and reproduction. Through close attention to shifts in pronouns, representation, and the unrepresentability of normative gender, and each text's careful play on genre conventions, I explore how antidevelopmental temporalities of repetition and revision model queer relations of care that exceed carceral epistemology in their insistence on nonreproductive futurity.

In the end, this is a book about close reading, and thus a book about method, as much as it is a book about abolition work. But this is not a book about "method wars." I am not concerned with positing *the* method that will save or invigorate an academic discipline subjected to constant attacks by neoliberal austerity governance and to racist and sexist and queerantagonistic attacks on fields of study that are perceived as antiwhite, anti-American, or otherwise antinormative and thus immoral. Indeed, that is the terrain of labor action and political solidarity more so than of academic monographs. The fight to keep structurally conservative campus governance networks, increasingly right-wing state legislatures, and growing fascist pressure from dismantling entire departments of humanistic inquiry is a fight that must be fought by labor action and solidarity, not by making better arguments about the proper relationship of reader to text or the relevance of any particular field of study or the transferability of any particular set of skills. Having the best argument in the method wars is not what will allow us and our students to have material support to study together, and so this book is not concerned with such fights, even as it is deeply concerned with method.

Rather, I submit *Abolition Time* as an offering and an invitation. My hope for the book is not so much that it will convince readers that I am correct in positing the best possible readings of the texts herein or that my theory of time is ironclad. Instead, my hope is that readers find in this examination of time, law, ethics, justice, and, of course, literature a way of reading texts in their own chosen archives for tools that might help us liberate our imaginations from the cages of law's grammar.

It is abolition time. I hope you will join us in the chorus.

J. M. W. Turner, *Slavers Throwing Overboard the Dead and Dying—Typhon Coming On (The Slave Ship)*, 1840.

ONE

Accumulation

THE EXCESSIVE PRESENT, THE MIDDLE
PASSAGE, AND THE JURIDICAL EVENT

There is a before and an after to the earthquake: but there is no before the ongoing event of the disaster. How, after all, to split time?

—Christina Sharpe, *In the Wake: On Blackness and Being*

What is at stake here is more than exposing the artifice of historical barricades or the tenuousness of temporal markers like the past and the present. By seizing hold of the past, one illuminates the broken promises and violated contracts of the present.

—Saidiya V. Hartman, "The Time of Slavery"

Why does Claudia Rankine's otherwise self-consciously contemporary and self-specified *American* book of poetry published in 2014, *Citizen: An American Lyric*, end with the image of British artist J. M. W. Turner's 1840 painting *The Slave Ship*? Why is *that* painting appearing at the end of *this* book?

When I first read *Citizen* in early 2015, I was arrested by the appearance of the painting in the final pages of the book before the closing paratext of permissions, references, and acknowledgments. *Why is this here?* On the final page of text before the painting appears, Rankine writes, "I don't know how to end what doesn't have an ending."[1] In grammatical terms, it seemed to me that in grasping for how to end a project without an ending, Rankine had gone back to a precursor to give her readers a capitalized noun which *Citizen* instantiates as pronoun, rather than the finitude of closure implied by a period. It looked like a rupture, an intrusion of the past into the present. And perhaps that is one interpretation: Turner's *The Slave Ship* is the return of the repressed traumatic past, the history that hurts, which precedes the racism Rankine recounts throughout her book.

But another way of observing this eruption of the past is to read it in view of this chapter's epigraphs from Saidiya Hartman and Christina Sharpe. In thinking slavery, Hartman asks us to do more than simply point out, again, that the separation between past and present is not as clear as some may think. And in thinking the devastation of the 2010 earthquake in Haiti, Sharpe poses the impossible question that situates the (un)natural disaster as another iteration in the ongoing disaster of Western modernity and all its attendant violences: *how, after all, to split time?* Reading Hartman and Sharpe together, I look again at *Citizen* to read it as a text that might do something other than simply communicate that the past of slavery is still influencing the racism of the present, such that, in order to redeem the present of *Citizen's* scenes of quotidian violence, we have an obligation to remember or to recover the past that we find in the violence of Turner's painting. I intend for the arguments about temporality in *Abolition Time* not to be reducible to the familiar logic that the past is still with us in the present. That is true enough, but as both Hartman and Sharpe insist in their work, that is a departure point for thinking, not a conclusion.

In excess of the framework of memory, remembering, and forgetting, through which we might see the emergence of *The Slave Ship* at the end of *Citizen* as confirmation of Joseph Roach's insistence that "while a great deal of the unspeakable violence instrumental to this creation [of the so-called New World] may have been officially forgotten, circum-Atlantic memory retains its consequences . . . the unspeakable cannot be rendered forever inexpressible," I read the presence of Turner's painting in Rankine's book as indexing what I theorize in this chapter as the *excessive present*.[2] Following Hartman's "afterlife of slavery" and Sharpe's "wake" as models of temporality that can be historicized against periodization, the excessive present names the folding of the past and future into a single, dynamic *now* that unfolds into an unbearable ethics irreducible to the juridical.

The excess of all that is present in the *now* means that the law, in its desire to impose teleological order through the violence of linear time leading from a moment of harm to a moment of redress by way of police and penal force, remains antithetical to ethics as the practice of justice. Instead of a list of axioms or knowable-in-advance propositions about moral right and wrong, the ethics of the excessive present demands abolition as the everyday practice of bringing a different world into being. The generative ethics unfolds against the World imposed by the "quotidian violence" holding together the "spatiotemporal catastrophe we call modernity," Man as the Overrepresentation of the Human, and Civilization as a genocidal project of White Being that forces life to be lived in atmospheres of violence.[3] Turner's *The Slave Ship*, when read as a sign of modernity emerging in the figuration of the excessive present, appears to mark the Middle Passage not as a historical event but as an ongoing disaster that does not so much pass as it does accumulate, to borrow Ian Baucom's language: "time does not pass or progress, it accumulates."[4] Rankine's *Citizen*, then, does not "end" with an event of rupture when the painting appears so much as its poetics of accumulation reveal themselves in a different form.

This chapter traces a poetics of accumulation in *Citizen* as well as in Suzan-Lori Parks's 1986 play *Imperceptible Mutabilities in the Third Kingdom* for the ways that such a formal strategy can rupture the framing device of *the event* for which the law can account. I argue that through complex and layered modes of address, as well as repetition and revision, the poetics of accumulation offered by Rankine and Parks rupture a specifically juridical conception of *the event* into a model of ongoing catastrophe that can be addressed only through the extrajudicial ethics of abolitionist world-building. A poetics of accumulation that indexes an excessive present, then, distinctly models the abolitionist ethic of *building as we tear down.*

DISPOSABILITY:
RANKINE, TURNER, AND THE *ZONG* MASSACRE

Citizen: An American Lyric utilizes poetic catalog, repetition and revision, and the conventions and history of lyric poetry to mark an "ongoing present of subjection and resistance."[5] Throughout the text, writes Anthony Reed, "racist microaggressions accumulate . . . as a kind of somatic archive . . . that makes it difficult to mark the beginning and end of events."[6] This accumulation incorporates not only moments of quotidian harm that might get called microaggressions but also moments of more spectacular violence, such as murder, assault, and state violence. Rankine's poetry, then, is thinking with and against the law. *Citizen* manipulates the lyric "I" in conjunction with a hailing "you" through repetition and revision across scenes of racist violence ranging from the linguistic to the bodily. As this manipulation occurs, I argue, time itself accumulates, but not merely teleologically in a linear path from lack to abundance. Instead, Rankine's poetics of accumulation gather in multiple temporal directions. As she writes, "a similar accumulation and release drove many Americans to respond to the Rodney King beating. Before it happened, it had happened and happened."[7] That is, in *Citizen*, what seem like ruptures in the time line are accumulated repetitions. These poetics mark the "time of slavery" as an ongoing reality in which "then and now coexist," but one in which "a utopian kernel and an anticipatory illumination" cannot be completely extinguished by the World inaugurated by the Middle Passage.[8] The resulting excessive present dis-orders the order imposed by law's conceptualization of the juridical event—that moment of violation for which law's own structures can account using its technologies of violence.

On its front cover, *Citizen* begins its temporal shuffling with a photograph of David Hammons's 1993 sculptural work *In the Hood*. Hammons's sculpture is a green hoodie torn (or cut?) at the bottom, severed from the rest of the article of clothing it implies, and given shape by wire so that even though there is no body wearing it, it holds shape as if there is. When its photograph is reproduced on *Citizen*'s cover, the green hoodie appears gray and can be

identified as Hammons's work only in small paratext on the back
cover of the book, leaving the observer or reader uninformed of
the image's origin unless they turn the book over.[9] This obfuscated
citation of Hammons's *In the Hood* begins the work of accumulation. Many critics and reviewers have observed that the cover
immediately invokes, through the figure of the hoodie as mimetic
symbol made ubiquitous by the Movement for Black Lives, Trayvon Martin and his murder by self-appointed vigilante George
Zimmerman in 2012. By an accident of the time line, 2012 is also
the year that Rodney King, whose vicious beating in 1991, two years
before Hammons's sculpture's appearance in a gallery, by members of the Los Angeles Police Department, recorded on video by
George Holliday, and to whom Rankine herself refers when writing about a conversation between a Black American writer and a
white British writer about the police murder of Mark Duggan in
London, died.

My use of clumsy, noun-filled, interruptive parenthetical
clauses in that last sentence is an intentional attempt to get at
the poetics of accumulation that begin to stir before language begins to work its magic in the written poetry of *Citizen*. When we
encounter the hoodie's image in 2014 (or whenever we read *Citizen*), we are brought back to 2012 when we think of Martin's death
(or 2013? the year of Zimmerman's acquittal, largely credited as a
moment of so-called origin of what gets periodized as the Black
Lives Matter movement). And 2012 folds Martin's death, by a coincidence of the calendar, with King's death, an event that brings
us back to 1991 (or 1992? the year of the LA Rebellion, or LA Riots,
depending on who you ask, in response to the acquittal of the officers who beat King). And that date is so close but still off the mark
of the sculpture's time stamp of 1993 (or 2013? the year when it ap-
peared in an exhibit at the New Museum of Contemporary Art and
the year of Zimmerman's acquittal—another coincidence).

Rather than asserting the "correct" time stamp of the cover
image, my reading practice in this chapter follows an impulse to
notice the gathering and refuse the imperative to choose a single
moment in which to contain the site of the gathering. This refusal
of choosing a single time stamp for a floating signifier is related to

another fundamental part of my practice throughout this book: I am always reading both with and against the grain of authorial intention. This may seem like an old-fashioned or obvious point to make, but there will be moments in *Abolition Time* when I make a claim about a text's possible meanings or provocations that seems to depart from what we (think we) know about the politics or even vocabularies of the author. Such claims are not purely innocent but rather do come with the risk of allowing my own political desires to overdetermine my readings (as much as I insist that my reading is *of the text* and *not* of the author, how can I be sure part of me is not reaching further than evidence allows?). I make this comment now, early in the first chapter, in the body of a paragraph rather than in a note, to begin a thread that will continue throughout *Abolition Time*: aligning with the deconstruction-like impulse of abolitionist practice to defer notions of arrival in order to remain in perpetual, collective self-interrogation, an abolitionist reading practice continuously questions its own methodology's effectiveness, shortcomings, and risks.

In this chapter, an abolitionist reading practice attuned to accumulation looks at the hoodie on *Citizen's* cover as an insight into how, in Sharpe's words, "the means and modes of Black subjection may have changed, but the fact and structure of that subjection remain."[10] The sweatshirt hoodie, decontextualized, also appears as the KKK hood, or as the executioner's hood, and its suspension by wire recalls the white supremacist violence of lynching, with the body removed in a way that opens up that memory to both its particular anti-Black history and its historical use against non-Black people of color (including Indigenous peoples, Mexicans, and Chinese immigrants), especially in the American West. By way of accumulation, excessive iterations of racist violence gather onto the cover of the book in the form of a singular figure, inaugurating the troubling poetic utterances to come as the subject position of the "I" so important to the tradition of lyric poetry is thrown into relief by Rankine's accumulating subjects/objects of speech. If the speaker of the *American Lyric* is situated on the cover in the form of an empty hood (is the book's title a caption to the appropriated image of Hammons's artwork in how it is positioned under the hood?), perhaps it is no-body who utters such a lyric. Or is it all of the accumulated subjects and objects of extra/legal violence that such a symbol gathers as a citation of America? Either way, before even invoking the lyrical "I" in linguistic form, the cover image destabilizes its singularity through a visual poetics of accumulation.

Before it happened, it had happened and happened. What is the *it* in that formulation? Is it the beating of King? Or is it the "accumulation and release"? Or is it the response(s) to King's beating? Or the acquittal of those who beat him? What happened? When? These questions, set in motion by and gathered back to the book's cover, model questions that run through all of *Citizen's* poetry. In many of the scenes painted by the prose poems, these kinds of questions are directly asked, and in many, they play out in literal ways.

For example, section II of the book focuses on tennis great Serena Williams as both embodiment of athletic excellence and constant target of misogynoir. Rankine traces an infamous history of Williams getting the wrong end of bad referee calls throughout her career and recalls a moment when Williams snapped at a particularly egregious call:

> She says in 2009, belatedly, the words that should have been said to the umpire in 2004, the words that might have snapped Alves back into focus, a focus that would have acknowledged what was actually happening on the court. Now Serena's action is read as insane.[11]

In this moment, Rankine's poem literalizes "accumulation and release" by repeating and revising an account of a scene that appears five pages earlier:

> And insane is what you think . . . watching the 2009 Women's US Open final, when brought to full attention by the suddenly explosive behavior of Serena Williams. . . . Serena's behavior, on this particular Sunday afternoon, suggests that all the injustice she has played through all the years of her illustrious career flashes before her and she decides finally to respond to all of it with a string of invectives. . . . Oh my God, she's gone crazy, you say to no one.[12]

In the passage of time it takes a reader to travel through five pages of poetry, the 2009 moment gathers the 2004 moment as well as a 2001 moment to it. So upon reencounter, the repeated scene emphasizes not the excess of Williams's actions but the excessiveness of the racism that has made that single moment not only about the single moment. After all, before it happened, it had happened and happened. (The bad call? Serena's reaction? The racist commentary? Yes.)

This shift in emphasis is tracked by the repetition and revision of how the word *insane* is used. In the first use, the speaker of the poem, who is invoked via a second person *you* "that thrusts every reader into the position of speaker and addressee simultaneously,"[13] views Williams as "insane" and "crazy." At this earlier moment, it is possible (though not guaranteed, and neither invited nor forestalled) that the reader slips into identification with the speaker and glides by this judgment of Williams. In this earlier moment, then, the words on the page focalize on Williams as "crazy" in her behavior. But five pages later, after accumulating multiple moments of injustice, instead of the speaker hailing the reader to label Williams as "insane," the ableist word appears in the subject-secreting passive voice: "Now Serena's action *is read as* insane."[14] As the subject doing the "reading" disappears and the reader of the poem is left with an accumulation of injustice, the word *insane* is revealed as a tool of what Liat Ben-Moshe calls "racial criminal pathologization," a logic by which Williams can be policed as the source of (potential) harm.[15] The accumulation of narrative, in the form of naming more moments in time between the two iterations of the scene, and the accumulation of language, in the form of repeated words with revised syntax, work together to conjure an excessive present in which the carceral logic of the law's imposition of order (fine somebody for acting "insane") is revealed as contingent upon the erasure of time's accumulation. That is, Williams can only *be read as* "insane," if she can at all, when her actions are isolated as an *event* with a discernable beginning and ending to which the law can respond. But Rankine's poetics explode impositions of boundaries around singular events.

In fact, in between these two iterations of the 2009 scene with Serena Williams is where the reader of *Citizen* actually first encounters J. M. W. Turner's *The Slave Ship* (the full title of which is *Slavers Throwing Overboard the Dead and Dying, Typhoon Coming On*) well before the image of it appears at the end of the book:

> For years you attribute to Serena Williams a kind of resilience appropriate only for those who exist in celluloid. Neither her father nor her mother nor her sister nor Jehovah her God nor NIKE camp could shield her ultimately from people who felt her black body didn't belong on their court, in their world. From the start many made it clear Serena would have done better struggling to survive in the two-dimensionality of a Millet painting, rather than on their tennis court—better to put all that strength to work in their fantasy of her working the land, rather than be caught up in the turbulence of our ancient dramas, like a ship fighting a storm in a Turner seascape.[16]

Perhaps Turner's painting, on page 160, appears as it should have on page 27 in the book, similar to how Williams says in 2009 the words she should have said in 2004. In this passage, Rankine uses the second person *you* to bring together readers with "people who felt [Williams's] black body didn't belong on their court," who would prefer to relegate Williams to a nineteenth-century French painting of a peasant farming scene that could remain removed from the "ancient dramas" continuing to cause turbulence as the wake of Turner's nineteenth-century *The Slave Ship* in the twenty-first century. This passage thus conjures an excessive present in which the "now" of Serena Williams playing tennis contains within it the storm of a Turner seascape, itself a complex layering of accumulated time.

Turner painted *The Slave Ship* after reading the 1839 reprint edition of Thomas Clarkson's 1808 book *The History of the Rise, Progress, and the Accomplishment of the Abolition of the Slave Trade.* Among the overwhelming accounts of the path toward abolition in British law, Clarkson's book includes reflection on the infamous 1783 British court case *Gregson v. Gilbert.* The case adjudicated a battle of insurance claims by white shipowners and underwriters waged over the 1781 *Zong* Massacre, in which an order was given (by whom, exactly, was disputed throughout the case) to throw 132 enslaved Africans overboard, for which the shipowners expected to be reimbursed via their insurance policy for lost cargo.[17] Although the *Zong* Massacre is the most famous, it was not the only case of slave ship crews throwing enslaved people overboard during the transatlantic voyage on the genocidal foundation of Western modernity archived as the Middle Passage. As Sharpe writes, "Turner's unnamed slave ship stands in for the entire enterprise."[18] In the excessive present, in which Turner's ship can represent a single real vessel as well as the entire enterprise of the genocidal kidnapping euphemistically called the transatlantic slave trade, the eruption of Turner's painting at the end of *Citizen* is prefigured by the presence of the "ghosts" of the Middle Passage lurking in the text's accounts of racism, even when slavery is not named. When we watch Serena Williams playing tennis against the backdrop of a Turner seascape, we might wonder, again with Sharpe, "how does one account for surviving the ship when the ship and the un/survival repeat?"[19]

I want to be clear in my citation of Sharpe's question: I am not, and I do not believe Rankine's invocations are, asserting easy equivalence at the level of lived experience between traveling as legal cargo in a slave ship across the Atlantic Ocean and being subjected to (witness) a massacre, on one hand, and being officiated unfairly while playing tennis because of racism, on the other. My invocation of the excessive present as a folding together of disparate historical moments, and thus of different iterations of racist violence, is neither an exercise in flattening ("X is *the same as* Y") nor thin analogy ("X is *just like* Y"). As Hartman writes in *Scenes of Subjection*, "it is not my intention to argue that the differences between slavery and freedom were negligible; certainly such an assertion would be ridiculous."[20] Instead, I understand the anti-Black racism aimed at Williams as *qualitatively* different from the murderous violence of the *Zong* Massacre, but *structurally* the same.

In the passage that textually invokes Turner's *The Slave Ship*, Rankine also invokes Jean-François Millet, famous for realist

representations of rural peasant farming, in an attempt to contain
Williams's Black body in a scene of unprofitable farmwork—to
render her, through an imaginative pathway divorced from the Atlantic Ocean, as nothing more than slave *labor*. But Turner's ship
shifts the history of slavery as it is imposed onto the Black body
from an emphasis on *labor* vis-à-vis farming (it should go without saying that agricultural labor was not the only kind of labor
to which enslaved people were put) to the *fungibility* and *commodification* that come through the thingification that makes *chattel*
slavery—the kind inherent in the Middle Passage—distinct from
wage slavery; as Jared Sexton puts it, "it is not *labor* relations, but
property relations that are constitutive of slavery."[21] The shift from
images of (white) poor agricultural laborers in a Millet painting to the image of a massacre of enslaved (Black) people *at sea*
in a Turner painting performs this distinction particularly well
because, as Stephanie Smallwood argues, "the business of the
Atlantic market in Africa, in other words, was production not of
bonded laborers but of human commodities."[22] The "rough demo-
graphic specifications" were exactly what was being calculated
by formulas of slave insurance being considered in the "violent
arithmetics of the archive" visible in *Gregson v. Gilbert*, a direct in-
spiration of *The Slave Ship*.[23]

There is no doubt that the unpaid labor of the enslaved was a
necessary condition for the development of modern capitalism
and an inextricable condition for the expansion of the Industrial
Revolution's augmented capital accumulation and resource extraction that lead directly to contemporary conditions of climate
catastrophe that render global warming as a literal, not meta-
phorical, iteration of the ongoing disaster of slavery and colonial
conquest.[24] And yet, labor is still an insufficient framework for understanding slavery.

Rankine's book, intentionally or not, articulates this in its demand for readers to think the Middle Passage, rather than the
scene of the laboring body, as paradigmatic of the history of slavery. This makes the racist figures (and by way of the lyric *you*,
perhaps the reader) in Rankine's poem uncomfortable, because
if Williams's physical strength could be imaginatively projected

into a painting of poor white agricultural labor, then she remains a body that can be corrected, moved from one improper place (the tennis court) to a proper one (a site of labor). This puts a damper on the political demand that white power structures might read as threat, because the laborer transgressing into an improper place is simply demanding *access* or recognition, whereas the thingified chattel demands the implosion of the entire structure. Rankine's shift from a Millett painting of an agricultural scene to a Turner painting of a massacre at sea inaugurates the possibility of reading *Citizen* as doing something more radical than demanding the inclusion of Black people in the category of American or re-forming the logic of citizenship.[25]

This shift from Millett to Turner, from agricultural labor to oceanic massacre as paradigms for understanding slavery itself, has particular resonance in contemporary abolitionist thought and debate. There is contention among prison abolitionists about the appropriate way to articulate the relationship between chattel slavery and the prison–industrial complex (PIC). On one hand, scholars such as Joy James and Dennis Childs posit the carceral formation of the prison as a direct afterlife of slavery. Then, on the other, scholars like Ruth Wilson Gilmore and Jennifer James caution against moving too quickly to draw a clean continuity from slavery to prisons.[26] As I read these debates in scholarship and hear them manifest in activist and organizing conversations when the phrase "modern-day slavery" comes up, I ultimately think that the divergent framings of the question of continuity pivot on which attributes of *slavery* are emphasized as defining characteristics.

Incarcerated organizer Stevie Wilson has worked on gathering data on prison labor and insists that most incarcerated people in the United States do not perform labor while in prison. So it is not true that the PIC is primarily a mechanism of extracting *labor* in the way that chattel slavery is.[27] As an organizing strategy, it is tremendously important, if we are to organize around the conditions on the ground rather than our abstractions of them, to move away from "prison slavery" as *the* evil of the PIC. Without disputing that, what I am arguing is that the continuity between slavery and the PIC is to be found elsewhere, not in labor.

I am discussing this debate that occurs both within and well beyond the academy over the question of prison labor and slavery-PIC continuity here in this chapter because I believe that a reading of *Citizen* attendant to Rankine's invocations of seascapes and oceans as indexes of the Middle Passage helps us understand the nature of chattel slavery as residing in the thingification and disposability of the enslaved, rather than in the extraction of their labor. An understanding of slavery that emphasizes these characteristics is able to more rigorously account for the complex continuity between slavery and the PIC. Incarcerated people may not labor *in the same way* as the enslaved, even as the Thirteenth Amendment retains its infamous exception clause, but incarcerated people do become, as Angela Davis puts it, the "detritus of contemporary capitalism."[28] It is in the process of being produced as excess, as waste, and ultimately as disposable population that the incarcerated are positioned as continuous with the enslaved. It is *disposability*, and not labor extraction, that is the strongest thread of connection between slavery and the PIC. *Citizen*, then, even without ever explicitly mentioning prison abolition, in its invocation of the history of slavery and its afterlives, is a text that resonates with contemporary abolitionist thought, whether Rankine intends so or not.

REFERENTIAL FLUIDITY:
RANKINE'S ACCUMULATING ATLANTIC

If it seems I am making much out of a couple of references to a singular famous painting in my analysis of *Citizen*, this is because I believe that the poem's recurring references to oceans, as recurring iterations of accumulated histories of the Middle Passage, work in conjunction with the much more frequently analyzed poetics of Rankine's lyric pronouns to set in motion some of *Citizen's* most radical, abolitionist theorization.

I am guided in my focus on the oceanic in *Citizen* by Rinaldo Walcott—both his insistence in *The Long Emancipation* that the "Middle Passage cannot be pluralized; its uniqueness as the ongoing project of coloniality demands otherwise" and his ongoing work on the "black aquatic."[29] In a so-far unpublished paper,

Walcott writes, "Tides and waves both bring in and take out elements from the shore to the sea but importantly tides and waves leave elements behind as well resulting in new and different formations."[30] His work helps me differentiate the poetics of accumulation in *Citizen* from the logic of capitalist accumulation. Unlike a movement toward (profit as) abundance (which we might call theft), the accumulation happening across Rankine's poetry is akin to the "new and different formations" brought by the accumulating motion of tides onshore. Iterations of words, phrases, and images mingle with each other to produce not merely lists of possible readings for particular words, lines, or poems but dynamic fields of possibility that are more than the additive sums of their parts. It is with this model of tidalectical accumulation that I look to textual iterations of the sea.

There is of course the poem in section v of *Citizen* that directly borrows the phrase "the Atlantic Ocean breaking on our heads" from Robert Lowell's *Life Studies*.

> Listen, you, I was creating a life study of a monumental
> first person, a Brahmin first person.
>
> If you need to feel that way—still you are in here and here
> is nowhere.
>
> Join me down here in nowhere.
>
> Don't lean against the wallpaper; sit down and pull together.
>
> Yours is a strange dream, a strange reverie.
>
> No, it's a strange beach; each body is a strange beach
> and if you let in the excess emotion you will recall the
> Atlantic Ocean breaking on our heads.[31]

Citizen's shifting and accumulating first and second person pronouns invite multiplicity here. One exercise is to read the pronouns as shifting among referents throughout a single poem. So we could hear this passage as beginning by ventriloquizing Lowell as a lyricist concerned with "a monumental first person" who is impatient with his interlocuter—*Listen, you*—who is perhaps Rankine. Or perhaps the reader. Perhaps a layered *you* of (an) earlier speaker(s) in *Citizen* combined with the reader. The following lines can be read as a Lowell-figure continuing his impatience with his interlocutor's feelings, and perhaps "you are here and here is nowhere" is a put-down of his interlocuter. Or perhaps the *you* shifts, and "If you need to feel that way" is the interlocuter's response to the Lowell-figure, where Lowell becomes the *you*. We can continue returning to these lines and changing the point at which the "dialogue" they may be staging shifts between speakers, and ultimately what I think we see is a *you* that shifts among a (racist, white) Lowell-figure and a *you* that has existed and shifted embodiment throughout *Citizen* in ways that include incorporating the reader. Swimming in oceanic imagery, we might call this referential fluidity.

An abolitionist reading of a poetics of accumulation traffics in the open, speculative realm of *perhaps* as possible readings form into a field of possibility. So here, when the poem reaches the stanza of the Atlantic Ocean, Claudia Rankine, Robert Lowell, their poeticized lyrical speakers in their respective works invoked via Rankine's use of allusion, the *you* who identifies with Serena Williams's anger and the *you* who is asked to identify with the racist people who desire that Williams's body disappear from "their court," are all part of the *our* over whose heads the Atlantic Ocean breaks. And here, the Atlantic Ocean appears as a repetition of the sea in Turner's seascape, itself an image of the Atlantic Ocean as geography of the Middle Passage's murderous logics, the sea doubling as a graveyard, reappearing as the Atlantic Ocean *breaking* upon the heads of all of those possible subjects enveloped by the poem's *our*.

Kamran Javadizadeh reads this moment as Rankine's "historical" refutation and revision of Lowell's "figurative" Atlantic Ocean with her own. For him, "Rankine's evocation of 'the Atlantic Ocean breaking on our heads' asks us to imagine not the impersonalizing (and yet singular) wash of Lowell's poem but instead the particular (and plural) injuries of the Atlantic slave trade."[32]

I find Javadizadeh's reading insightful, but limiting in its oppositional structure between Lowell's Atlantic and Rankine's Atlantic,
which I believe comes out of an understanding of whiteness as essentially definable by *privilege* rather than by *violence*. That is, in
this reading, *Citizen*'s citation of Lowell's "Man and Wife" works
in the tune of a number of interpretations of the book that see
Rankine's *American Lyric* as applying a historical corrective. To
paint with a broad stroke, what we might call "reformist" readings
of *Citizen* posit that the book critiques the legal and social exclu-
sions of American citizenship that mainstream white discourse
erases through its self-mythology. In this reading, *Citizen* provides a corrective through revealing alternative understandings
of the category from its constitutive outside. This often results in
a hopeful gesture that the category of *citizen* can be opened to include those who have been excluded. And then, by this inclusion,
American citizenship can be re-formed into a more just structure
of collectivity that might be called a new *America* whose lyrical "I"
is a democratically open, historically self-conscious subject that
works to redress the injurious past. In this specific poem of *Citizen*,
such a reading allows us to see how different subject positions like
Lowell's whiteness and Rankine's Blackness cohere *differently* via
the Atlantic Ocean.

But I think that if we follow Rankine's poetics of accumulation and see both Lowell and Rankine, and more generally both
purveyors and victims of racism as defined by Gilmore as "the
state-sanctioned or extralegal production and exploitation of
group-differentiated vulnerability to premature death,"[33] as being
subjected to the Atlantic's waves breaking over their/our heads,
we can see whiteness differently. We can see whiteness as cohered
by and indistinguishable from the very violence that produces
it. That is, the Middle Passage, in Rankine's poem's invocation of
Turner's seascape as the latter indexes the *Zong* Massacre as both
singularity and synecdoche, creates whiteness as much as it creates Blackness *as racial positions*. Not only can Lowell speak his *I*
into being because privilege assures him of standing but the Atlantic Ocean he invokes is actually *exactly the same* as the one that
Rankine invokes, even and especially as he does not realize it.

The Atlantic Ocean becomes, in Rankine's poetics of accumulation, not a particular iteration of history of which some are afforded the white privilege of disavowing but what Toni Morrison might call an "Africanist presence" that allows whiteness to cohere its meaning at all.[34] Here emerges an abolitionist understanding of whiteness *as* violence, as inseparable from violence, as only ever defined by violence, and, as violence, as a structure of law itself that requires abolition, not reform. Instead of telling Lowell to check his privilege (and, by proxy, canonical conceptions of American poetry), *Citizen's* poetics of accumulation demand the end of whiteness itself.

Citizen continues to invoke the ocean. There is the situation video script on Hurricane Katrina in which quotations from an archive of 2005 footage are presented with their speakers' identities secreted by pronouns whose antecedents are not to be found in the pages of *Citizen* itself.[35] In this script-poem, the line "we are drowning here" arrests with its reverberations of Turner's seascape as the figures in the painting drown alongside residents of New Orleans whom an unnamed Wolf Blitzer calls "so poor and so Black" to index the Atlantic Ocean as what Baucom calls "this moment of drowning, and drowning, and drowning."[36]

This reencounter with an Atlantic Ocean that accumulates the racist violence of the Middle Passage spectacularized by Turner's painting with the racist violence of the unnatural disaster of Hurricane Katrina gathers to the institution of policing through the specific practice of stop-and-frisk in another situation script. "In a landscape drawn from an ocean bed, you can't drive / yourself sane—so angry you can't drive yourself sane."[37] Here *driving while black* gathers to it the anger read and pathologized as the insanity of Serena Williams. And it is given historical substance by the recognition of the ocean bed—a graveyard holding the memories of the figures in Turner's painting, which stand in for the real lost lives of the enslaved on the *Zong* who index the humans designated as cargo as they were jettisoned from the Human even if they weren't thrown off a ship—as the condition of possibility for the very landscape on which driving happens. The violence of the law in a policy like stop-and-frisk is continuous with the violence of the Middle Passage that gives it coherence (we can think about Walter Benjamin's "founding violence" here).[38] Beyond the juridical logic of *precedent* or *event of injury* for which remedy must be made by the law acting to correct for past violence, an abolitionist reading of *Citizen*'s poetics of accumulation reveals the Middle Passage as ongoing disaster for which the law cannot account without disarticulating itself.

This is the key point at which *Citizen*'s poetics of accumulation truly illuminate as a poetic of justice against the (reformist) grammar of the law. As an instrument for bringing something it calls justice, the law works in two ways, temporally understood as *before* or *after* specific moments of harm or injury. First, as Jacques Derrida explains in "Force of Law: The 'Mystical Foundations of Authority,'" law is defined by its enforceability. This means that law maintains social order through the constant threat of its use of violence.[39] That is, the law strives to cut off moments of injury before they happen through deterrence by way of its ubiquitous and ostensibly monopolistic capacity to use violence on behalf of the state to incapacitate. Or, on the other side of the moment of harm, the law can use its capacity for violence to enact punishment and restitution on the harmer(s) as a *response* to the injury.

In both cases, whether acting before or after the moment of harm, injury is treated as *a juridical event*. As an event, injury is bounded by a temporality with a beginning and an ending that can be known only through discovery and investigation after the event has ceased. The bounded temporality of the juridical event as the *knowable and known moment to which the law responds* is a fundamental organizing thread of legal temporality and the ordering power that I call *law's grammar*. Against this grammar, which places juridical events in their place in order to bring justice for them through the state's instruments of violence (incarceration, fines, restraint, death), the texts I study in *Abolition Time* offer poetics that reconceptualize justice precisely by rupturing the temporal organization of law's ordering capacity, the juridical event.

Here in *Citizen*, Rankine's poetics of accumulation do so in the form of the Atlantic Ocean as the ongoing catastrophe of the Middle Passage which refuses containment in a bounded temporality to which the law can respond. Rankine's poetry expands the the-orization toward which Smallwood works throughout *Saltwater Slavery,* culminating in the "impossibility of narrative closure" in her final analysis of the recorded testimony of an enslaved woman called 'Sibell.[40] Hartman's analysis in *Scenes of Subjection* takes this nonclosure into the nineteenth-century United States and across the temporal divide of the end of the Civil War, which she desig-nates as the "nonevent of emancipation"; Sharpe's theorization in *In the Wake* delineates how "the semiotics of the slave ship con-tinue"; and Walcott's arguments in *The Long Emancipation* further extend Smallwood's nonclosure to the twenty-first century as it continues her insistence on the Atlantic as a framework for a di-aspora that exceeds nouns which refer to land.[41] Within *Citizen's* poetics, the insistence on the Middle Passage, rather than labor, as the framing image of slavery as an ongoing catastrophe that ex-ceeds the bounded temporality of the juridical event pushes one step further through the accumulation of first and second person pronouns eventually to shatter the self that an "American Lyric" might call *America.*

SHATTERING (SINGULARITY:) *CITIZEN'S* LYRIC SPEAKER AGAINST TURNER'S SEASCAPE

In an often-quoted poem in *Citizen,* Rankine writes, "However, sometimes your historical selves, her white self *and* your black self, *or* your white self *and* her black self, arrive with the full force of your American positioning."[42] It is Rankine's layering of *and* and *or* here that coalesces into what I keep calling accumulation and that sets in motion my reading practice of lingering in the potential of the *perhaps.* It is also in these lines, when read as accu-mulating to the phrase *historical selves* the resonance of Rankine's Atlantic Ocean, where the poem's accumulations push the *Lyric* of *Citizen's* subtitle against the *American* found there, rupturing the latter as *America* is displaced to *Atlantic* and *citizenship* is displaced to the massacre of Turner's seascape.

Against the backdrop of a Turner seascape, we see how, as Evie Shockley argues, "with her 'lyric-You,' [Rankine] achieves a full-throated polyvocality . . . that thrusts every reader into the

position of speaker and addressee simultaneously."[43] Across a series of poems documenting racism against Black subjects/objects,
readers are asked to identify both with the speaker and with the
addressee, dislodging the separation between discrete selves that
could be positioned on opposite ends of an adversarial judicial
process. Sharing this point with Shockley, I sharply depart from
a reading like Nikki Skillman's, in which there exists "an inexora-
ble boundary between readers who have been subjected to racial
dehumanizations and who therefore recognize their own experiences reflected in the anecdotes and those who have not."[44] Rather
than absolute boundaries, Rankine's poetics of accumulation
gather subject positions across boundaries; both white people and
Black people are present on board Turner's slave ship, on board the
Zong, are part of the nonevent of massacre as the ongoing disaster
of modernity, even and especially as race overdetermines the role
each enacts.

The centrality of the Middle Passage as a/the historical process that solidified Blackness into a racial position, and not just a
phenotypical marker of geographic or visual difference, has been
thoroughly addressed in scholarship on the historical, social, and
legal constructions of race.[45] But what *Citizen* does, in my reading
of this moment of historical selves confronting each other with
the full force of their American positioning framed by Turner's
seascape, is reveal that whiteness, too, is historically solidified as
a racial position through the violence of the Middle Passage. So
when readers encounter the racist image of white tennis player
Caroline Wozniacki stuffing her uniform in mocking imitation of
Serena Williams's "excessive" figure to the old tunes of blackface
minstrelsy and in citation of the old story of Saartje Baartman, we
are encountering *both* the consolidation of the white subject as
the consolidation of white gender *and* the dissolution of that gendered subject.

The sneer that we can see in Wozniacki's "I'm just joking"
smile in the image with which Rankine concludes the section on
Serena Williams betrays that the innocence that accrues to Wozniacki's white femininity is made possible by the process of what
Sarah Haley calls "carceral gendering." Haley writes, "Carceral

gendering reveals that gendered knowledge is produced not merely through male/female binaries, but also through a complex of material and discursive knowledge projects; normative female gendering was produced through the spectacular cultural and legal production of the black female invert as a relational and trammeled social category."[46] That is, rather than understanding "woman" as a gender produced in binary opposition with "man," Haley's analysis of racialized carceral power reveals "white woman" as a particular, always already racialized gender that consolidates through the violent production of its inversion in the category of the Black woman.

In contrast to Williams, who Tyrone Palmer notes in his reading of *Citizen* and critique of affect theory "is indicative of the ontological ungendering and deindividuation of the Black under modernity . . . [and so] there is no gendered integrity to Serena's affectivity," Wozniacki becomes and remains legible in her white gender so that she can, in Rankine's words, "finally giv[e] the people what they have wanted all along by embodying Serena's attributes while leaving Serena's 'angry . . . exterior' behind."[47] But, *Citizen*'s poetics tell us through the collision of historical selves that may switch places, Wozniacki can never actually leave Williams behind. Her entire performance can only cohere as a "joke" against the backdrop of Turner's seascape, can only have meaning as a sick joke in the context of slavery as historical precedent that refuses to be merely precedent. She appears, in Rankine's text, as an image accumulating the violence of its scenes and the multiple subject positions hailed by its lyric address. She appears as the grotesque image of Dylan Rodríguez's White Being, "the militarized, normative paradigm of human being that inhabitants of the ongoing half-millennial civilizational project have involuntarily inherited as a violent universal."[48] She appears as the embodiment of gender as always already a racial category under settler colonialism and in the afterlife of slavery. That is, Wozniacki's joke hides and reveals the truth that the gender category of "woman" is not simply "problematic" because of historical exclusion of women of color but rather that the category is, in the so-called West, constitutively racialized as white. The joke only makes sense because everybody knows but nobody says out loud (except when they do, such as when they call Williams's physique "manly" or when Black women, both cisgender and transgender, are disproportionately targeted by trans-exclusionary athletics rules) that only white women are women.

The grotesqueness of the image explodes off the page if we follow how the grammar of Wozniacki's joke—Wozniacki disappears the Black body to present her own in mocking triumph—mimics the grammar of the edited lynching photograph in section VI of *Citizen*, at the end of "In Memory of Trayvon Martin."[49] In the latter photo, the body of a lynching victim is removed, leaving only the white people gathered for the occasion. These people are not wearing hoods to hide their identities. Many are looking at the camera, one person extending a hand to point at the body. With the removal of the murdered human being, the white person's pointing finger registers the absent presence that gives the whiteness of the crowd meaning as whiteness—not simply privilege but Black death. Though white people and all non-Black people bear a starkly different relationship to the ship, its hold, and the Middle Passage as the very difference imposed by racialization, it remains the case that all subject positions that emerge within Western modernity as it imposes the hegemony of its World on the worlds of the globe are formed in the wake of slavery's ongoing catastrophe. In short, white people, too, live in the wake, precisely because whiteness and the legibility of white gender depend on the deadly machinations of anti-Blackness for their coherence. *Citizen*'s radical act is not in imposing absolute boundaries between subject positions but in demonstrating the falsity of such boundaries.

This is certainly not to say that *Citizen* implies that there is no difference between white subjects and Black subjects under the ongoing regime of race; rather, through the Middle Passage, subjectivity is both forged and perforated for more than just Black subjects.[50] The lyric *I* and *you* throughout the text, as they accumulate both white and Black historical selves, sometimes shift mid-stanza, and this shifting can spill across individual scene-poems such that the lyric speaker remains constantly unable to cohere into individuality or stability. One scene goes as follows:

The man at the cash register wants to know if you think your card will work. . . . [Your friend] says nothing. You want her to say something—both as witness and as a friend. She is not you; her silence says so. Because you are watching all this take place even as you participate in it, you say nothing as well. . . . What is wrong with you? This question gets stuck in your dreams.[51]

Who is the target of that last interrogative *you*? Is it uttered by the lyric speaker *you* who wonders what their friend was thinking in keeping silent? Is it an indictment of the friend? Or is it an internalized question, the speaker asking themselves the question of why they did not speak on their own behalf, or why they keep this person as a friend, or what they did to deserve to be treated the way they were by the racist store clerk? I think we can answer yes, as we see the multidirectionality of accumulation gather this moment to an earlier scene when a woman calls the lyric speaker *you* by the name of the only other Black woman in their workplace. At the end of that scene of misrecognition, the poem asks, "What did you say?"[52] Who is being asked that? Is it the *I can't believe you just said that* question that recurs throughout the text? Is it the question that the speaker in the cash register scene wants to pose at her friend as she fails the ethical task of witnessing and intervening? Is it a question for the reader as a (failed) witness? Again, I think we can answer this list with yes. Against the backdrop of a Turner seascape, the field of ethics implied by questions of witnessing and intervention cannot be mapped across an adversarial investigation of a singular juridical event. The splitting open of subjectivity engendered by Rankine's multiplying lyrical pronouns opens ethical ground beyond the juridical. A poetics of accumulation, as a poetics of justice, disarticulates one of the most fundamental grammars of law: individuation.

Picture a courtroom. In front of the judge sit two teams of lawyers, each with a client. On one side, the prosecution. On the other, the defense. So long as the judge can differentiate between the two sides, they are capable of issuing justice in this adversarial system. Metaphysically, then, in this model, justice depends on the differentiation and the individuation of the accuser and the accused.

Without these two separate sides, the judge cannot do their duty. What I am saying is that *Citizen* turns both the accuser and the accused—and even the witnesses being called to the stand—into a chaotically excessive singular pronoun: *you*. The poetics of justice deployed in that small, simple pronoun's gathering together of the accuser and the accused prevents the individuation that the judge needs to be able to make sense of whatever case is being decided, because the law's grammar is ultimately governed by a principle of individuation. *Citizen's* poetics of justice wash away the boundaries between discrete subjects in the waters of the Atlantic Ocean in Turner's bloody seascape.

There is one final moment of *Citizen* that I wish to address: the situation script titled "In Memory of James Craig Anderson," specifically when the poem addresses Anderson's murderer, Deryl Dedmon. The script begins with a *you* that retains the ambiguity of *Citizen's* earlier poems. But following an expanse of white space on the page and the personification of the pickup truck that Dedmon used to run over Anderson, the *you* specifies an addressee: "Do you recognize yourself, Dedmon?"[53] As I have argued, Rankine demonstrates through a poetics of accumulation how whiteness itself is inseparable from the "ongoing history of the destruction of black life,"[54] and I suggest here that one of the effects of that poetics in this particular poem is that the reader is asked—demanded—to identify with Dedmon, a white man who pled guilty to a federal hate crime charge for killing Anderson.

This insistence of identification happens because the force of Rankine's *you* has throughout the book tugged the reader into its scenes. But unlike most of the other poems, here the reader encounters a proper noun. Isolated, this encounter could merely reinforce the logic of the kind of hate crime legislation under which Dedmon was prosecuted: that it is the exceptional individual doing an exceptional act of monstrous evil who commits an action that we call a *hate crime*. Such an individual can be separated from our realm of the social as an aberration, their act framed as an exceptional juridical event to be remedied by the law.[55] That is, the logic of *hate crime* is a juridical grammar of individuation, exceptionalism, and containment. It is therefore a logic that rehabilitates dominant social structures by way of expelling the pathologized individual, because, as Eric A. Stanley writes, "if we end at singularity, we, too, have ensured there will be yet another beating tape by refusing to eradicate the conditions of its reproduction."[56] Hate crime legislation secretes the conditions of violence's reproduction by displacing them onto an exceptional individual. *You, reader, are not Dedmon, law's grammar of individuation assures. Dedmon is an exception, we can get rid of him, and the rest of us will be secure.*

I want to be absolutely clear here that my reading of oceans has led to hate crime legislation both because Rankine herself draws these parallels through invoking Anderson's literal hate crime and because *Citizen's* poetics of justice, as demonstrated, particularly displace law's grammars of individuation. And the pinnacle of such grammar is found in the logic of hate crime legislation, which depends on the figure of the exceptional individual. While often thought of as politically progressive because it presumes to "protect" minoritized categories of people, the logic of hate crime legislation so thoroughly exceptionalizes targeted violence that it reifies a false image of the status quo as not itself fundamentally unevenly violent. That is, if the law were to recognize that the *order* that it was preserving was a status quo of distributing violence unevenly through the matrix of racial capitalism, settler colonialism, and cisheteropatriarchy, then the act of committing violence against a marginalized person could not be framed as anything other than what is already always happening.

But in this moment in the text, *Citizen's* poetics of accumulation explode individuation and exceptionalism. *Citizen* refuses the possibility of containing the pathologically hateful murderer at a distance. *Citizen* reveals that Dedmon's act of murder is visible in Turner's seascape. It reveals that the whiteness that Dedmon secured through murdering Anderson cannot escape the violence of the Middle Passage that gave and gives it coherence. In the excessive present of Rankine's *Citizen*, of Turner's *The Slave Ship*, of the *Zong* Massacre, of the ongoing disaster of modernity, justice cannot come as a response to a singular moment of injury, cannot be an accounting for a singular juridical event, because the catastrophe is ongoing.

Thus, though the interpersonal intimacy of the poems in *Citizen* may, on one hand, invite readers to ask questions about repair or recovery at the scale of the damaged, wounded, mutually dependent, or morally responsible self, on the other hand, the poetics of accumulation across its invocations of first and second person pronouns snatch that invitation mid-delivery. The law, as the ordering force that responds to an injustice like Anderson's murder *after the moment of harm* in an attempt to repair or redress that harm by imposing violence on the singular subjects who committed it, is powerless in the face of subjectivity shattered by time's refusal to periodize. The judge has no power in a courtroom without two discrete sides. Hate crime legislation is rendered nonsensical by a text that traffics so powerfully in the affective force and language that feeds the very logic of hate crime legislation in the first place. That is, in presenting individual scenes of racism with a lyrical *you* that invites the reader's affective engagement, *Citizen* sets in motion the sentimental logic of exceptional tragedy. But through the force of repetition and revision, these individual scenes gather together into an ongoing, transhistorical structure—an excessive present. And this gathering is *Citizen's* radical refusal of the grammar of law and the poetry's opening toward other ethical horizons, for as Mumia Abu-Jamal writes, "attention to the episodic elicits tears, while contemplation on the systemic brings the challenge of change."[57] Accumulation refers both to buildup and to rupture in this way. All of the affective force of *Citizen* can in one instance lead directly to the individuating logic of "hate crime" as a framework for protecting victims of gendered-racist violence but, in the very same instance, can rupture that framework.

Here we see that abolitionist close reading commits without reservation to the importance of formalism and aesthetics while also remaining open to reading against the grain of the text at hand, recognizing that symptomatic reading may shift into counterreadings toward possibilities opened by the text working against itself and the very assumptions it may invoke via its genre and shape. When it comes to *Citizen,* this means staying with the text's commitment to reconfiguring the lyric as an investigation and reformulation of the speaking subject with a discernable interiority not only as a porous subject but as a nonsubject. If the presence of *The Slave Ship* recalls a history of forging individuated identity necessary for conceptualizing private property as the ground zero of chattel slavery and colonization's genocidal violence against the no-bodies jettisoned from the Human, and of individuation as the original logic of whiteness and of incarceration, then *Citizen* both inscribes in itself the ongoing disaster of that history as the struggle with the legacy of the lyric "I" *and,* against itself, flashes inward toward a horizon of antisubjecthood in which carcerality, without an "I" or a "you" to contain, is unthinkable.

On the terrain of the unthinkable subject, an extrajudicial notion of justice emerges. Employing similar poetics of accumulation to Rankine, Suzan-Lori Parks stages meditations on slavery and the Middle Passage as ethical crises that exceed the framework of the juridical event and remain, instead, as ongoing disasters in which abolitionist thought emerges alongside the emergency of genocidal violence.

THE NONEVENT OF EMANCIPATION AND THE CARCERAL AFTERLIFE OF THE MIDDLE PASSAGE

In its final turn, this opening chapter of *Abolition Time* makes one more push against the juridical event by way of the ongoing catastrophe of the Middle Passage as indexed by a poetics of accumulation, though this time in drama rather than poetry: Suzan-Lori Parks's 1986 play *Imperceptible Mutabilities in the Third Kingdom.* The structure of Parks's play reveals the Middle Passage as what Dennis Childs calls a "carceral model" that persists beyond Hartman's "nonevent of emancipation."[58] And the poetics of accumulation achieved by the dialogue's "rep & rev" reveals abolition as an unruly energy that, too, persists in the excessive present that cannot be periodized by the grammar of juridical events—be they events of injury, such as the Middle Passage, or events of redress, such as emancipation.

Imperceptible Mutabilities takes on the disaster of the Middle Passage as part of Parks's project to "creat[e] history where it is and always was but has not yet been divined," as she puts it.[59] The play is broken up into five pieces we might view as vignettes—four "parts" and a "reprise." Part II, "Third Kingdom," and "Third Kingdom: Reprise," which occurs between parts III and IV, take place on a slave ship on the Atlantic Ocean. In these vignettes, four enslaved figures discuss their displacement in both material and psychological terms as an authority figure threatens to "jettison" them from his ship before the whole boat sinks at the end of the reprise. (I hope that readers will hear my own repetition of *jettison* in this chapter as my invocation of the lines in *Imperceptible Mutabilities*, accumulating the figure of the Human as well as the drowning figures of Turner's painting and the literal victims of the *Zong* Massacre to the "glass-bottom boat" of the slave trade from which the enslaved are thrown in Parks's play.) Parts I, III, and IV take place at different times both before and after emancipation, but they bear the weight of the Third Kingdom through the play's implementation of what Parks calls "rep & rev." By having words and phrases repeat across scenes that are not set in chronological order, Parks disrupts linear time lines, eschews the separation of the past and the present, and highlights the Middle Passage as paradigmatic disaster while refusing to give the Middle Passage the temporal frame of juridical event.

Imperceptible Mutabilities begins with "Snails," in which Molly, Charlene, and Veronica are living in what could be interpreted as a shared apartment that is infested with cockroaches, one of which is an instrument of surveillance constructed by The Naturalist, who doubles as Dr. Lutzky, the exterminator. Throughout "Snails," characters utter phrases like "should I jump should I jump or what?" and "Eat. Please eat" that are repeated and revised in later parts of the play, most notably in "Third Kingdom" and its reprise. These "later" parts of the play, of course, are *historically* prior to "Snails," and so these phrases in part I both repeat what has come historically before and prefigure what comes narratively after their invocation, gathering and releasing in multiple directions across multiple timelinesscapes.

Because a play is a live performance, as Parks emphasizes in her essays "From Elements of Style" and "An Equation for Black People on Stage," language cannot be separated from its embodiment in the actors delivering the lines. "I am most interested in words and how they impact on actors and directors and how those folks physicalize those verbal aberrations," she writes.[60] Following this, we can see how in *Imperceptible Mutabilities*, by having actors speak the same words while playing different characters in different contexts, language becomes a medium through which time itself exceeds not only the difference between individual characters but also the demarcations of discrete dramatic units, be they scenes or acts or vignettes or parts, as well as discrete historical moments, be they past, present, or future. Each instance of "should I jump should I jump or what?" or each utterance of a form of the word *wave* or *splat* or *kin* is a moment when the actor's body indexes the fictionality of bounded iteration, as multiple characters and multiple times gather to it and pull it to other parts of the play before and after the audience even "gets" to those parts. If the Middle Passage, as represented in "Third Kingdom" and its reprise, can be read as the play's force of coherence, given its titular significance and explicit repetition, it spills into each of the other parts of the play even as those other parts spill into it. Thus, even though there are two units of dramatic time—part II and its reprise—that directly represent the Middle Passage, the Middle Passage refuses containment in these units of time. It exceeds its own framing through the poetics of accumulation achieved by language's embodiment in live performance. *Imperceptible Mutabilities* stages, perhaps as literally as possible, an excessive present in which the past, present, and future fold into a dynamic, undifferentiated *now*.

Audience members or readers, of course, do not know this about the language of the play upon first encounter, but "Snails" does complicate temporality within itself in addition to how it echoes across other parts. In section C of part I, Charlene refers to events that have yet to happen (for the audience, at least) in the past tense, as if they have already happened:

CHARLENE: Once there was uh one named Lutzky. Uh exterminator professional with uh Ph.D. He wore white cause white was what thuh job required. Comes tuh take thuh

roaches uhway. Knew us by names that whuduhnt ours.
Could point us out from pictures that whuduhnt us. He became confused. He hoses us down. You signed thuh invoice
with uh X. Exterminator professional with uh Ph.D. He can
do thuh job for $99.

This is quickly followed up with Charlene's suggestion to call Lutzky, hinting to the audience that the visit is yet to be staged.[61] Sure
enough, Lutzky arrives at the house, becomes confused, and hoses
down Molly, Charlene, and Veronica with his antiroach chemi-
cals. Or, to be very heavy-handed, he shoots them, his squirt gun
exploding the linear foreshadowing temporality of Chekhov's famous gun by going off before it comes on the stage.

Within the first part, then, the language of the play refuses the
linearity of a progressive time line that can order past and present
and future, instead using the past tense to refer to future action.
Playing with different grammar rules than Rankine, who worked
her poetics of accumulation through repetition and revision of
pronouns and concealment of antecedents, Parks interrupts normative grammars of tense while repeating and revising lines across
and within scenes so that the ordering grammar of linear progression that sets in motion the juridical event is disordered. That
is, instead of setting up a situation in which Lutzky first arrives
onstage, draws his gun, and shoots the women, which would be a
standard juridical event with a beginning and an ending that the
law could examine and rectify, Lutzky is onstage and has shot them
before he is physically onstage through his conjuring by Charlene,
if we take seriously Parks's phrase that "words are spells in our
mouths."[62] That is, the violence that Lutzky brings precedes his
presence so that when he does arrive, his arrival is the continuation
of an ongoing violence, what Sharpe's language helps me figure in
direct opposition to a juridical event as, instead, *catastrophe.* The resulting temporality of the play in the wake of this improper use of
tense is thus unstructured by the grammar of what Parks calls the
Standard Time Line and Standard Plot Line and instead can open
itself to the antigrammar of disaster as voices cross between the
no-longer-discrete moments of past and present and future.

This antigrammar of disaster, through its refusal of linearity and, thusly and more importantly, of beginnings and endings, opposes the ordered grammar of the juridical event. It also doubles as an anticolonial antigrammar by way of the juxtaposition of Charlene's antilinear temporality with The Naturalist's rigidly ordered, heavily periodized teleology. In section D, which directly follows Charlene's remixing of past and future tense, The Naturalist takes the podium to deliver a monologue that in Parks's signature irreverent style satirizes "scholarly" and "authoritative" language and those who speak it. He eventually pontificates on the vast separation between "us" and "our subjects":

THE NATURALIST: Having accumulated a wealth of naturally occurring observations knowing now how our subjects occur in their own world (mundus primitivus), the question now arises as to how we of our own world (mundus modernus) best accommodate them. I ask us to remember that it was almost twenty-five whole score ago that our founding father went forth tirelessly crossing a vast expanse of ocean in which there lived dangerous creatures of the most horrible sort tirelessly crossing that sea jungle to find this country and name it. The wilderness was vast and we who came to teach, enlighten, and tame were few in number. They were the vast, we were the few. . . . Information for the modern cannot be gleaned from the primitive.[63]

In this monologue, The Naturalist relegates Molly, Charlene, and Veronica, whom he, as Dr. Lutzky, renames Mona, Chona, and Verona, to primitive time—literally to a separate world from the one in which he and those included in his "we" exist. This severing of the primitive world from the present and future modern world maps an ontology of primitiveness, a stuck-in-time-ness, onto the three other characters. This markedly Hegelian conjuration of people without history is followed up with classic "White Man's Burden"–style rhetoric to establish a colonial epistemology through which the present hierarchical order of power is justified. Insofar as The Naturalist is the gatekeeper of knowledge, and insofar as his double Dr. Lutzky's chemical assault on Mona, Chona, and Verona does not register as a violation punishable by law, The Naturalist/Dr. Lutzky embodies the law against which Parks is writing her play. In the essays "Possession" and "Elements of Style," Parks argues that history is not simply a matter of fact but rather is a result of selective remembering and dismembering, of archiving and erasing, in order to tell what becomes the Standard story along a Standard Time Line. In breaking up the time line in her play, Parks is breaking up the Standard Time Line and intervening in the ordering episteme of Western modernity as it has been structured by slavery and colonization. In staging the excessive present, a temporality that resists the ordering grammar—the rules, the law—of the Standard Time Line, Parks revises the past as present to stage a possible world beyond the reach of the law imposed by the grammar of linear time.

As mentioned, the temporality of *Imperceptible Mutabilities* further exceeds linearity when considering the characters' speech across parts, not only the juxtapositions of speech within part 1. For Parks, the structure of repetition and revision "creates a drama of accumulation."[64] This is because when a reader encounters a sentence or a phrase or a scene again after an initial iteration, that repetition in the text appears to the reader as a signifier that has gathered multiple signified meanings to it, resulting in each latter repetition carrying with it the meanings that previous iterations have already established. Repetition as a literary strategy is thus inseparable from accumulation. Parks asks, "What does it mean for a character to say the same word twice? 3 times? Over and over and over and oh-vah?"[65] And what, *Imperceptible Mutabilities* asks, does it mean for *different* characters to repeat the same words and phrases, twice, or three times, with different emphases and speeds, over and over and over or overandoverandohvah?

In the fourth line of the play, Molly asks, "What should I do Chona should I jump should I jump or what?"[66] At this initial hearing, it is not apparent what Molly could mean in asking if she should jump. The line is quickly bypassed as Charlene asks Molly if she would like eggs before Molly shifts into recounting how she lost her job after being thrown out of a grammar class for being unable to pass the teacher's tests. She is literally expelled (*thrown out* of class) because of a refusal to follow the rules of grammar, which in the play act as a force of law imposing Standard order from which most characters are jettisoned/expelled.

MOLLY: They—expelled—me.

CHARLENE: Straight up?

MOLLY: Straight up. "Talk right or youre outta here!" I couldnt. I walked. Nope. "Speak correctly or you'll be dismissed!" Yeah. Yeah. Nope. Nope. Job sends me there. Basic skills. Now Job don't want me no more. Closely-behind-at-Marys-heels. HHH. Everythin in its place.[67]

On its own, this exchange makes plain the material effects of enforcing standard English and refusing to recognize nonstandard forms of expression or knowledge as Molly loses her job over her inability to pronounce words "correctly" or use standard grammar. Insofar as grammar denotes rules, we can interpret the expendability of Molly in the face of a law into which she cannot fit. But it accumulates more resonance when audiences hear the phrase "should I jump or what?" again in part II, "Third Kingdom."

"Third Kingdom" stages the transatlantic journey of four enslaved figures, Kin-seer, Shark-seer, Us-seer, and Soul-seer, under the authoritative eye of Over-seer. Throughout, the five characters discuss how "thuh world had cleaved intuh 2," leaving two cliffs on either side of the world, the second of which being further divided in two, and an enormous gap in between the cliffs.[68] Over-seer tries to summarize the discussion: "Half the world had fallen away making 2 worlds and a sea between. Those two worlds inscribe the Third Kingdom."[69] Then Shark-seer revises this account: "Black folks with no clothes. [Audiences recall this phrase from the first part as a way of referring to the African continent.] Then all the black folks clothed in smiling. In betwen thuh folks is uh distance thats uh wet space. 2 worlds: Third Kingdom." But during this conversation, Over-seer interjects the threat of being jettisoned from the ship multiple times, first in response to a story Kin-seer tells about waving across the ocean at himself and then in response to Soul-seer. "Quiet, you," Over-seer says, "or you'll be jettisoned!"[70] So it is within these conversations and among these threats, on this ship that is not a ship, in the Third Kingdom that is the Middle Passage, that Kin-seer asks, "Should I jump? Shouldijumporwhat?"

And in that moment, the audience hears again Molly's speech from the first act, now with the desperately quicker, perhaps even breathless delivery of a character who has experienced his sense of self being torn in two, giving the phrase a suicidal note. Mapping back onto the opening moments of the play—or mapping forward, because time works in multiple directions at once in the sense that part I comes before part II in the order that the audience experiences them, but part II precedes part I in linear historical setting—audience members may question whether Molly was contemplating suicide herself, having been thrown out of a class that she needed to keep her job. This possibility re-sounds in the sound of eggs cracking into a frying pan, bursting open like a body "splatsplatslpat[ing]" on the ground after falling from a high-rise apartment building or splashing against the surface of the sea upon leaping overboard a ship. Additionally, her story about school gains a new inflection as "Third Kingdom" is gathered into Molly and Charlene's home via the language of the play, since, as Parks writes elsewhere, "Because words are so old they hold."[71] (Ships also hold. As do prisons. Sharpe: "Semiotics of the slave ship." But also, so do we. We hold each other. Hold on to that. I promise.) The event of the Middle Passage gathers to the event of Molly's breakfast and produces resonances between her teacher's expelling of her from the class and Over-seer's threat to jettison slaves from his ship, transforming both from events into iterations of the same disaster.

This throwing out of bodies rendered disposable by the law becomes the common condition of Molly and Kin-seer and Soul-seer. Disposability is revealed as the crux of carceral epistemology cohering in the "carceral model" that Childs names the Middle Passage as exemplifying: "[The slave ship] functioned as an un-precedented penological configuration of early modernity, one that turned the Atlantic into a *necropolitical* geography."⁷² Again like Rankine's incorporation of Turner's painting to index slavery, the slave ship in "Third Kingdom" indexes necropolitical expendability, not labor, as the ongoing disaster of slavery. As Rodríguez writes, "the continuity of the chattel relation does not pivot on the reproduction of the 'involuntary servitude' as prison labor, but rather on the subjection of targeted, criminalized beings to a carceral logic of anti-Blackness that renders them *available* as fungible chattel. It is the terror of this availability that primarily defines the aftermath of U.S. slavery's (non)abolition."⁷³ Rather than a technology of extracting labor, incarceration is the extraction of *time itself* vis-à-vis the grammars of disposability and individuation. It is that strand of logic that connects incarceration to slavery, *not* the thread of unpaid labor. Thus *The Slave Ship* and Over-seer's "glass-bottom boat" make this connection because they stay with slavery as a project of building modernity through the disposability of the enslaved, rather than just by way of enslaved labor. The ship itself is a technology of extraction; the slaves are resources to be used and/or disposed of as the ultimate nonselves, the no-bodies, the others beyond the borders of the Human who therefore create those borders and produce the Human.

Thus Molly is not literally in the hold of the ship, but she does (have the "freedom" to) attend school and eat breakfast and look for jobs to pay bills in its wake. She thus bears the mark of fungibility targeted by the word *jettison* and its always imminent enactment, even as her very insistence against grammar cuts the thread between "the hold" and "the wake" such that, as Sharpe observes, "to be in the wake is also to recognize the ways that we are constituted through and by continued vulnerability to overwhelming force though not *only* known to ourselves and each other *by* that force."⁷⁴ She can be thrown from the ship, but its hold cannot hold her.

"Third Kingdom" gathers in multiple directions throughout the play as a whole. Not only does "should I jump" bring the Middle Passage to the time of Molly, Charlene, and Veronica but Kin-seer's "wavin" reverberates into part IV, "Greeks (or The Slugs)." Part IV tells the story of Sergeant Smith, Mrs. Smith, and their daughters

Buffy, Muffy, and Duffy. Sergeant Smith is constantly away from his family, seeing them only rarely because of his military duties, which the audience comes to learn boil down to keeping a rock clean. He is obsessed with earning a "distinction" from the officers above him and finally does when he is either wounded by a mine or killed as he breaks the fall of a soldier thrown (jettisoned?) from the air. There is much more to say about this particular part of the play and how it situates *Imperceptible Mutabilities* in discussions of military violence and imperialism, and there are numerous details—such as the slippage between defining a mine as a thing that remembers versus one that dismembers—that could offer further evidence of the play's antilinear temporality. But the most salient detail for my current line of inquiry comes in section C. While presumably writing a letter to his family, Sergeant Smith says, "Next time your mother takes you to visit the ocean, Buffeena, look very far out over the water and give me a wave. I will waaaave back! . . . Next time your mother takes you to visit the ocean, Buffeena, throw me a kiss and I will throoooow one back!"[75]

These instructions from father to daughter are given heft by "Third Kingdom" and its reprise. In the first iteration of "Third Kingdom":

KIN-SEER: My uther me then waved back at me and then I was happy. But my uther me whuduhnnt waving at me. Mu uther me was waving at my Self. My uther me was waving at uh black black speck in thuh middle of thuh sea where years uhgoh from uh boat I had been—UUH! [Parks defines this "UUH!" sound as "Deep quick breath. Usually denotes drowning or breathlessness."[76]]

OVER-SEER: Jettisoned.

SHARK-SEER: Jettisoned?

KIN-SEER: Jettisoned.

US-SEER: Uh-huhn.

SOUL-SEER: To-the-middle-of-the-bottom-of-the-
big-black-sea.

KIN-SEER: And then my Self came up between us. Rose up
out of thuh water and standin on them waves my Self was
standin. And I was wavin wavin wavin and my Me was wavin
and wavin and my Self that rose between us went back down
in-to-the-sea.[77]

In the wake of this waving in witness to the tearing apart of self-
hood by the violence of the Middle Passage, audiences are left
questioning the efficacy of Sergeant Smith's command to his
daughter, especially after he returns home to meet uncertainty
about his own identity in his now blind wife and one child who
is convinced her father does not know her name. This attempt at
cross-generational recognition is interrupted by the way in which
the actors' words and gestures gather to their moment the catastrophe of the Middle Passage represented in previous iterations
of those words and gestures. As repetition and revision gather moments together, the Middle Passage ceases to begin or end, because
through this gathering across antilinear temporalities swirling
in the play's stage time, the event exceeds itself and its own ending. The Middle Passage is both event and nonevent, because
immanent to its very event-ness is the capacity to gather and be
gathered which renders its singularity already dispersed, even as
the historicity of singularities remains imperative to any analysis
that seeks to understand how Molly, Kin-seer, and Sergeant Smith
can all be marked by fungibility, while only Kin-seer is enslaved.
Ultimately, the Middle Passage emerges in *Imperceptible Mutabilities* as unceasing reverberation.

The Middle Passage is the violence that tears the Wor(l)d in two,
emerging from that tearing as modernity itself. The Middle Passage is the event of the end of the world and the ongoing disaster
of continuing apocalypse. This ongoing apocalypse is the current
World ordered by the carceral logic of the law's grammar of juridical events. The Middle Passage thus ends worlds—the worlds of
Black and Indigenous peoples, the worlds of (non)genders beyond

a male–female binary, the worlds of interspecies thriving—and also unceasingly calls for the World's ending. This is the Abolition Time that emerges as the demand of the ethical problem of the excessive present. Without discernable beginning or ending, without splitting time, staying with the devastation of disaster, lingering with the possibilities of futures spoken against linear tense, Abolition Time is after, and before, the end of the world.

LEAP, CATCH, HOLD

What if Mona's jump, what if Kin-seer's jump, which would be different from Over-seer's or Captain Luke Collingwood's "jettisoning" of them because it would be self-propelled, were a leap for freedom? What if the ship held the promise of movement rather than the hold of a cage? I end with these questions thanks to the students in my Black Plays and Performance class that I taught while I was still in graduate school. In that course, I arranged the plays we read chronologically, despite my own inclinations against linear time, and near the end of the semester, as we read Parks's play, I asked students, "Where have we heard about a jump before?" in an attempt to lead them to connect Kin-seer's "should I jump?" to Mona's earlier iteration of the phrase. In one semester, a student "broke the rules" of close reading and, instead of staying in the text slated for that day's discussion, dragged us back to the very first play on the syllabus by responding, "*The Escape.*"

That course began with William Wells Brown's *The Escape; or, A Leap for Freedom*. Brown's play employs comic melodrama to tell the story of enslaved people escaping their enslavers via the Underground Railroad. *The Escape* portrays the journey of Glen and Melinda—two enslaved people who are in love with each other but who are legally property of two different white men—as well as Cato, another enslaved man on the same plantation as Melinda, along the Underground Railroad. Although there is much to say about the problems and possibilities of performativity, the signification of sexual violence, and the representation of dialect in the text, what was on my student's mind in class on the day I asked about *Imperceptible Mutabilities* was Brown's play's representation of the *event* of emancipation—what its title calls "a leap for freedom."

There are two literal "leaps" in Brown's play: first, when Glen strikes Dr. Gaines's overseer over the head when he is sent to whip him and then leaps out of the window of a tobacco house, and second, in the play's closing moment, when Glen, Melinda, and Cato leap into a ferry crossing the Niagara River into Canada. Recalling Frederick Douglass's fight with Covey in his 1845 *Narrative*, the first f(l)ight is a paradigmatic enactment of bodily self-defense as catalyst toward emancipation. The second leap occurs at the very end of the play, when Glen, Melinda, and Cato have made it to Buffalo, New York, and are just about to take a ferry to Canada. Dr. Gaines and some police officers find the self-emancipated characters and attempt to recapture them, and Mr. White, a white northern man who was earlier portrayed in the play as a well-meaning but ineffective abolitionist, runs to help prevent this. The final words of the play's text are stage directions:

> The fight commences, in which Glen, Cato, Dr. Gaines, Scragg, White, and the Officers take part.—Ferryman enters, and runs to his boat.—Dr. Gaines, Scragg, and the Officers are knocked down, Glen, Melinda, and Cato jump into the boat, and as it leaves the shore and floats away, Glen and Cato wave their hats, and shout loudly for freedom.—Curtain Falls. THE END. [78]

This second leap, like the first, is preceded by violence, this time in a collective fight between enslavers and the formerly enslaved assisted by a white abolitionist, as opposed to the singular act of self-defense Glen takes up earlier. Significantly, this final set of stage directions signifies the first instance of staged physical violence in the play, because previously, Glen's self-defense is rendered in flashback and the whipping, beating, and assault of enslaved characters are pushed offstage. Inscribed in the title of the play and the historical context of its performance—Brown was himself a self-emancipated Black man and would read the play aloud as a call to abolition in the years before that all-too-foreseeable-in-hindsight event of the Civil War—this leap for freedom structures the meaning of all that comes before and after it.

At the same time, it is itself structured by a geography of slavery that seems to make the event of emancipation not only possible but necessary. Perhaps the most significant part of those stage directions is that Glen, Melinda, and Cato *"jump into the boat,"* because the moment their feet touch that ferry, they are being moved toward freedom. Written after the passage of the Fugitive Slave Act but before the advent of the Civil War, *The Escape* positions its protagonists as able to change their own political ontology from property to personhood by changing their location on a map. And it represents that move as the most significant moment of its plot—a dramatic finish to a high-stakes chase. Then, once the characters touch down on freedom, the stage directions call for gestures of victory as Glen and Cato turn, shout, and wave their hats. At the end of Brown's play, a leap *into* rather than *from* a boat is the event that changes everything for these three characters, and it is given the theatricality it well deserves.

So when my student mentioned this leap in response to my question about Kin-seer's jump, I was thrown off my expected course for the day's discussion and waited to see how the class would consider this point. In class that day, our discussion consisted mostly of contrasting the plays: Glen, Melinda, and Cato jump into a boat in the hope to live in freedom, whereas Kin-seer contemplates jumping out of a ship, which would ostensibly mean death by suicide. As I consider this contrast again, or, more accurately, as my student's response to my question and my unpreparedness for it continue to haunt me, I am thinking about Rinaldo Walcott's insistence that "if the sea has been death, it has also been life, too";[79] of Hartman's "critical fabulation";[80] and of Sharpe's "anagrammatical blackness that exists as an index of violability and also potentiality," which transforms the slave ship's *hold* into the language of *beholding.*[81]

What if it is not just the case that linear retrospection lets us see the futility of Glen, Melinda, and Cato's leap for freedom as we recognize the nonevent of emancipation and the ongoing disaster of the Middle Passage that would overdetermine the boat into which the characters leap as yet another iteration of Turner's ship, of the *Zong* from which they might be jettisoned? What if, following the *perhaps* of abolitionist literary studies as I am trying to develop it here, Kin-seer's and Mona's *jumps* can be *leaps* too? What if, like Derrick Bell's insistence on continuing to work toward freedom in the face of the permanence of racism, Glen, Melinda, and Cato continue to be held by the hold of Over-seer's ship, of Turner's seascape, of Captain Collingwood's *Zong, and still* they hold each other, knowing themselves as more than the law's declaration of property? Can we imagine, in a play that explodes linear time, that the body that Sergeant Smith catches as it falls from the sky at the "end" of *Imperceptible Mutabilities* is the body of Kin-seer? Or Mona? This would not save the enslaved from their drowning, of course, but as a "queer utopian memory," to invoke José Esteban Muñoz, it might perforate a hole through which we might glimpse the future in the present that abolition time indexes in its demand to end the end of the world.[82] Could the jump or the leap be a gesture of world-making and an invocation of death? In a World held together by the quotidian violence of carceral technologies of disposability, I think so. The leap *into* the boat, as that future which could have been but was not and yet remains as possibility in the excessive present, is inseparable from the jump *from* the ship, as that future nullified by the elimination of the present in the past.

Grant Farred asks about Rankine's book, "Is this how, we are provoked to wonder, the Middle Passage ends, without the possibility of exit? Is *Citizen* the recognition that, at the end of the road, at the end of that journey the black body has undertaken by sea, by land, by air, it culminates in its absolute dissolution?"[83] Perhaps. But perhaps there is something else happening on those famous pages of the book, which change with every new printing, where Rankine writes *In Memory of* moving down the page, each printing adding more names to a list, eventually dropping the *of* to leave *In Memory* in ink that fades lighter and lighter, from black into the white of the page. This technique, Shermaine M. Jones argues, "underscore[s] the ever-present threat of violence and death that permeates black life" and, as Sarah Nance demonstrates, "creat[es] a list that is both limited (by the page itself) and limitless, lingering in the moment of terrible potential between near-death and actual death."[84] I agree that the fading into white and the dropping of the preposition can be read as Rankine's lamentation that the death will continue, that there will always be the necessity of one more name to add to the list of the jettisoned. But at the same time, not in distinction from that possibility but alongside it, the fading into white is also the disappearance of the list. It is the nonarrival of the future dead.

The field of ethics opened by abolitionist reading is not a list of answers to the questions of ongoing catastrophe but an insistence on thinking in excess of law's ordering grammars. In the excessive present, we are coeval with the dead, but we cannot save them. The ethical demand of Abolition Time is not a rescue mission by some saviors of the present. It is the attempt to do the work of deferring the arrival of the future dead. It is the refusal of any more referents that the law can capture in its grammar. It is the affirmation to hold the future open, now, by beholding each other in order to hold the blank space of the death ledger open, all at the risk of not knowing in advance what the leap might hold, should we jump.

TWO

Perforation

INHABITATION AND THE
VULNERABILITY OF THE LAW

Thus the question remains as to what exercise of the
will, forms of action, or enactment of possibility is
available to animate chattel or the socially dead or to
the excluded ones that provide the very ground of
man's liberty. The double bind, simply stated, is: How
does one account for the state of domination and the
possibilities seized in practice? How does one represent
the various modes of practice without reducing them
to conditions of domination or romanticizing them as
pure forces of resistance?
       —Saidiya V. Hartman, *Scenes of Subjection: Terror,*
   Slavery, and Self-Making in Nineteenth-Century America

Ana- as a prefix, means "up, in place or time, back,
again, anew." So, blackness anew. Blackness as a/tem-
poral, in and out of place and time putting pressure on
meaning and that against which meaning is made.
       —Christina Sharpe, *In the Wake: On Blackness and Being*

While it was the presence of J. M. W. Turner's *The Slave Ship* at the
end of Claudia Rankine's *Citizen: An American Lyric* that inaugurated the project that has become *Abolition Time,* it has been one
particular antecedent of Turner's painting that has most solidly
grounded my project: the 1781 *Zong* Massacre. I first encountered
the story of the *Zong* Massacre in Ian Baucom's *Specters of the Atlantic: Finance Capital, Slavery, and the Philosophy of History* while

doing research focused on the racial history of finance capitalism, and I became obsessed with the fact that the archival touchstone for the mass murder was not a murder trial but a legal fight over insurance payments. My obsession led me to M. NourbeSe Philip's *Zong!*, a text that I begin to write about in this particular chapter but which in many ways is at the very heart of *Abolition Time*. In that book, Philip and her ancestral coauthor Setaey Adamu Boateng pull apart the words found in the court record of the insurance case and anagrammatically rearrange them to compose the poems that make up *Zong!* That is, the words used to record the massacred Africans as nothing more than cargo are decomposed at the source and recomposed into poetry that rejects the Africans' objectification in order to do justice to the being that law's ordering declarations of who was and wasn't Human could never fully extinguish, even as the law succeeded in its obliterative capacities. At the same time, because *Zong!*'s poetry is formed out of the exact linguistic "stuff" of the Africans' subjection (the text's "poetics of justice" are materially of the same stuff as "law's grammar," here), it cannot leave behind the violence of the law.

The way that Philip's poetry inhabits an archive of ontological evisceration but, from that very vantage point of necro-carceral inhabitation, mounts a deconstructive attack on the power of the law itself recalls, for me, one of the most remarked upon scenes in the African American literary canon: the "loophole of retreat" in Harriet Jacobs's *Incidents in the Life of a Slave Girl*. In that nineteenth-century autobiographical text, Jacobs recalls, through her pseudonymous protagonist Linda Brent, how she spent seven years hiding in a cramped attic in her grandmother's shed, remaining a stone's throw away from her enslaver while he searched the far northern corners of the country, thinking she had run away. Like but different from Philip inhabiting the murderous language of the legal archive to craft her poetry, Jacobs inhabits carceral confinement as a portal to "something akin to freedom." Through inhabitation, both authors illustrate forms of freedom dreaming that never leave the surveilling reach of the law but that nevertheless undo the law's ordering grammar precisely by inhabiting it.

This chapter thus proceeds in two movements. First, across three sections, I read Jacobs's narrative alongside Sutton Griggs's novel *Imperium in Imperio* to sketch what I call *perforation* as a conceptual apparatus traceable to embodied and enfleshed practice against law's grammars. Then, in a final section, I read Philip's direct disarticulation of the law in *Zong!* as an enactment of a poetics of perforation that shifts the grounds for theorizing justice and temporality.

THE LOOPHOLE OF RETREAT: ESCAPING WITHOUT LEAVING

In this chapter, I trace, after Christina Sharpe, a particular "anagrammatic" poetics that I name *perforation* in the work of Jacobs, Griggs, and Philip.[1] These writers occupy distinct temporal and geographic nodes of the African diaspora, but their texts share a common investment in direct confrontation with the force of law. In this confrontation—be it, in Jacobs's case, the law of inherited slave status or, in Griggs's case, the law of national citizenship or, in Philip's case, the legal archive of slavery and insurance—each writer employs anagrammatic poetics that highlight that "as the meanings of words [like *woman* for Jacobs, or *nation* for Griggs, or *murder* for Philip] fall apart, we encounter again and again the difficulty of sticking the signification."[2] Law's grammar of order, then, seeks to contain and *correct* (hear the resonance of "department of corrections") the anagrammatic because, as Grant Farred concisely tells us, "the law knows itself as, before all else, vulnerable" in the face of the contingency of its own coherence.[3] Within this dynamic of law's ordering grammar and the anagrammatic poetics of justice we can see in Black Atlantic literature, this chapter theorizes perforation as a particular mode of breaking down the unlivable world held together by the law's violence.

In *Incidents in the Life of a Slave Girl*, Jacobs expresses how she journeyed from enslavement to legal emancipation while arguing that readers ought to join in the work of abolition. In approaching a goal that itself was deemed an impossibility within the terms of the legal enslavement in which she lived, Jacobs's pseudonymous protagonist Linda Brent performs acts that may not strike readers with the (violent) heroic imagery of her contemporary Frederick Douglass grabbing his overseer by the throat but that nevertheless enact "something akin to freedom" by moving through the perforations in the fabric of the law.[4]

In fact, while hiding in the garret of her grandmother's shed, she literalizes perforation in a quiet act of seemingly inconsequential—or almost certainly undetectable, at least by Dr. Flint—resistance: "I bored three rows of holes, one above the other; then I bored out the interstices between. I thus succeeded in making one hole about an inch long and an inch broad."[5] What she does with these small actions is remarkable as theory-in-practice—as an embodied practice of being within and yet in excess of law.[6] She does not leave the South, but she escapes the reach of her enslaver. Taking Jacobs's carving as paradigmatic example, *perforation is the possibility for and the enactment of escape without leaving.* Or, to further problematize "escape" alongside Tina Campt and Stephen Dillon,[7] who both theorize *fugitivity* in complex ways that situate the now common term in Black studies as exceeding the grammar of resistance or reaction to domination and violence, *perforation is a practice of freedom that can neither destroy nor be captured by law's ordering force.*

Of course, Jacobs's "loophole of retreat" is one of the most often remarked upon scenes in African American literary history, so it is not to say anything new to point out that the garret is a site of resistance or life lived in defiance of the death-bound ethos of slavery, however liberatory or futile such resistance can be.[8] Saidiya Hartman's *Scenes of Subjection* remains an imperative framing of Jacobs's enactments of resistance and possibility. Writing about sexuality and the discourse of seduction in Jacobs's text, Hartman reminds us that in our recognition of Brent's resistance to slavery, "it is important to note that it is not equality or the absence of constraint that is celebrated in this inscription of 'calculation' but the *possible gains to be made within the context of domination.*"[9] Hartman's larger claim is that there is no absolute distinction between enslavement and freedom so long as anti-Blackness is intact and that scenes of Black performance signify doubly as both emancipatory and imprisoning. This argument is embodied by

Brent as she spends three years in the garret, since on one hand, she is able to reverse the gaze of anti-Black surveillance—she can watch without being watched—and yet, on the other hand, she is confined to a dark, imprisoning space both materially damaging her body and symbolically highlighting her inscription within slavery's structures of domination. Neither her surveillance of Dr. Flint and his estate nor the loving bond she is able to sustain with her children through this hole in the wall is a liberatory reversal of the terms of enslavement, because they never escape the reach of the law. Rather, *Incidents* "suggests that surrender and resistance may operate in tandem."[10] So while Jacobs is certainly able to use the loophole of retreat to actively resist her enslavement, there remains tension between these enactments of agency and the structures of domination in which they take place.[11]

I return to Jacobs's text not to posit a new definitive reading but to ask how her documentation and critique of a carceral slave past might also, to follow Kara Keeling's extension of C. L. R. James, Gary Wilder, and David Scott, articulate an abolitionist "future past."[12] If with Hartman we can, in retrospect, see the end of the U.S. Civil War not as a moment of *abolition* as much as a "nonevent of emancipation," where the distinction between emancipation and abolition is the distinction between juridical freedom and something far more expansive, we might see the eventual failure of Reconstruction as an abolitionist future that might have been but was not and yet must be.[13] Jacobs's poking of holes in the wall of her grandmother's attic is, thus, *a pulling into the present* (emphasis on the verb form *pulling*) of a future that has yet to materialize, such that that future (which we might call *total abolition,* as distinct from emancipation) remains both just out of reach and in Jacobs's hands, in her *now,* or our *then.* Jacobs's seven years in the garret are a unit of abolition time, and her injured body indexes that such an assertion is not at all celebratory or victorious but rather is a recognition of the demarcations of the law's grammar that persist even as they are deformed by poetics of justice.

Thinking with Hartman's questions in the epigraph to this chapter, *perforation signifies the vulnerability of the law that can neither fully disarticulate nor be disarticulated from the overwhelming force of law.*[14] That is, inherent to the existence of "law" as the force that orders society is the possibility for law's force to be interrupted or mitigated, and it can never be separated from its vulnerability to interruption or mitigation. More than just a notation that there are holes in the arguments put forth by law, *perforation describes the ways in which law's very own limits inscribe within themselves spaces that allow passage between zones of distinction* (e.g., past-present, illegal-legal, civil-criminal), *as well as the forces within and outside the law that perforate the barriers erected between those zones of distinction.*

C. Riley Snorton's analysis of Jacobs's "fungible fugitivity," in conjunction with Alexander Weheliye's theorization of "habeas viscus" as an extension of Hortense Spillers's flesh-body distinction, help clarify how I read *Incidents* as theorizing law's vulnerability. Snorton writes:

> Just as the "loophole" refers to both the small space in Brent's/Jacobs's grandmother's attic that contains the protagonist for seven years and the hole that Brent makes in that space in order to see outside, the swamp stages the transversal relationship between fugitive life and death, as it also allegorizes *how fungibility emerges as a tactic of maneuvering from within the morass of slavery's identity politics.* To and from the Snaky Swamp Brent moves in "disguise," and in these "cross-dressed" perambulations enacts a fugitive plot that stages through Brent's ungendered body the various ways fungibility and fugitivity pass into one another.[15]

Here Snorton demonstrates how Jacobs retreats into one of the characteristic vulnerabilities of enslavement—the fungibility of the enslaved—rather than resisting it to set in motion a flow beyond the sight of the law even without leaving its site. A hallmark of slavery was the production of Black bodies as interchangeable commodities through the violation of the flesh. But as Weheliye theorizes flesh, it is not merely the object of violation, because "violent political domination activates a fleshy surplus that simultaneously sustains and disfigures said brutality," thus enabling us to "reclaim the atrocity of flesh as a pivotal arena for the politics

emanating from different traditions of the oppressed."[16] Thus
Jacobs mobilizes a precise vector of the law's ostensible obliteration of her subjectivity—the ungendering of her flesh through
the magic of unmaking her as a person vis-à-vis the transforma-
tion into a commodity—as an avenue of fugitivity.[17] This fugitivity,
though, "only makes sense in the space of unfreedom and thus
cannot be constituted as freedom"—it is no "big narrative."[18] Instead, it is a space of freedom out of sight of the law but still on
the site of law's violence. In *Abolition Time's* terms, Jacobs's mobilization of flesh is a manipulation of law's grammar, maneuvering
within its terms of order beyond the designs of that order. If, for
Snorton, "fungible fugitivity" and, for Weheliye, "flesh" index the
maneuverability of the subjected within the terrain of subjection,
then *perforation* for me is the flip side of that coin; it describes *the
pressure that such maneuverability exerts on the law itself* as always
under the state of *being disfigured by its own terms of coherence*. The
grammar of the law is both sustained and cut by the anagrammatic
movements of Blackness. The coconstitutive sustaining and cutting is what I refer to as perforation.

SPECTERS OF REVOLUTIONS TO COME:
MR. LITCH'S GHOSTS AND THE
IMPERIUM IN IMPERIO

While Linda Brent's presence in the garret as she perforates the
walls of her hiding place is undetected, Jacobs describes one plantation owner who fears a presence he detects all too powerfully:
Mr. Litch is afraid to walk his own property at night. Such a fear is
a manifestation of the law knowing itself as vulnerable, and it is a
fear that makes Sutton E. Griggs's first novel, *Imperium in Imperio,*
an interesting case of a literary mobilization of the logic of perforation. In this section, I pair Jacobs's autobiographical narrative
with Griggs's post-Civil War novel to supplement Jacobs's insight
about the working of fear as an affective ecology of plantation life
with Griggs's novel's manipulation of that fear in service of a political analysis that shifts focus from the terrain of psychological
or libidinal anti-Blackness to the terrain of the force of law as expressed in the geopolitical formation of the nation-state itself. In

other words, both Jacobs and Griggs drill down to the fundamental fear that is inextricable from white supremacy, and it is in considering their two texts' different deployments of perforation that a full analysis is most visible, even as we cannot erase the significant differences between the antebellum autobiography and the turn-of-the-century novel.

Published in 1899, *Imperium in Imperio* tells the story of two Black men, Belton Piedmont and Bernard Belgrave, and their divergent but complementary lives defined by their work on behalf of achieving freedom for their race. The narrative is an alternative history, its title alluding to a secret shadow government of the United States organized to legislate over and protect the African-descendant people within U.S. borders. Called the "Imperium in Imperio," this secret organization of Black people was structured by a constitution modeled, for the most part, after the U.S. Constitution. Griggs's characters go to great lengths to emphasize the heavy-handed point of his title—that this shadow government exists *within* the very terms of the dominant order rather than outside of it. In the framing schema of my chapter, the grammar of law that *Imperium in Imperio* inhabits is the grammar of citizenship. By situating a shadow government within the bounds of the U.S. government, Griggs is able to inhabit the legal conception of citizenship precisely in order to perforate it, even, perhaps, beyond his intentions.

Upon introducing Bernard to the existence of the Imperium, Belton explains that "this flaw or defect in the Constitution of the United States is the relation of the General Government to the individual state."[19] What follows is a thorough indictment of federalism as a sham of reciprocal governance. With the Civil War as background, Belton conjures the voice of the U.S. federal government calling on its people to fight for the preservation of the union, even if they must fight against their own individual states. He then points to the obvious hypocrisy of how the federal government will then turn around and tell Black people that it cannot protect them from those individual states when they implement discriminatory laws or allow racist extrajudicial killing. Even though their citizens are supposedly obligated to the unified

federal government, under federalism, the individual states maintain sovereignty in such a way that allows them to violate the
liberties of individuals who are supposedly under the jurisdiction
of the federal government when their labor is necessary for the
survival of the union. Naming the condition out of which the Imperium arises, in language that anticipates Malcolm X's "The Ballot
or the Bullet," Belton declares, "The Negro finds himself an unprotected foreigner in his own home." Recognizing this, "in order to
supply this needed protection, [the Imperio] has been formed."[20]
Again in the register of a preemptive echo—this time of James
Baldwin's declaration that "it was *inevitable* that the fury would
erupt, that a black man, openly, in the sight of all his fellows,
should challenge the policeman's gun, and not only that, but the
policeman's right to be in the ghetto at all"[21]—Belton recognizes
the perforation through which the Imperium develops. The U.S.
Constitution itself, in establishing federalist governance while
declaring itself as the supreme law of the land demanding the defense of all those subject to its jurisdiction, is thereby structured
by perforated limits through which Griggs's imagination moves.

In fact, Griggs's novel, written as it was in the decades following
the war and published the year after the 1898 Wilmington massacre, is one of the key texts of the nineteenth century outlining
the ways in which the Civil War was not an aberration in democracy but rather the inevitable outcome of the perforated structure
of the U.S. Constitution. Although the scale and scope of the war
were unknowable before and during its duration, the possibility
of a general conflict over the question of slavery, or, to be more
faithful to Griggs's terms, the question of Black freedom, is inscribed within the U.S. Constitution and made inevitable by the
very tools of the law that sought to prevent all-out war. That is, the
U.S. Constitution inscribes the very possibility, even the promise,
of a war between the states over the questions of slavery and freedom, and the legal compromises of the early and mid-nineteenth
century all but usher in the event they seek to prevent. After all,
"the event is only partially—and very rarely—the product of
chance. It also marks that not entirely random moment when various historical forces (often antagonistic) come into an unforeseen

(unforeseeable), unavoidable conflict."[22] In other words, the event (war) does not come out of nowhere. It can be traced, even if only after the fact. In the case of the legal inscription of Black subjects in the United States, the federalist structure, as Griggs demonstrates through Belton, marks one set of perforations at the law's limits. And then when the law acts to defend itself against invasion through these perforations by passing the Missouri Compromise or the 1850 Fugitive Slave Act, for example, these attempts at self-defense ultimately attack the integrity of the law's own body. In guarding the pores of its own skin, the body of the law threatens itself with being torn apart.

Of course, the tools of achieving the destruction of the dominant order do not always necessarily come from within the order itself. Whether intentionally or not, Griggs's *Imperium in Imperio* is insightful on this point, if only because of the ignorance of one of its briefly appearing though heavily emphasized white characters. Early in the novel, Mr. V. M. King, editor of a national newspaper, takes a great interest in Belton after his paper reprints the young man's graduation oration on "The Contribution of the Anglo-Saxon to the Cause of Human Liberty." He takes home a copy of the issue in which Belton's oration is printed to show his wife and declares to her that "it has come at last."[23] By "it," Mr. King means the promise of conflict between the Anglo-Saxon and Black races:

> He argued that, living as the negro did beneath the American flag, known as the flag of freedom, studying American history, and listening on the outer edge of Fourth of July crowds to eloquent orators discourse on freedom, it was only a matter of a few years before the negro would deify liberty as the Anglo-Saxon race had done, and count it a joy to perish on her alter.[24]

For Mr. King, the Anglo-Saxon people of the United States have sown the seeds of racial conflict by way of their very best articulations and celebrations of democratic freedom. The coming conflict, which he believes is embodied in Belton, will, like the Civil War, be an event inscribed within the very terms of freedom that America had itself written. The only problem comes when one seeks after what is insistently present in its absence in Mr. King's reasoning—namely, Black self-emancipation, slave revolts, and the kind of Black political praxis that W. E. B. Du Bois elaborates in his account of the general strike that ensured the North's victory in the Civil War.[25]

Mr. King cannot imagine Black political thought and instead believes that Black people will get ideas of freedom from hearing them articulated by white people. In fact, he refuses to utter his warning to his fellow white folk in plain terms of rebellion or armed conflict "for fear that the mention of it might hasten the birth of the idea in the brain of the negro."[26] It is probably not difficult to imagine readers both in Griggs's time and today scoffing at this sentiment, not least of all in the shadow of Nat Turner, the *Amistad* case, or the Haitian Revolution. And it is probably difficult to imagine readers *not* scoffing at Mr. King's belief that "the negro . . . should recognize that the lofty conception of the dignity of man and value and true character of liberty were taught him by the Anglo-Saxon."[27] To believe such a thing is to believe that Africans had no conception of freedom until they were taught it by their enslavers, and such a belief is unsustainable in the face of slave rebellions and maroon communities as well as careful readings of slave narratives that identify how self-emancipated individuals imagined themselves moving about the world in ways other than what the world had to offer in its own terms.

By way of its narrational structure, *Imperium* both begins and ends with a promise and a threat. The premise of the entire novel is the hypothetical existence of an organization of African Americans plotting to secure their rights secretly within the borders of the United States. By the end of the novel, the Imperium has been dismantled by the betrayal of the fictional narrator Berl Trout. But Berl ends his narration with the declaration, "I only ask . . . that all mankind will join hands and help my poor downtrodden people to secure those rights for which they organized the Imperium, which my betrayal has now destroyed. I urge this because love of liberty is such an inventive genius, *that if you destroy one device it at once constructs another more powerful.*"[28] With this declaration, the novel thus reassures readers that the Imperium is not real and at the same time leaves off with the spectral presence of the Imperium's aftermath—its ghost in the real, its potentiality beyond the page—the more powerful device which may, like the Imperium itself, already be under construction without detection.[29] This is the fear of the slave revolt that outlives the end of legal slavery and manifests in Black Codes forbidding public gatherings of more than two Black people after sundown and in early twenty-first-century practices of stopping and frisking groups of Black youths as part of "broken windows" policing. It is a fear built on the unspoken knowledge that the law is not as omnipotent as it claims; it is the fear of what flows through perforation. And this fear is what allows Berl's warning to read as a threat—and for the warning-as-threat to be read as promise.

The promise of the threat of power's dissolution is constitutive of the vulnerability that is constitutive of power. And it is this web of power, vulnerability, and the threat of dissolution, not merely an idiosyncratic, pathological paranoia, that culminates in the fear of Mr. Litch in Harriet Jacobs's "Sketches of Neighboring Slaveholders," the chapter into which Lydia Maria Child as editor condensed Jacobs's accounts of the bodily torture of enslaved peoples on plantations.[30] In short, the social structure as it is maintained by law is haunted by the very specter the law seeks to keep at bay: the Black revolution that would literally undo the World as it is known.

In *Incidents*, Jacobs recounts two enslaved men who brought (or, in the language of the law, stole) some ham and liquor back to their homes and who were subsequently killed by Mr. Litch.[31] Directly following this, she writes, "Murder was so common on his plantation that he feared to be alone after nightfall. He might have believed in ghosts."[32] The first sentence is striking precisely because it is the murder of enslaved Black people that is so common on his plantation, so why need he, the white, wealthy enslaver, fear being alone after nightfall? Is he not the murderer, rather than the potential murder victim, in this scenario? Is he not the embodiment of the power to murder on the plantation, beyond the reach of those he murders?[33] What ghosts did Mr. Litch fear?

I would suggest, following Jacobs's own text, that Mr. Litch feared the specter of Black revolutionary violence promised at the end of *Imperio* or the threat of self-defense levied by the two "leaps" in William Wells Brown's *The Escape*.[34] This is a literal instance of the law knowing itself as vulnerable: Mr. Litch knows that he is outnumbered by the enslaved people on his plantation, knows they have reason to kill him, and knows that in the dark of night, while he is asleep, he is helpless to protect himself from a hidden show of force. He has no way to know whether there is a double of Linda Brent hidden away in an attic on *his* plantation, waiting for the right moment to end his life.

The law of the plantation, over which Mr. Litch as master holds complete sovereignty, is the law of white supremacy. And yet, the law of the plantation, even as it strives to enforce order through maintaining a zone of distinction between white masters and Black slaves through the execution of its force via physical and mental torture, contains within its own limits the possibility of nullification in the form of *partus sequitur ventrem,* or "the child shall follow the condition of the mother." Jacobs explains this grammar of law: "if the white parent is the *father,* instead of the mother, the offspring are unblushingly reared for the market."[35] The law of white supremacy, then, seeks to keep white and Black distinct, thus the existence of specific antimiscegenation laws, and at the same time contains in this limit a perforation in the form of the principle of *partus sequitur ventrem,* so that when miscegenation does occur in the form of rape by white people against enslaved Black people, there is legal precedent for how to proceed with the children, who are property. In other words, the zone of distinction is a zone of indistinction, because any child may have both white and Black parents, whatever its legal status. As Sharpe demonstrates in her readings of Jacobs's *Incidents* and Gayl Jones's *Corregidora* in *Monstrous Intimacies: Making Post-slavery Subjects,* the "monstrous intimacies" of the plantation render white supremacist imaginings of free subjects always already tenuous.

Once this hole is thrown into the open, it may be possible to do as Jacobs does in her garret and carve the interstitial space between it and another to create a larger puncture. The specter of such a puncturing hand—a Black hand holding a knife that could puncture his white skin, perhaps—is the ghost in which Mr. Litch believes. As he kills enslaved Black people, he is aware, because he knows well the perforation of the law's limits against miscegenation, that he may be killing his own child—a child with "white blood."[36] Because the perforation of the law allows the possibility that any Black body on the plantation may bear the trace of white parentage and sexual violence, each murdered Black body signifies the possibility of the master's own murder. And in the other direction, the legal acknowledgment of Black children with mixed parentage implies without naming the possibility of white children-become-adults with mixed parentage. Brigitte Fielder attends mostly to the (re)racialization of white women and mixed-race Black characters as she analyzes how "through acts of conceiving and carrying mixed-race children, white women literally embody Blackness, containing the racial Other in their own bodies."[37] In the bodies of white men like Mr. Litch, there is not the *literal* embodiment of Blackness that Fielder describes, but there is the specter of Black flesh within their white bodies. As Fielder argues, "the theory of hypodescent is not just one of reproducing oppressed races, then, but also a theory of how whiteness might be absorbed, erased, folded into racial nonwhiteness. Hence white racist anxieties about racial mixing are always predicated upon not only others' racial proliferation, but of whiteness's disappearance."[38] Because plantation law is structured by the knowledge that interracial reproduction is fundamental to slavery's (libidinal) economy, white men like Mr. Litch can never be certain that somewhere in their genealogical ancestry, some "drop of Black blood" didn't enter their bloodline. If, within the grammars of law on the plantation, white = sovereign and Black = murderable, but at the same time the grammar of hypodescent plus the secrecy necessitated by *partus sequitur ventrem* means that racial purity is everywhere under threat, then every sovereign is not only a possible object of retributive justice but also a possible object of the violence of the law. Mr. Litch can never know if, on one hand, his white violence may be responded to with Black self-defense or, on the other hand, if he himself, like the Black people on his plantation bearing traces of white descent, bears traces of Black descent, leaving him vulnerable to the very grammar of legal violence he deploys.

Under the cover of night, when so many subversive acts of fugitivity, marronage, or resistance took place, Mr. Litch had every reason to believe that his ability to enforce the law would run out or, worse yet, the prerogative to extinguish life would turn against him and be his own, and his World's, undoing. So while Jacobs herself did not overturn the order of slavery or abolish the law of the plantation in her time in the garret, she found herself moving through the perforations in the law's limits, embodying the possibility, even if not the reality, of Dr. Flint's murder by a secreted presence moving about under the cover of night.

In the next section, I follow the thread opened here by attending to the necropolitics of reproduction under slavery to read Jacobs's *Incidents* as a nineteenth-century articulation of abolition feminism. My reading will serve as a transition from describing perforation as a conceptual apparatus to tracing it as a textual poetics through attention to layers of meaning packed into pronouns and the ambiguities of language, not unlike my readings of *Citizen* in the first chapter.

SECURITY, SAFETY, AND THE UN/GENDERING OF RACE: INHABITING LAW'S GRAMMAR OF *PARTUS SEQUITUR VENTREM*

Incidents in the Life of a Slave Girl points not only toward juridical emancipation that might be described in its own famous words as "something akin to freedom" but also toward a more expansive liberation in the mode of what Angela Davis, Gina Dent, Erica Meiners, and Beth Richie identify as a connective force in a long genealogy of abolition feminism.[39] Bridging contemporary prison abolition with nineteenth-century abolitionist politics through Black feminist and queer theory, I read Jacobs's *Incidents* as theorizing abolition as a demand for liberation that is incompatible with liberal conceptions of the rights-bearing subject granted the "burdened individuality of freedom."[40] That is, even as *Incidents* directly critiques the law through engaging its own terms of evidentiary analysis and grammars of order to demand what we can recognize in juridical terms as civil rights, its demands for justice exceed the terms of law's order in their conjuring of a world beyond the horizon of rights-based frameworks. Significantly, my reading moves both with and against Jacobs's own intentions and sometimes against the grain of her rhetorical situation as autobiographical writer, but it is precisely in reading both with and against the grain of the author's intentions, rhetorical choices, and received historical vocabulary that a poetics of perforation mobilizes through inhabitation.

When I teach *Incidents*, rhetorical analysis has been an initial way into the text for students. By attending to the ways in which Jacobs carefully crafts her narrative with white women as her audience in mind, a general trend I have noticed is that students interpret the text's argument as making three major points: (1) slavery is morally wrong even and especially when it is backed by law, (2) enslaved Black women experience motherhood and "womanhood" itself differently from white women, and (3) slavery is "even worse" for enslaved women than enslaved men. Students often bring up the term "intersectionality" without being prompted and turn the conversation to why it is important to attend to both race and gender rather than elevating one or the other. Often, this thread leads to students gesturing toward the common liberal framework (institutionalized within the setting of the university itself) of *inclusion as remedy* in response to the text.[41] Within such a framework, exclusion is the wrong for which inclusion is the redress. In applying their already-existing inclusion framework to the text, students project onto Jacobs that she is arguing for Black women to be *welcomed into womanhood* to experience the *protections of gender* in the same ways as white women.[42]

In dialogue with my students, and against inclusion-framed readings of the text, I develop an interpretation of *Incidents* that does not displace Jacobs's appeals to white women's reason and sympathies for recognition in her own womanhood but supplements that important reading of Jacobs's rhetorical skill with the thesis that *Incidents* argues for the obliteration of the existing field of racialized gender altogether as a condition of true abolition. That is, *emancipation* from slavery might mean delivery into the security of existing binary parameters of colonial Gender, but because, as Patrice Douglass argues, "Black gender is constitutive of the paradigm of enslavement," *abolition* means something more liberatory—a move in excess of the grammars of colonial Gender.[43] In other words, I argue that at the same time that Jacobs rhetorically deploys the grammar of womanhood to build political allegiance among white and Black women—a deployment that reifies the grammar it inhabits—*Incidents* (as a text that exceeds the intentions of its author) articulates, in Marquis Bey's words, "a recognition of 'female' [as] a vehicle for whiteness, patriarchy, and the gender binary, which are violent apparatuses."[44] The text therefore opens space for thinking beyond the very grammar its author deploys. I develop this argument by thinking with the distinction between *safety* and *security* in contemporary abolitionist thought, Spillers's body–flesh distinction, and Snorton's and others' extension of the concept of "ungendering" in Black feminist, queer, and trans theory.[45]

Incidents presents readers with an abolitionist feminist argument insofar as Linda's vulnerability and subjection to rape—what Spillers names as "an amazing stroke of pansexual potential" and what Aliyyah Abdur-Rahman demonstrates as indicative of the "collective raped subjectivity of the enslaved"—index the monstrous intimacy of slavery that both made possible and was made possible by the ungendering of Blackness kept captive by the property (re)productive capacities of gender's ability to possess unprotected female flesh.[46] That is, Linda as property is held captive by gender as much as by race, even as—or perhaps *precisely because*—she is herself ungendered. Thus her call for the sympathy of white women readers is not (only) a call for inclusion in the realm of women and thus the universal grammar of gender but also a call for the abolition of that grammar so that intimacies less monstrous might emerge.

Incidents makes these two simultaneous arguments—one for inclusion and one for generative obliteration—through the mobilization of simultaneous theorizing in the body and through the flesh. Tracing these two distinct arguments, I draw on a genealogy of Black feminist scholarship that has long grappled with the ramifications of what Sarah Haley calls "gendered racial terror"

for understanding Blackness and gender in slavery and its afterlife.[47] Writing while incarcerated in 1971, Angela Davis notes that
"in order to function as slave, the black woman had to be annulled
as woman," but also argues that sexual violence was deployed
against Black women as a form of "counterinsurgency."[48] This
is why, for Spillers, it is true both that under slavery, "we lose at
least *gender* difference *in the outcome*," because "under these conditions, one is neither female, nor male, as both subjects are taken
into account as *quantities*,"[49] *and* that "[the Black woman, specifi-
cally] became instead the principal point of passage between the
human and the non-human world."[50] Building on Davis and Spillers, Hartman shows that "in the confines of chattel slavery, gender
is discernable primarily in terms of the uses and conveyances of
property, calculations of sentience, evaluations of injury, and de-
terminations of punishment," such that "the captive female does
not possess gender as much as she is possessed by gender—that
is, by way of a particular investment in and use of the body."[51] Jennifer L. Morgan's historical research gives this insight material
texture, as she "locate[s] the exposure of female captives to sexual
predation and violation as foundational to the production of race
and racial hierarchy, rather than as its horrifying culmination,"
adding to Davis's analysis of sexual violence as counterinsurgent
terrorism the extrapolation that even in their ungendered removal
from the province of legal personhood, Black women's perceived
capacity for biological reproduction meant that sexual violation
became a central economic logic of slavery.[52] This line of analysis provides frameworks for thinking gender both as that terrain
from which Black subjects have historically been denied access
as a constitutive component of the terrain's very legibility *and* as
a deployable violence of capture differentially applied to Black
bodies. On the other side of this terror that, as Bey puts it, "gender is one of the chief forms through which coercive, compulsory
violence and captivity are carried out," it is also possible that, as
Snorton argues, "the ungendering of blackness, then, opens onto a
way of thinking about black gender as an infinite set of prolifera-
tive, constantly revisable reiterations figured 'outside' of gender's
established and establishing symbolic order."[53] It is within this

rich tapestry of Black feminist theorization that my reading of *Incidents* develops.

As I read this genealogy of Black feminist scholarship on ungendering as an arc of a long history of abolition feminism, the very process through which Blackness is gendered—a process set in motion by mathematics of violence and property accumulation—is the process through which Blackness is ungendered. Thus gender difference is lost, but at the same time, gender difference becomes property quantification, appearing in the arena of race as the reproductive portal marking the distinction between the human and the nonhuman. This is all to say that I recognize in Spillers's term *ungendered* a complex account of racial-sexual violence that can be rendered neither simply as the negation of gender as a relevant axis for Black subjectivity nor as an assertion of a bio-essentialized particularity of Black *women* as exceptional subjects.[54]

Following Dorothy Roberts's theorization of "prenatal property," through which she unpacks the implications of how "the law granted to whites a devisable, *in futuro* interest in the potential children of their slaves," for me, *partus sequitur ventrem* is the law's grammar that violently produces Black gender as ungendered fungibility and vulnerability to what Sharpe marks as perpetually "imminent and immanent death."[55] Through this ordering principle, the ostensible ambiguity of racial "mixing" is conjured into the certitude of category distinction. While the translated phrase "the child follows the condition of the mother" points to the child as the subject of the law's force, as the antecedent of the child's condition, the mother is ordered by the law here as well. If enslaved, the mother is simultaneously a viable human sexual partner for the enslaver and a non-Human commodity-machine for (re)producing more commodities that will then accumulate as the increased property and wealth of the enslaver. Both gendered sex object capable of reproduction and thingified commodity without a Human Gender, the Black mother is ungendered through the ordering capacity of *partus sequitur ventrem* as the law's grammar of gender. My contention is that in her narrative's focus on Linda's role as mother, Jacobs's text *inhabits* the law's grammar of gender to simultaneously demand inclusion within it *and* to deconstruct it as a necessary clearing-away for the realization of total abolition.

At the level of experience, Jacobs registers the simultaneity indexed by *ungendering* throughout her text. For example, when she learns that her second child has been assigned female at birth, she writes, "Slavery is terrible for men; but is far more terrible for women. Superadded to the burden common to all, *they* have wrongs, and sufferings, and mortifications peculiarly their own."[56] I am struck by the doubleness possible in the unspecified pronoun *all* here. This declaration can be taken to mean that in addition to the burden common to *all enslaved Black people,* enslaved Black women experience additional horrors that enslaved men do not. But it can also be taken to mean that in addition to the burden common to *all women,* Black women are targeted by additional abuses unknown to white women. If we read along the terms inaugurated in *Abolition Time*'s first chapter regarding poetics of accumulation, then the undecidability of *all*'s referent signals the simultaneity of the gendering and ungendering of Blackness, where the first interpretation recognizes the differential production of gender within a raced population and the second interpretation recognizes the differential production of gender between raced populations. This simultaneity also points to the racialization of gender in that white women can only be "women" so far as they are not Black, such that the historical production of racial Blackness is also the historical production of the gendered category of the Western, modern woman.[57]

Even as I insist on the undecidability of *all*'s referent in that textual moment, I think there is evidence in *Incidents* that it is *women* rather than *slaves* who are being invoked. Abdur-Rahman has written about the sexual abuse of Luke by his male enslaver, and I would add that Jacobs generalizes from Luke's experience when she writes, "[The white daughters of slave owners] know that the women slaves are subject to their father's authority in all things; and in some cases *they exercise the same authority over the men slaves.*"[58] That is, it is not even secreted in code that white women are sexual abusers in Jacobs's text; it is right there on the surface to be read by those paying attention. Of course, as Spillers insists upon not allowing us to forget, Linda herself is abused by *both* Dr. Flint and his wife. Thus I think we can read *Incidents* as delineating how, for the enslaved, Blackness is ungendered, not despite but because of the word "Girl" in the title. The lives of enslaved girls might be subject to rape more *often* than the lives of enslaved boys because of the capacity for property reproduction into which their bodies are conscripted by their enslavers and the law's grammar of *partus sequitur ventrem*, but because there is also a libidinal and not only a monetary economy to slavery, enslaved boys and men are *ontologically* and *juridically* equally vulnerable to rape. Sexual assault, then, cannot be counted as a mortification not suffered by enslaved men. This racialized vulnerability to sexual violation indexes for Hartman the difference between the "captive female" who is "possessed by gender" and the white woman who "possesses gender."[59]

Hartman's distinction between the capacity to possess gender and the capacity to be possessed by gender links *ungendering* to Spillers's flesh–body distinction in "Mama's Baby, Papa's Maybe: An American Grammar Book":

> But I would make a distinction in this case between "body" and "flesh" and impose that distinction as the central one between captive and liberated subject-positions. In that sense, before the "body" there is the "flesh," that zero degree of social conceptualization that does not escape concealment under the brush of discourse or the reflexes of iconography.[60]

Throughout her essay, Spillers mobilizes this distinction to disarticulate the projection of pathology onto African American social and familial structures by discourses exemplified by Daniel Patrick Moynihan's *The Negro Family: The Case for National Action*. She builds on and lays groundwork for theorizing in the fields of Black feminism and Black queer studies through her articulation of the ungendering of Black subjects through the Middle Passage and the potentiality for occupying an insurgent, alternative conceptualization of gender or humanity.

On my reading of this distinction, flesh emerges as the material stuff of human beings and bodies as the conceptually knowable, legible, and order-able subjects/objects that discourse—primarily what I would identify as grammars of law—shapes out of flesh. That is, there is flesh in the world, and the words that are used to represent flesh are the discourse that "cuts up the continuum of beings into a pattern of characters."[61] Black flesh is not, therefore, inherently enslaveable; rather, discourse "brushes" Black flesh to create Black bodies that are enslaved and treated as chattel, such that the flesh under these bodies can be violated in any way deemed permissible by the "master's will." But this body is constructed by cultural forces such as law, and so social death is imposed upon Black bodies without ever being able to reduce Black flesh to the status of a capital-S Slave. Weheliye and Snorton help us see that this is the point in Spillers's theory that flesh exceeds the reach of the whip or the sight of the law, as flesh becomes an excess into which Black(ened) subjects may flow to engender fugitive movement that disfigures even as it sustains the violence of the law. The Black body is molded by discourse; it is not preordained, predetermined, fixed in place, or naturally occurring. Of course, this holds true for the white body as well, because flesh is not naturalized as Black, nor is Blackness naturalized as flesh. The brush of discourse that forms the Black body in the early stages of modernity as slavery solidifies as global practice also crafts white bodies, marking white subjects as also bearing the mark of discourse and therefore, as I argue in my reading of Claudia Rankine's Atlantic Ocean, meaning that white subjects do not escape living in the excessive present of slavery after the historical moment of emancipation.

In short, we might say that the flesh exceeds the capture of discourse even as it is mortified by the assaults of material violence, while the body coheres its legibility by way of the (enforced) articulations of discourse. The distinction is not a neat racialized distinction, wherein Black people have only flesh and white people get to have bodies, nor a relationship of unidirectional linearity in which flesh becomes body, but rather a recognition of simultaneously operating vectors of power's reach and limits. What this means for Jacobs is that she writes and theorizes along both vectors. On one hand, as a theorization within the parameters of the discursively recognizable *body* with a gender that is legible according to the grammars of law manifest in *partus sequitur ventrem*, *Incidents* is a critique of the terms of exclusion that separate Black women from the realm of womanhood enjoyed by the white women of Jacobs's audience. That is, if, in the grammar of law, on one hand, women get to mother their own children and, on the other, objects of property have no "right" to the objects they produce for their owners, then *Incidents* argues for Black people who produce children to be included in the law's grammar of "women." At the same time, as a theorization in the *flesh* unbound by the terms of discursive order in which bodies emerge as recognizable within existing structures of power, and thus ungendered insofar as flesh *exceeds* gender discourse, *Incidents* can be read as a rebellion against the recognition of the gendered body by way of critiquing the very violence that holds the body together for *both* white and Black "women."

This, finally, steers my reading of Jacobs's theorization of racial-sexual violence as a form of ungendering squarely into contemporary abolitionist thought as expressed in the distinction between *safety* and *security*, which I think can be mapped in parallel onto Spillers's landing in and on "*insurgent* ground" in the closing passage of "Mama's Baby, Papa's Maybe."

Stephen Wilson, an incarcerated educator and organizer, writes that "as prisoners, we live in a very secure environment. But security doesn't mean safety. There are barbed-wired fences, concrete walls, locked doors, cameras, gun towers and officers with riot gear, shock shields, tear gas and metal batons. . . . Being incarcerated, we know firsthand that policing and surveillance might create security, but they don't create safety."[62] Abolitionist thinker and activist Mariame Kaba expands on this:

> Security and safety aren't the same thing. Security is a function of the weaponized state that is using guns, weapons, fear and other things to "make us secure," right? All the horrible things are supposed to be kept at bay by these tools, even though we know that

horrible things continue to happen all the time with these things in place—and that these very tools and the corresponding institutions are reproducing the violence and horror they are supposed to contain. . . . Safety means something else, because you cannot have safety without strong, empathic relationships with others.[63]

For contemporary abolitionists, we want to get rid of a world in which people invest in *security* to protect their well-being and create in its stead a world in which people invest in *safety* to continuously sustain our (collective) well-being. And I'm not so sure this project is distinct from the one in which Jacobs's text is engaged as it perforates the limits of white supremacy, as it fails to cohere in the gendering and sexualizing law of *partus sequitur ventrem.*

Throughout *Incidents,* Jacobs repeatedly invokes the motif of protection, mostly in the form of law: "there is no shadow of law to protect [the slave girl] from insult, from violence, or even from death."[64] She often compares this status of unprotection to the relative protection afforded white women: "[your children, white women,] are your own, and no hand but that of death can take them from you."[65] At the same time, she expands the zone of nonprotection to include Black men, both enslaved *and* "free," when she tells how Dr. Flint threatened to shoot on sight the ostensibly free Black man with whom Linda had fallen in love. One might thus read *Incidents in the Life of a Slave Girl* as Jacobs's plea for Black people to be included within the bounds of protection.

Because she is writing to white women, rhetorically she deploys law's grammar of gender in a strategy of what Imani Perry might identify as "sympathetic occupation" to make this point. "Sympathetic occupation," Perry writes, "is at once the occupation of a normative notion of personhood or citizen in society, and the use of that occupation as a context in which to evoke sympathy from a potential readership."[66] The technique functions by way of denying expectations by confronting assumed universalisms with abrupt particularities. In other words, a reader may bring to an African American literary text their own notions of universal justice—notions about how the world is supposed to work. On this axis of interpretation, Jacobs's abolitionist feminism might be read as a political demand to abolish slavery so that Black men and women may enter into the law's grammar of gender—so that Blackness may cease to be *un*-gendered—in order to be within the zone of juridical bodily protection. And yet, as Spillers demonstrates, "this materialized scene of *unprotected* female flesh—of female flesh *'ungendered'*—offers a praxis and a theory, a text for living and for dying, and a method for reading both through their diverse mediations."[67] At the same time that Jacobs intends to argue for her inclusion within the protection of womanhood, if we linger with the text's considerations of *unprotected* female flesh as female flesh *ungendered,* to follow Spillers's parallel, other interpretive possibilities emerge.

On one hand, Jacobs sees white women as possessing a gender that grants them protection in the form of *security.* But, as the innumerable white women who themselves were victims of the sexual violence of white men could attest, that security granted by their gender was not, and still is not, genuine *safety.* As Kaba reminds us, security is protection against material violence that is made possible by the threat and enactment of material violence. It is thus an illusion of safety, as the protection is paid for by instruments of violence that can always be turned back on those whom they ostensibly protect. Additionally, those who believe themselves protected are protected only insofar as there exist objects of those instruments of violence that can be violated to maintain the machinations of security.

In contrast, safety is protection against harm made possible by maintaining interdependent relationships that materially and spiritually sustain mutual thriving through the sharing of resources and support structures without resorting to technologies of violence. *Incidents* clearly shows, through not only Mrs. Flint but also examples like Mrs. Wade, that white women's social positions were *secured* through their material violence against Black women.[68] But Jacobs makes clear that white women are not actually safe, themselves, in her repeated articulations of the dispossession of white women of their political agency and property rights by white men. White women are secured protection in their

gender through violence enacted against Black people of all genders, and at the same time that white women's security grants them
the juridical authority to mortally and sexually abuse Black flesh,
white women's gendered bodies cohere their meaning within the
terms of patriarchal order that dispossess them of the very rights
to the property that they "enjoy" in Black flesh. Womanhood, as a
race-gender position produced through the violences of modernity's ongoing Civilization project, is a *carceral technology of security*.
Here is an opportunity to follow Sharpe's directive to "think the
ways the hold cannot and does not hold even as the hold remains
in the form of the semiotics of the slave ship hold, the prison, the
womb, and elsewhere in and as the tension between being and in-
strumentality that is Black being in the wake."[69] As a poetics of
perforation, the ambiguity of *all*'s referent inhabits a carceral
technology written by law's grammar in order to undo its terms,
holding it together to make its argument and simultaneously rupturing it through a poetics of justice that the law cannot hold.

The law's grammar of gender that consolidates in *partus sequitur ventrem* and which was made possible by and in turn made
possible the violence of slavery is ultimately incapable of granting
something like safety even though it can, to a degree, bestow protection in security. This is why I believe we can see in Jacobs's text
not only her intended argument to be included in the law's arms of
protection but also a feminism that is focused, not on inclusion or
equality, but on *liberation*. This feminism, an abolitionist feminism
that may not at all be what Jacobs intended, would seek to create a
new universe of genders that would make possible the cultivation
of relationships that sustain safety. I think that Jacobs's analysis,
even if beyond her rhetorical intentions, might be, in Spillers's
words, "less interested in joining the ranks of gendered female-
ness than gaining the *insurgent* ground as female social subject."[70]
Gender equality as a political destination might not only be a false
horizon, but Jacobs's text helps us see colonial Western Gender
as a form of what Dylan Rodríguez would recognize as *counterinsurgency*—as a force meant to arrest the liberatory flows of flesh
that exceed the terms of law and order that demand technologies
of security.[71] Rather than juridical emancipation in the form of

recognizing her "rights" as a liberated subject of the state's "protection," Harriet Jacobs demands abolition of the full coalescence of forces that impose racialized gender violence.

The poetics of perforation in *Incidents* mobilizes Jacobs's skillful and dexterous manipulation of nineteenth-century literary and rhetorical conventions to craft an argument in the precise terms through which her audience would recognize a call for immediate political action while simultaneously starting a flow of the imagination toward terms that cannot fit those existing grammars. We add here another meaning to the "loophole of retreat." In addition to referring both to the literal garret in which Jacobs hides and the hole she carves in the attic's wall through which she watches her children, Jacobs's inhabitation of law's grammar of gender is a loophole through which a vision of justice not bound by the technologies of security called *man* and *woman* emerges. Just as she inhabits the crawl space above her grandmother's shed in order to leave the law's sight while still in its site, her text inhabits law's grammar to escape without leaving its terms of order, still under the constraints of her audience's expectations but never only defined by those expectations. As Jacobs inhabits the law, her text imagines beyond it.

METHOD MEANS MURDER: INHABITING LAW'S ARCHIVE IN PHILIP'S *ZONG!*

Perforation is tethered to inhabitation. Griggs's deployment of the promise of the threat and Jacobs's double-pronged call for inclusion within terms that her ambiguous pronouns destabilize are poetics of perforation enacted from authorial subject positions that inhabit rather than escape the targets of their critique. We might say that *perforation as a poetics mobilizes against the ordering capacities of law's grammar precisely by inhabiting that grammar.* The final section of this chapter thus stays with the difficulties of inhabitation in order to extrapolate the paradoxes of temporality and violence laid bare in Philip's *Zong!*

You have heard this story before. In November 1781, the British slave ship *Zong* was nearing the end of its water supply after overshooting its destination at Black River, Jamaica, while making a trip back from the African coast to sell enslaved people. Confronted with this depleting water supply in the face of his financial responsibilities to the owners of the ship, captain Luke Collingwood (or one of his subordinates—the archive is unclear on who made this decision) decided to dispose of one-third of the ship's cargo, which meant throwing 132 enslaved Africans overboard to their deaths. (Or 133—the archive is not definitive on the exact number. There is also evidence that one jettisoned African climbed back on board, and there are accounts of perhaps a dozen Africans throwing themselves into the sea; the mathematics of murder are hard to pin down.) This mode of killing was not uncommon as slave ships crossed the Atlantic and turned the ocean into a mass grave out of which Western modernity would grow, but this particular instance becomes an infamous event in the history of slavery because of how it so visibly enters into the archive.[72] James Walvin observes, "The atrocity might have passed virtually unnoticed [here I intervene into Walvin's sentence to ask, Unnoticed by whom?] but for one extraordinary fact: the syndicate of Liverpool businessmen who owned the *Zong* took their insurers to court to secure payment for the loss of the dead Africans."[73] The owners of the ship wished to be paid the value of the lost "cargo," but the insurers did not want to pay for what they argued was an unnecessary disposal of "goods."

I should say before moving on that every act of writing *about* the *Zong* Massacre is done in complicity with the legal archive's obliteration of the personhood of the enslaved. To write literary criticism about texts that take the massacre as their occasion is to repeat the jettisoning of the enslaved from the ship—and from the category of the Human. The desire to resolve this complicity, I argue here and more forcefully in *Abolition Time*'s third chapter, must be resisted as we read and act against law's violence.

The ensuing legal trial, *Gregson v. Gilbert*, was not a murder trial; it was an insurance case. There was no attempt to prove or disprove the killing of persons because the law did not register the bodies of human flesh that died to be persons. As Philip observes, the law "attempts to extinguish being": the legal documents in the archive do not record the being of the persons thrown overboard, only their monetary value as units of property. This is one reason that Philip says, "I don't trust the archive."[74] Philip's interview, her essays in *Zong!*, and the poetry itself reveal the way in which law is the archive (though, importantly, not the *only* archive). So it makes sense that if law is that which transforms human flesh into enslaved bodies and therefore ought not to be trusted, and *law,* given its existence *as a body of documents* that sets the parameters for interpreting future events based on the recorded past, *is the archive,* then one ought not to trust the archive itself. Philip encounters the law's attempt to extinguish being, but she sees that "where the law attempts to extinguish be-ing, as happened for 400 years as part of the European project, be-ing trumps law every time."[75] She sees that law can mark flesh with hieroglyphics and create bodies that are enslaved and reduced to nothing other than objects, but law cannot touch flesh's excess, despite its greatest fantasies of omnipotence.

What Philip exposes in seeing the law as itself the archive is the theoretical point that Renisa Mawani makes in "Law's Archive." Mawani's essay is a concise distillation of what she calls the "archival turn"—including Jacques Derrida's *Archive Fever: A Freudian Impression* and Michel Foucault's *Archeology of Knowledge and the Discourse on Language*—into a simple but profound observation that Philip's poetry stretches to its limits and possibilities, namely, that "law is the archive."[76] In attending to law as "(il)legitimate force of command," Mawani moves to think the archive not only through Derrida's *Archive Fever* but also through "Force of Law."[77] Derrida insists that "there is no such thing as law that doesn't imply *in itself, a priori, in the analytic structure of its concept,* the possibility of being 'enforced,' applied by force."[78] Because the law is *always* bound up with violence, Derrida argues, it becomes impossible to distinguish between the violence that "founds" law and the violence that sustains it. Mawani puts this together with Derrida's focus on the "archiviolithic" force of the archive in *Archive Fever* to herself conclude that "the double logic of violence that underwrites law as archive is not solely grammatological or epistemological but also ontological and material."[79] That is, the law is both discursively and materially violent, its grammar of order inseparable from the material enforcement of *corrections*. (Insofar as it is grounded in such an observation, *Abolition Time*'s designation of "law's grammar" is not mere metaphor.)

Yet, in the face of this double violence, it is precisely law's archive that is the site to which Philip goes to render poetically the enormous wound of the Middle Passage. The poetry in *Zong!* is made up of rearranged words found in the literal text of *Gregson v. Gilbert*, which Philip reproduces at the end of her book for reference. In an interview with Patricia Saunders published in 2005, when *Zong!* was still a work in progress, Philip said, "I have locked myself in the text in the hope of discovering something that remains hidden below the surface of the legal document. . . . I am rewarded by the fact that although I have imposed the limitation of the text on myself, I have been able to find a lot of freedom within those limitations."[80] Through her inhabitation of the very discursive force that sought to obliterate the being of African peoples, Philip crafts poetics of justice out of the anagrammatic rearrangement of law's archive, indexing through perforation that the body from which law derives violent force is itself defined by its own vulnerability to undoing.

Zong!'s poetics of perforation emerge *as* the text's very methodology of emergence—that is, its inescapable intertextuality with *Gregson v. Gilbert*. In a sense, *Zong!* is law even as it undoes law. *Zong!* both sustains and rends apart *Gregson v. Gilbert*; it both enlivens and undermines law's archive. Philip's book has been read variously as fugue, lyric or postlyric, ecopoetics, (anti-)elegy, and counterarchive, and critics have also written about her performances of the poetry.[81] Without discounting these previous framings of *Zong!*'s poetics, I attend in turn to how the poem's anagrammatic rearrangement of text; its shapes, spatial arrangement, and typography; and its wanderings through partial narration provoke practices of reading that illustrate the simultaneous power, seduction, and vulnerability of law, twisting law's grammar into a poetics of justice that highlights complicity and uncertainty as much as it suggests reparation.

Writing about *Zong!*, Anthony Reed argues that "in addition to positing a legal framework . . . the poem attests the necessity of invention."[82] I would add that the necessity of invention comes, partially, from the fact that the poetry of *Zong!* can never escape its own temporal out-of-jointness. That is, because it is written through the inhabitation of law's archive, it always explicitly marks the asynchronicity of its writing as its complicity with law's violence. There is no separation between the so-called past and present in the text of *Zong!* as the text of *Gregson v. Gilbert*. Building on Reed's thoughtful analysis of Philip's craft, I argue that invention is twinned with inhabitation in a poetics of perforation revealed by abolitionist close reading by considering the anagrammatic rearrangement of *Gregson v. Gilbert* that readers encounter in the first section of *Zong!*, titled "Os," meaning "bone" in Latin. The invention in these poems—numbered 1 through 26 and often recognized by students when I teach Philip's book as the "least intimidating" or "most recognizably structured" poetry in *Zong!*—is both noun and verb, refiguring *time* and *justice* as processes enacted by the *doing* of poetics.

Appearing at a distance to mimic the columnal textual arrangement of a ship ledger (like numerous poems in "Os"), "Zong #18" vibrantly illustrates the simultaneous mattering of nouns and verbs. The poem disarticulates the words of *Gregson v. Gilbert* into a poetic form that initiates movement against the stagnation of law's archive, which then multiply invokes the word *means* for its denotations of method, interpretation or definition, and mathematical averages.

Only two words are repeated in the poem: "water" appears twice, and "means" appears nineteen times. In the archival text of *Gregson v. Gilbert* that Philip provides in *Zong!*, the word "water" appears fifteen times, while "means" appears just once. In the paragraph summarizing the argument put forth by Davenport, Pigott, and Heywood—the lawyers for the insurers—the word appears in this sentence: "The truth was, that finding they should have a bad market for their slaves, they took these means of transferring the loss from the owners to the underwriters."[83] This sentence does tremendous work explaining the legal argument against paying insurance money for the jettisoned cargo without arguing that mass murder took place. Most literally, the

Zong! #18

         means

truth

means   overboard

         means

sufficient

means   support

         means

foul

means   three butts

         means

necessity

means   provisions

         means

perils

Toyin Sipho Adelabu Lisabi Fayemi Eki

31

"Zong! #18" by M. NourbeSe Philip. Courtesy of the author.

word *means* is used in the sentence to refer to the *methods*—both plans made and actions taken—that the captain and crew used to shift the financial burden of mismanaged resources from the ship owners to the underwriters. The first three words—"the truth was"—as a transitional phrase signaling contrast with preceding sentences, announces that this sentence reveals through *interpretation* the proper *meaning* of events aboard the *Zong.* And the question at hand that the subjects of the sentence—the crew who were using the *means* that the sentence interprets into *meaning*—act upon is a question of balance sheets organized by the mathematics of racial terror: who will bear the economic cost for so much property jettisoned from a slave ship?

Philip's poem tracks all three of these strands of *means* tied together in this sentence through its use of repetition, structure, and interruption. At an immediate first glance, there are at least two readily apparent ways to read the poem: you can read top to bottom and left to right, as one conventionally does in English, starting with "means/truth/means/overboard" and so on, or you can read down the left-hand column first before reading down the right-hand column, as if it were a table of lists, which would give "truth/means/sufficient/means." Of those two choices, the latter is the first to offer words in an order that forms a grammatical sentence—"Truth means sufficient means," as in the truth is defined as having methods adequate to the question at hand. But what methods are adequate to the question posed by law's archive of the *Zong* Massacre? "Zong #18" does not readily offer a string of sentences like this first one, but a number of word strings yield provocative phrases ("necessity/means/provisions" on a slave ship because you better have enough supplies to meet the needs of everyone on board). Mining the text for these phrases leaves a reader wondering whether finding "meaning" through stringing together phrases from an exploded text is an adequate means for confronting the law's violence, when all of the pieces through which we are sifting are tools of that very violence. To repeat, this poem is crafted out of a sentence that encodes without question the object-status of the enslaved as cargo. And by directly drawing attention to the *means* of deciphering *meaning*, the poem demands that we as readers take stock of our own reading, our own inhabitation of the poem as it inhabits the legal archive. The poem's poetics inhabit our time and act of reading, as our reading selves inhabit the archival time of *Gregson v. Gilbert* while face-to-face with the inadequacy of our methods for accounting (finding the *mean?*) for the enormity of the ontological violence of the law in the history of slavery as a history of jettisoning and drowning.

The last lines of the poem, perhaps—at the risk of searching too hard for definitive meaning—swallow the reader in the enormity of the stakes of the questions at hand. Having established a visual and syntactical pattern wherein "means" is every other word unit, whether reading conventionally or down columns, the poem interrupts its own pattern in the final three "rows" of its structure when "means" meets "water." On the left is how the final five words of the poem are arranged in the text, and on the right is how they would be arranged (with an additional "missing" "means") if the spatial pattern of the poem were continued uninterrupted:

means	want		means	want
water				*means*
means	water		water	
			means	water

My preoccupation with the Atlantic Ocean from chapter 1 resurfaces here in my reading of this interrupted pattern as perforation by submergence. While at sea, fresh, drinkable water falls down from the sky onto the ship, while undrinkable saltwater seeps in through pores or holes or cracks, rising from the bottom of the boat. At the bottom of the ship/ledger that is "Zong #18," "water" gathers to itself a double, becoming the only word besides "means" to appear more than once, the second "water" seeping into the sentence from law's archive now that Philip's inhabitation has allowed her to perforate its grammar. Comparing the left (actual) and right (if the pattern were to continue) versions of the poem, we see that "water" has moved upward, washing out an iteration of "means" that should have been there to continue the poem's means evidence

means

mortality

means policy

means

voyage

means market

means

slaves

means more

means

dead

means want

water

means water

Okeowo Sonubi Modele Madoda Chenzira

“Zong #18” by M. NourbeSe Philip. Courtesy of the author.

pattern and shifting the spatial configuration of the poem's shape. Order has been established and interrupted by water creeping up to submerge the *means* of "Zong #18." Method, interpretation, and mathematics disappear into water, remaining irretrievable, but not without leaving a trace in our noticing of the pattern's break. Law's grammar, as the ordering force of law's archive, is anagrammatically rendered into a poetics of perforation that lets the sea seep in, resulting in ...?

Here I lose my grammar as a literary critic, stewing in the openness of ellipses, grasping for the ribbon of a question mark to signify my reluctance to end that sentence, as the poem forces me to face the limits of my methods' inadequacy. What means for making meaning out of human lives reduced to arithmetic means can possibly do something like justice here? The best I can say is that Philip's poetics of perforation, crafted through inhabitation, open space. Perhaps perforation transforms the periods of law's archive—the punctuation mark that defines the event of a sentence as *over*—into ellipses?

Zong!'s first page suggests how the book as a whole will resist the "ordering mechanism" of grammar that Philip herself identifies as the "mechanism of force."[84] In "Zong #1," the phrase "want of water" is stretched, folded, interrupted, and scattered into a poem that immediately escapes the textuality of the printed page by the way it demands—in a way similar to Suzan-Lori Parks's dialogue-writing, which draws our attention to annunciation—to be spoken aloud through the body, drawing breath, gasp, and gurgle out of the throat of the reader. Beginning in a moment wherein, according to Sharpe, "thirst dissolves language," "Zong! #1" confronts the reader with a page of mostly empty space, with letters scattered throughout, almost to the point of looking like a connect-the-dots puzzle or like leaves scattered by wind over the surface of water or bodies floating on the surface with the swelling of death before sinking to the bottom to be lost forever.[85] A puzzle, a scattering, a death scene: these are some of the possible re/dis-formulations and dis-articulations Philip carves out of *Gregson v. Gilbert.* While the rest of the poems in "*Os*" after this first one are more akin to "Zong #18," the spatial dis/organization of stretched and torn-apart archival material remains prominent. As readers move through *Zong!* from "*Os*" through "*Sal*," "*Ventus*," "*Ratio*," "*Ferrum*," and "*Ebora*," the spatial arrangement of the words and letters on the page appears to loosen further, spreading across the paper as, in Philip's words, "each cluster of words is seeking the space or the silence above."[86] Flipping the pages from front to back cover, readers' eyes watch as the words of individual poems move, sometimes in what appear to be the neat lines and columns of a ship's ledger or poetic catalog, sometimes in pockets of textual density surrounded by blank space, sometimes in seemingly random distributions of letters, sometimes in what look to be discernable shapes that mimic the movement of fish or debris through water, sometimes in what looks like smoke billowing up through the air or bubbles rising through water, and then, near the end, in "*Ebora*," in what appears to be the fashion of pools of oil seeping into each other, becoming darker in some places than others, before finally letters in different fonts and of different shades overwrite each other on the excessively cluttered final page before the glossary of terms.

This final page renders visual the palimpsestic nature of *Zong!*, which in turn renders poetic the palimpsestic nature of *Gregson v. Gilbert*. As the words on this final page bleed ink into each other and make it nearly impossible to tell which layer of letters is "on top of" which, Philip's poetry writes over the text of law's archived documents, muddying the clarity asserted in the insurance case. That is, whereas the insurance case as it is recorded in law's archive gives a simple equation wherein the bodies of the enslaved people equal property, as if the question were decided, Philip's overlaying of words and letters and bleeding together of lines of ink break that equation. This is an instance in which excess is not only the phenomenon of oppression established in the so-called past exerting force on the present; rather, here, the excess of ink dilutes the certainty of the hold that mechanisms of oppression established in what is thought of as the past can assert on the present. Of course, that asserted clarity in *Gregson v. Gilbert* was itself a palimpsest, a rewriting that covered up the being in the flesh of those bodies thrown overboard. *Zong!* explodes the text of *Gregson v. Gilbert* from the inside and scatters its raw material. Law's archive, *Gregson v. Gilbert* in this case, as the body of law's force, is revealed in all of its vulnerability to be the contingent force that it is, incapable of omnipotence even as it retains its capacity for world-destroying violence.

The exploded text of *Zong!* un-tells the story that the legal text tells and renders the meaning of that court case into unmeaning: "The disorder, illogic, and irrationality of the *Zong!* poems can no more tell the story than the legal report of *Gregson v. Gilbert* masquerading as order, logic, and rationality. In their very disorder and illogic is the not-telling of the story that must be told."[87] Reading *Zong!* is thus a task of searching for a method of responsibly encountering unmeaning presented through not-telling, and such a task may remain irresolvable.

Philip recounts throughout her essay at the end of *Zong!*, "Notanda," a number of "characters" and incomplete narrative threads that emerge in the text. This includes the name Dido, an unnamed white man with authority on the ship, and "women's voices." We can add the names Ruth, Ade, Sade, Wale, and Claire, as well as discernable scenes of violence, to the flashes of narrative representation that flicker across the surface of *Zong!*'s untelling. Like I have done in my attempt to close-read the repetition, structure, and ambiguities of "Zong #18," scholarship on *Zong!* often engages in a kind of search for meaning in a text that resists the ordering logic of grammar that Philip equates with the force of law. These readings often uncover discernable scenes and voices. Sarah Dowling alerts us to a "narrative of sexual assault" that "is intertwined with descriptions of throwing someone, probably the victim, overboard,"[88] and Anne Quéma outlines further instances of violence to show that "central to Philip's critique is rape, which is all at once a singular act of violence and a collective trauma."[89] Sasha Ann Panaram highlights "audible enactments of Black breath—songs, shouts, cries, moans, and groans—in and through Black women whose breath interrupts atmospheric conditions" of violence,[90] and Nicole Gervasio traces the name "Ruth" through three different iterations in the text that elaborate this centrality of sexual violence. Dowling ultimately argues that *Zong!* is not a project of mere recovery of voices but instead "break[s]" the association of voice with personhood,"[91] and Gervasio self-reflexively posits that "the irony of Philip's text is that readers *must* violate her disorder by wrenching her verse back into the constraints of narrative logic. . . . Where Philip's rules affirm incoherency, irrationality, and circularity, the reader's instincts search for coherency, rationality, and linearity."[92] I ask, even as I do it myself, *must* we?

I refuse to suggest here that such scholarly endeavors are incorrect or simply ethically dubious—indeed, I believe our collective thinking is enriched by close, critical readings of *Zong!* that examine moments of discernable meaning. At the same time, I follow Philip's model in "Notanda" of explicitly foregrounding the complicity of the writer and the critic with the violence of law's archive as we examine law's grammar for the possibilities opened by poetics of justice. Philip writes:

> And since we have to work to complete the events, we all become implicated in, if not contaminated by, this activity. . . .
>
> The half-tellings, and un-tellings force me to enter the zone of contamination to complete it; in so doing I risk being contaminated by the prescribed language of the law—by language in fact. . . .
>
> And, by refusing the risk of allowing ourselves to be absolved of authorial intention, we escape an understanding that we are at least one and the Other.[93]

Abolition Time's third chapter will directly take up questions of contamination and risk by way of a critique of witnessing as a mode of ethical reading, but I end the current chapter here, staying with the difficulty outlined by Philip, to underscore that abolitionist literary studies is not simply applying a political desire to a text to produce the reading that we might want ahead of time—*look, this is how this text models liberation.* Instead, a commitment to abolitionist close reading means checking our own desires and highlighting the limits of our methods—not merely in the footnotes or asides but as an integral part of the methodology itself. We may want to read Jacobs as escaping the enslaver's surveillance or successfully evading the reach of *partus sequitur ventrem,* and we may want to read Philip as repairing the harm done to those enslaved persons jettisoned from the *Zong,* and we may want to tell ourselves that our scholarship itself produces something like justice for the dead, but if we are to inhabit the violence of an ongoing archive and its ordering force, we must account for our contamination by implication.

My reading of Jacobs's, Griggs's, and Philip's poetics of perforation has insisted that by inhabiting various instantiations of law's grammar of violence, the texts at hand produce poetics of justice that open space for thinking and doing *livability* in an unlivable world, even as the inhabitation that is the condition of possibility for perforation is also that which winds up sustaining the structures of unlivability that the poetics undermine. Perforation both undermines and sustains law's grammar. And this chapter, as a reading of perforation, both sustains and undermines literary criticism as a practice. *Abolition Time*'s poetics of perforation is a reading practice that opens space for thinking in excess of the ordering grammars of law, but by relying on the traditional tools of formalist close reading, it sustains the very ordering logics that *discipline* knowledge into carceral logics in the first place. This is a contaminated book, an implicated method. And yet, what might we glimpse through the holes that are opened?

Every time you see me, you want to mess with me. I'm tired of it. It stops today. Why would you . . . ? Everyone standing here will tell you I didn't do nothing. I did not sell nothing. Because every time you see me, you want to harass me. You want to stop me [garbled] selling cigarettes. I'm minding my business, officer, I'm minding my business. Please just leave me alone. I told you the last time, please just leave me alone. Please please, don't touch me. Do not touch me. [garbled] I can't breathe. I can't breathe. I can't breathe. I can't breathe. I can't breathe. I can't breathe. I can't breathe. I can't breathe. I can't breathe. I can't breathe. I can't breathe.

—Eric Garner

An Interlude on Method, or
Abolition Is Not a Metaphor

In the first half of *Abolition Time*, I have read poetics of accumulation and perforation as poetics of justice against the event-time of law's grammar of order. I hope to have shown by this point that close reading with and against the grain of literary texts can open up our ability not only to "imagine otherwise" through their representational content (e.g., slavery and abolition) but to see how texts' manipulations of temporality, genre conventions, and readerly expectations through their literary and rhetorical techniques sketch on the page philosophies of justice. Be it accumulation's shattering of the bounded juridical event and its attendant singular subject or perforation's escape from law's force while inhabiting its very grammars of violence, the poetics I have read thus far register that nonjuridical philosophies of justice exist in the excessive present of our *now*. But both accumulation's rupture and perforation's necessary inhabitation result in uncertainty and speculation. And neither mode of poetics is able, in M. NourbeSe Philip's words, which recall Walter Benjamin's Angel of History, to "defend the dead" in the wake of law's violence as it secures the afterlife of slavery as the ongoing terror of our present's catastrophic crises of settler colonialism, extractive racial capitalism, and carceral cisheteropatriarchy.

At the end of the previous chapter's reading of Philip's *Zong!*, I claimed that "abolitionist close reading means checking our own desires and highlighting the limits of our methods—not merely in the footnotes or the asides, but as an integral part of the methodology itself." This interlude is an attempt at continuing to name the limits of my book's method, which I do through reflecting on my own evolution of political consciousness into abolitionism and naming my desires so I might, if not undo, then at least check them as I turn to the second half of the book.

So I pause here to mourn Eric and Erica Garner. I pause here in the middle of *Abolition Time* to think about breath and the impossibility of resurrection, to consider again the limitations of abolitionist literary studies, to consider again abolition as a thinking of and with the impossible in the wake of the unbearable.

On July 17, 2014, Eric Garner was killed by New York Police Department (NYPD) officer Daniel Pantaleo. Officer Pantaleo used an illegal choke hold on Garner, who was unarmed, ending Garner's life as he stated eleven times that he could not breathe. The entire murder was captured on video that has been widely circulated, and the NYPD itself acknowledged the illegality of the choke hold, but in December 2014, a grand jury decided not to indict Pantaleo. What seemed like straightforward evidence of an excessive and improper use of lethal force—a video of a police officer escalating a situation in which nobody was using force approaching the threshold of lethal to the level of using lethal force on a citizen under no more than the suspicion of selling loose cigarettes—failed to register as cause for bringing the law's arm of punishment to bear on Garner's killer. This failure to register speaks to the underlying racist structure of U.S. law, which frames how objects of evidence can or cannot enter legal discourse to shape policy and decisions.

Although I was convinced that policing and the prison-industrial complex were structurally racist before Garner's death, it was the nonindictment of Pantaleo that finally broke my remaining faith in the possibility of reforming existing legal and political institutions to do something like justice in the face of anti-Black violence. In my naïvety, I thought that because we could see the murder on video, and because even NYPD policy itself forbade the choke hold technique that Pantaleo is seen—on video!—using, surely this time the legal system would have no choice but to hold a killer cop accountable. The evidence was just too clear. Working within a paradigm of "witnessing," whereby I believed that if injustice could be *seen*, it could be rectified, I was sure that because so many people could, via video, witness Garner's murder, the law would be forced into action.

But I was, of course, incredibly wrong. The problem was not a lack of evidence or an impossible barrier to witnessing injustice that could be rectified in the twenty-first century by the ubiquity of cell phone cameras but a grammar of law that could not witness the video *as* evidence of murder. Despite the nonevent of emancipation, the very same grammar of *Gregson v. Gilbert* that precluded the possibility of seeing the *Zong* Massacre as mass murder remained at play. It is a grammar elaborated by Sylvia Wynter's analysis of the Los Angeles Police Department's "No Humans Involved" designation, in Derrick Bell's diagnosis of the "permanence of racism," and in Dylan Rodríguez's explication of the "logics of genocide."[1] It is a grammar that cannot register Eric Garner as mournable, grievable Human life, and so it is a grammar into which the video of his death cannot discernably emerge.

In the case of the video of Pantaleo killing Garner, when that video enters into the realm of discourse structured by the law and its preexisting archives of precedent, it fails to become legible as evidence of either murder or manslaughter, not because of a literal failure to translate languages or a gap on the level of culture. Rather, it fails to become legible on the level of structure because of the antagonistic relationship between Blackness and the Human, since law is the purview of the Human.[2] Or, in Guitar's words in Toni Morrison's *Song of Solomon*, "ain't no law for the colored man except the one sends him to the chair."[3] Black people are not outside the law's protection because of *cultural* difference but because of the *structural position* Blackness occupies in relation to law. Namely, Blackness, and Black people's bodies in particular, is the ground on which the signpost of the law is raised. With Saidiya Hartman's argument that the policing power of white people during slavery translates into the police powers consolidated after emancipation underpinning my thinking with Bell and other critical race theorists, I have since come to argue that the video of Garner's death failed to act as evidence for an indictment not simply because individual members of the Richmond County grand jury were racist but because the structural position from which the video "testified" could not be recognized as a legitimate position from which to charge that an agent of the state's monopoly on violence had committed unjustified murder.[4] That position from which the video gives its evidence is the position still structured by *Dred Scott v. Sanford*—a position of unrecognizability before the law—even after the Fourteenth Amendment.[5] Because the law depends on its enactment of violence against Black bodies for its continued sustenance, if it were to recognize Garner's death as unjustified, it would thereby recognize its own "founding violence" as illegitimate, thus jeopardizing its own "mythical foundations of authority."[6] Therefore the video fails to translate, not across a gap in language or culture, but across a structural antagonism. The law's preexisting structures of reading prohibit the video from registering as evidence of murder, because 231 years after the law defined the *Zong* Massacre as *not* an act of murder, it is evident that when Black people die as objects of state violence, the script is that there are "No Humans Involved." This is a grammar of law that literally kills, and it requires nothing less than total abolition.

If we listen to Garner's final words to the police, we can hear the accumulation that Rankine illustrates through Serena Williams in *Citizen*. Garner was protesting his treatment in that moment, but he was also speaking to multiple nows:

> "every time you see me,"
>> "I'm tired of it,"
>>> "every time you see me,"
>>>> "I told you the last time."

In addition to registering the unjust treatment to which he is subjected in the singularity of the moment, Garner's last words register the nonsingularity of the moment and signal his refusal to be handcuffed (by moving his hands away) as a refusal of a continuously unfolding event of attempted capture.

This continuously unfolding event is what I saw when I first watched the video of Pantaleo killing Garner. I could not help myself from seeing the police officers as slave patrollers enforcing the 1850 Fugitive Slave Law, capturing Garner's body simply because he was Black and therefore not a legal citizen. As I have stressed repeatedly, such resonance does not erase the fact that Garner *indeed was* a legal citizen with a full set of human and civil rights that makes him *clearly distinct* from self-emancipated fugitives in the nineteenth century, and yet when his death enters into the legal archive *as a legal killing,* this distinction becomes less sharp. Like the murder trial that never happened for the 132 enslaved Africans thrown overboard the *Zong,* Pantaleo's nonindictment means that Garner's death is recorded forever in the legal archive as justified. It *should not* be the case that this observation could be made. It *should* be unthinkable that Garner's arrest bears resonance with slave patrollers' capture of the self-emancipated or that Pantaleo's nonindictment bears resonance with the nonquestion of murder in *Gregson v. Gilbert.* Slavery's presence in this present is excessive.

In the wake of Eric's murder, his daughter Erica took up the task of fighting the racist system that killed her father. Although the Garner family was awarded a financial settlement with the city of New York, Erica was steadfast in her radical activism to hold the NYPD accountable for its racism, pushing for a federal civil rights investigation of her father's death while refusing to have her father's memory incorporated into mainstream liberal politics.

Erica Garner died on December 30, 2017, after suffering a heart attack. She was a daughter and a mother as well as an activist, and she is survived by two children, whom she raised and nurtured while doing her tireless work for justice as a figure of what Joy James would name the "captive maternal."[7] Erica wrote of one meeting with U.S. Department of Justice officials:

> I wasn't enthused at all. They kept talking in circles, and not answering questions, until my son, who I was carrying in my arms at the time, told me that he would rather eat lunch than waste any more time watching our conversation go nowhere. It's frustrating, because while we waited to hear something new, what we got was

the same old "be patient" speech and vague comments like "we are working as hard as we can to ensure justice." But as the federal government is deciding if they are going to bring charges against my dad's killers, I have been working furiously to get justice somehow someway on my own.[8]

Erica's attention to mothering is not separate from her attention to activism. Her child is with her in the room while she is seeking justice for her dead father. It is not to romanticize Erica or to transform her into a superhuman savior-figure to observe that quite literally in this moment, in this quiet space of a procedural meeting with a team of investigators, she is simultaneously working to extend the life of her child, to nourish his body so that he may breathe into the future, in the wake of a moment when her father's breathing was so callously extinguished, and to pull the future into the present by pushing investigators to stop making vague promises of justice to come. Erica Garner was demanding justice now, and her daily living practices enacted a futurity in her here and now precisely because she found the notion of a then and there posited by the legal system to be so unacceptable as a horizon for justice. The last words of her posthumously published final essay on the federal civil rights investigation are "Now it's been three years later, and we're still waiting on justice." In her father's words, "this [waiting] stops today."

Erica Garner has joined her father, also too soon, in death. Her daughter Alyssa and her son, also named Eric, survive. Her family shared these words on the morning of her death: "When you report this you remember she was human: mother, daughter, sister, aunt. Her heart was bigger than the world. It really really was. She cared when most people wouldn't have. She was good. She only pursued right, no matter what. No one gave her justice."[9]

No amount of writing can give the Garners justice. My insistence on the presence of futurity is not a utopic imagining of salvation, redemption, or the deliverance of justice for the dead. It is merely an attempt to articulate the possibilities that exceed law's excessive violence.

I insist on placing this interlude at the center of *Abolition Time*'s four chapters to highlight, rather than hide in the footnotes or the preface, the limits of my project, as I believe it necessary in doing this work that I genuinely think of as important, even as I insist on its smallness. On the heels of chapter 2's interrogation of readerly or scholarly desire when encountering texts about slavery, of my thinking with Philip's meditations on the implication she and her readers have with the violence of law's archive and the risk she and we must take in embracing that implication as a condition of our work, I recall here the historical moment that I remember as the autobiographical moment at which I decided that reform was not enough. I will never write my way around the fact that my political consciousness has been formed through my processing of so much death—and through one particular death. If the *Zong* Massacre has been the object of my academic obsession for nearly a decade, Eric Garner's death and the history that haunts his last name have been the presence outlining the limits of my academic obsession (Christina Sharpe writes, "I am reading/hearing echoes of Margaret Garner in all of this" when Eric enters her elaboration of "aspiration" in *In the Wake*[10]). Nothing that I write, here or elsewhere, will ever do justice to the Garners' stolen lives.

Abolition is not a metaphor. It requires the literal dismantling of prisons, the literal disarming of police, and the literal end of settler-colonial racial capitalism's regimes of binary gender and private property. It is not a poetic figure. It is a method of living and acting in and beyond the realm of politics. It is not an academic field of study, even as it is itself inseparable from study. To the extent that it takes place inside universities and in scholarly books published by university presses, abolitionist literary studies, then, can have no illusions about what close reading does and doesn't do.

With the humility of all that *Abolition Time* is not seeking to do, I continue to write as an invitation. I write in the hope that more join in abolitionist study, in applying our various disciplinary methods of inquiry to investigating what models of thinking and doing justice beyond the juridical, the adversarial, or the penal exist. I write with the conviction that even though our methodologies are, taken individually, inadequate to the scale of the task at hand, they can be put to use in service of the abolitionist chorus.

Noting limitations is not the same as arriving at a trap. Ruth Wilson Gilmore offers the following interpretation of Audre Lorde's oft-quoted assertion that "the master's tools will never dismantle the master's house," which I find invigorating for both academic analysis and activist praxis:

> As with any theoretical premise, Lorde's caveat is useful only if the elements—whose paring away enables its elegance and urgency— are added back, so that the general truth of the abstraction has concrete meaning for day-to-day life. The issue is not whether the master uses, or endorses the use of, some tool or another. Rather, who controls the conditions and the ends to which any tools are wielded? Control is not easy. In the culture of opposition, control, tentative at best, results from risky forays rather than documentable ownership through capital accumulation. Lorde proposes a decisive seizure whose strategy works towards multiple ends. First, Lorde's focus on tools requires us to concentrate on fundamental orderings in political economy. If the master loses control of the means of production, he is no longer the master. Thus, relations of production are transformed in the process. Second, her focus on the master's house guides our attention towards institutions and luxury. The house must be dismantled so that we can recycle the materials to institutions of our own design, usable by all to produce new and liberating work.[11]

In this passage, Gilmore helps us understand that we may very well, like Philip rearranging the text of *Gregson v. Gilbert* into *Zong!*, have to work with contaminated tools. With a materialist commitment to reordering the distributions of resources and means of production of such tools, I write with conviction that even the highly disciplined and disciplining methodology of close reading, for all that it cannot do, retains utility as a contaminated tool that can be repurposed—a grammar that can be inhabited in order to perforate itself. The work that *Abolition Time* demands is always in excess of textuality and the task of reading, even as it remains focused on those planes of action. Refusing to resolve itself into either defeat or victory, abolitionist literary studies, as I am trying to practice it here, remains discomforting even as it remains invitational and welcoming. Let us be discomforted together so that our study might help us figure out where to go from here.

The final two chapters of *Abolition Time* take up, in turn, two problems for justice made all too real in the deaths of Eric and Erica Garner: the failure of witnessing as a mode of ethics and the simultaneous impossibility and necessity of Black futurity in the wake of extinguished breath. Staying with the discomfiture of the inadequacy of its methods, I continue in the second half of the book to close-read the poetics of justice at work in literary texts that refigure justice, not as juridical event, but as ongoing practice in excess of law's reach. First, as a way to think through the failure of witnessing made so obvious by Pantaleo's nonindictment, I examine a poetics of *witnessing* in late twentieth- and twenty-first-century neo–slave narratives. Then, in the final chapter, as a way of thinking in (*not* "through") the paradox of Black futurity as it exceeds without escaping Eric Garner's repetitions of "I can't breathe," I look to poetics of *breath* in the form of nonreproductive futurity figured through representations of childless mothering.

While abolition is not a metaphor, it may very well be an embodied poetics that manifests in breath, not as a figure, but as a literal practice threading through a Black radical tradition of abolitionist thought and action. A single breath is a connection to this present now that holds the potential but never the promise of the next breath to come, even as it gives life to the vibrant actions taken in its own *now*.

During the long nights I was restless for want of air . . .
Yet the laws allowed him to be out in the free air,
while I, guiltless of crime, was pent up here,
as the only means of avoiding the cruelties
the laws allowed him to inflict upon me!
—Harriet Jacobs

I had to leave;
I needed to be in a place
where I could breathe
and not feel someone's hand
on my throat.
—James Baldwin

To say we must be free of air,
while admitting to knowing no other source of breath,
is what I have tried to do here.
—Frank B. Wilderson III

When we revolt it's not for a particular culture.
We revolt simply because,
for many reasons,
we can no longer
breathe.
—Frantz Fanon

THREE

Witnessing

IMPOSSIBLE RECOVERY, FAILED
RECOGNITION, AND THE OBLIGATION OF RISK

> I put forth that black cultural production that attends
> to slavery not only involves the work of rememory and
> return but also contains within it an anticipatory ur-
> gency that looks forward, to the present, and surveys
> the unsurprising and mundane work of contemporary
> racial violences.
>
> —Katherine McKittrick, *"Dear Science" and Other Stories*

> The necessity of trying to represent what we cannot,
> rather than leading to pessimism or despair must be
> embraced as the impossibility that conditions our
> knowledge of the past and animates our desire for a lib-
> erated future.
>
> —Saidiya V. Hartman, "Venus in Two Acts"

If publicly bearing witness to the murder of Eric Garner could not
bring justice, then witnessing itself is thrown into crisis as a potential mode of ethics. This crisis is taken up by Saidiya Hartman
early in *Scenes of Subjection* when she critiques empathy as an act
of obliteration. It is one of the pillars on which the now familiar
dialogue that Fred Moten builds with Hartman concerning Frederick Douglass's recounting of his aunt (H)Esther's beating is built.[1]
And it is at the heart of ongoing debates concerning the efficacy
of body cameras on police officers as a solution to state violence.
At issue here are a number of interconnected ethical concepts
that are fundamental to liberal political and moral imaginations:

witnessing, empathy, and recognition. And in the context of reading modern and contemporary literatures of chattel slavery, including the genre of the neo-slave narrative, these ethical concepts are inseparable from questions of temporality.

On one hand, conventional liberal politics—as observable, for example, in "rights" discourse—is built on a faith in the politics of recognition, wherein to recognize the other as a fellow subject is to extend to them the rights of civil subjecthood. Along this thread, empathy as conjured through witnessing the suffering of the other is imagined as a reliable pathway to recognition, which, again, leads to "rights" and thus ethical engagement and political security. But on the other hand—as Hartman, Alexander Weheliye, Dean Spade, Glen Coulthard, Lisa Lowe, and others argue via various analytics—the recognition of the "other" as a liberal subject included within civil society itself entails violence that reinforces subjection.[2] On this axis, either witnessing in practice fails to conjure empathy or, if empathy is conjured, it winds up working to reaffirm the position of the observer and reinforce the inequitable structure that maintains the subjection of the object of the witnessing gaze. In short, the faith placed in witnessing's ability to conjure empathy, and the faith placed in empathy to conjure ethical relation and legal rights, is misplaced.

This ethical problem is at the heart of my pedagogy when I teach literatures of slavery. As such, this chapter of *Abolition Time* lingers with the crisis of witnessing that I recount in the interlude on Eric Garner's murder by way of a critical reflection on my practice of reading and teaching neo-slave narratives. When I teach this genre of texts—no matter the type of course in which I teach them—students consistently articulate the same initial responses to questions about what the texts are doing and/or what might be gleaned from engaging with them. These initial responses have become predictable (which I say without any value judgment) in the way that they are framed by linear models of temporality, assumptions about the redressive capacities of memory and remembering, and investments in witnessing and empathy as ethical frameworks for reading literature.

Broadly, my students consistently encounter neo-slave narratives as objects that fill in the gaps of history left by their formal education regarding the lives of enslaved Africans. They often see the filling in of gaps with new knowledge as, itself, an *ethical* act of redress for the wrongs of slavery, which are framed as terrible but ultimately in the past, even if said wrongs still affect the present. Reading neo-slave narratives, in this initial framing, is articulated as a form of witnessing, whereby we as contemporary readers are able to see and understand the violence and injustice of the past. And by bearing witness to it, so this reasoning goes, we are able to leave the text transformed for the better, able to "do justice" to that past from which we are separate even as heirs.

It is my goal to help students to read neo-slave narratives as doing something other than this familiar and, I argue, too-tidy ethical framing. Aida Levy-Hussen observes that "certain habits of reading black historical fiction have calcified into restrictive habit," and for me, "remembering," "acknowledging," and "witnessing" the past connote such calcified habits of reading, which are perceptible not only in my classrooms but at conferences, at roundtables, and in the pages of both academic journals and more public cultural criticism media.[3] I believe that part of what makes these habits attractive is that they offer clean and discernably progressive moral accounts of how to live in the wake of a history that hurts, within which "acknowledging" what happened becomes a fundamentally morally "good" act. Here I am after reading practices that get us beyond acknowledging harm into an ethical realm that is less tidy and more demanding.

While I do not dispute that there is dangerous investment—both discursively and materially—by the governing forces of settler-colonial racial empire to "silence the past," as Michel-Rolph Trouillot has shown, I believe that when we read Black historical fiction as overdetermined by the task of countering that silencing, we get ourselves "stuck," in Levy-Hussen's language, in a dialectic that ultimately winds up maintaining the ruling epistemic terms of order.[4] In contrast to this overdetermined reading, like Katherine McKittrick, I see Black creative work that engages slavery as "not only involv[ing] the work of rememory and return but also contain[ing] within it an anticipatory urgency that looks forward, to the present."[5] That is, I see historical fiction focalized on chattel slavery as being equally about the present and future as much as it is about the past. As Hartman asks in *Lose Your Mother: A Journey along the Atlantic Slave Route*, "to what end does one conjure the ghosts of slavery, if not to incite the hopes of transforming the present?"[6] In other words, literary engagement with the "past that is not past" of slavery, to continue echoing Christina Sharpe's phrasing, ought to be read as engagement with the *now* of writing, rather than as a preoccupation with the loss of the archive.

We know that slavery's archive is founded in violence and governed by erasure. Reading a literary text about slavery and interpreting it as reiterating this point, then, is too flattening. Therefore, when teaching, I help students read for the moments of difficulty in such texts, moments that call into question the efficacy of "acknowledging the past" as bearing any kind of redressive power, and I ask us all to dwell together in the discomfort of these moments. Together with my students, I ask, What might happen if we take seriously what literatures of slavery *fail to do* as a point from which to ask questions about ethical relationships with the past that is not past? (Because, after all, since the past is the present is the future, we cannot have any relationship to the past which is not ethical.)[7]

This question about failure returns me, yet again, to the *Zong* Massacre. In particular, I consider Fred D'Aguiar's novel *Feeding the Ghosts*, which reimagines the massacre to tell a fictional story wherein one of the 132 enslaved people thrown overboard climbs back on the ship and survives to live a full life. Beginning with D'Aguiar's novel and Hartman's essay "Venus in Two Acts" in tandem with a return to M. NourbeSe Philip's *Zong!*, the first section of this chapter unravels the impossibility of recovery and incompleteness of rememory as projects of literatures of slavery. Then the next section carries *Feeding the Ghosts* forward into a meeting with Toni Morrison's *A Mercy* in order to analyze the failure of recognition as a pathway to ethical redress for the immeasurable violence of chattel slavery alongside the future-oriented rhetorical device of the direct address. I am drawn to read Morrison's novel, which is not about the *Zong* Massacre, alongside D'Aguiar's novel and Philip's book, which directly engage and re-present the massacre, because of *A Mercy*'s poetics. Like *Feeding the Ghosts* and *Zong!*, *A Mercy* directly addresses its readers and problematizes literacy itself as a central concern of its narrative. (And there is a massacre by drowning in the novel, though it goes by the reader's attention quite quickly. We will return to that scene later.) Finally, Philip's writing resurfaces in a final section along with both D'Aguiar's and Morrison's novels as I examine how all three texts meditate on the necessity of risk for an ethics that exceeds the capacities of liberal subjecthood.

In reading the impossibility of recovery as a task of literary representation, the failure of recognition as a sufficient mode of ethical relation, and the obligation of taking on risk in the face of impossibility and failure, this chapter stays with the question, What does it mean to do justice to the dead? Such a question extends within itself the reflection on Eric and Erica Garner that I have centered in *Abolition Time*'s interlude. If, after the moment of harm, it is impossible to recover the stolen lives of the dead, and if recognizing the humanity of survivors does not prevent their lives from being stolen too, then what else might be demanded of the living to create a future worthy of both the names we remember and the names we do not, and can never, know?

RECOVERY (IMPOSSIBILITY)

In her essay "Venus in Two Acts," Hartman returns to a story that she could not tell in her then recently published *Lose Your Mother* to theorize, through reflection, narration, and self-reflexive methodological argument, how to encounter what is "a history of an unrecoverable past."[8] That is, because the very conditions under which slavery enters historical archives are conditions of erasure and dispossession, and because the lives of the enslaved are recorded in the interstice between social and literal death, when it comes to the Middle Passage and Atlantic chattel slavery, the "lost object" is unfindable. This therefore makes recovery an impossibility. The impossibility of recovery necessitates Hartman's deployment of what she calls "critical fabulation"—a historical methodology of constructing discernable narrative out of an archive defined by its gaps and enforced silences in a way that both dares to imagine unrecorded, unverifiable lives lived under conditions of erasure and insists on resisting the temptation or desire to fill in every gap.[9] Critical fabulation is a form of "impossible writing" in that it seeks to recover—while knowing it cannot do so—that which cannot be recovered: the extinguished and unrecorded lives of the enslaved.[10]

There has been tremendous critical attention to Hartman's methodology over the past decade and a half as she continues to experiment with it. In my present chapter, I want to ask what happens if we bring the ethical concerns of critical fabulation—a method of *writing*—with us to our encounters with creative texts. How can we bring critical fabulation to a method of *reading*? In asking this question, I return to Philip's *Zong!*, about which Anthony Reed argues, "in addition to positing a legal framework—where the poem bears witness (as testimony) in the place of those who cannot . . . the poem attests the necessity of invention."[11] That is, to trace Reed's "necessity of invention" to Hartman's attempt to "imagine what cannot be verified" through "an impossible writing which attempts to say that which resists being said," we can read *Zong!* as enacting critical fabulation in its writing such that we as readers need to take seriously, if we are to engage the text on its own terms rather than as a screen against which to project our own desires, that *unknowability* and the *impossibility of recovery* are the conditions of possibility inscribed within the poem's very capacity for invention.[12] In other words, if critical fabulation as a method of *writing* means synthesizing cohesive narrative out of violently carved gaps in the archive (the "fabulation") all while refusing to allow the narrative to consolidate (thus the appendage "critical"), then critical fabulation as a method of *reading* means assimilating literary knowledge as imaginative possibility that fills in gaps in historical knowledge ("fabulation") without accepting imaginative possibility as the suturing of an open wound ("critical").

In the essay "Notanda," appearing at the end of *Zong!*, Philip reflects on her own writing process through self-reflexive analysis of language, desire, and the yet unresolved ethical questions that she confronted as she drafted poetry out of law's archive. Her reflections describe the paradox of an imperative to tell a story that cannot be told but must be told through *un-telling*. From this paradox, the essay asks far more questions than it answers, underlining that a reparative reading of the book as a recovery of the lost lives of the enslaved or a re-membering—the hyphen there emphasizing hearing the word as the opposite of *dis*-membering, thus in terms of "putting back together," as in *repairing*—of the violence of the Middle Passage fails to take seriously the incalculability of the task at hand.

Philip earnestly asks, "What did, in fact, happen on the *Zong*? Can we, some two hundred years later, ever really know? Should we?" These three questions move through the realms of the factual (what happened?) to the methodological (how can we know?) to the ethical (ought we to know?). Philip ties them together: "These are the questions I confront. Although presented with the 'complete' text of the case, the reader does not ever know it, since the complete story does not exist."[13] She highlights the distance between what the archive has to *tell* (the complete text of the case) and what remains *untold* (the complete story). The story is not the text. There is a gap to be filled.

But Philip insists on asking not only *how* we might fill it in but *whether* we should even attempt to fill it in at all. I therefore agree with McKittrick's thesis that "to suggest that this poetry cycle is *only* reclamation (resuscitating the unliving) forecloses the ways in which the poet is, in my view, attempting to trouble practices of reclamation."[14] In other words, I am not denying *Zong!*'s interest in questions of reclamation, recovery, and re-presentation but rather pushing us to suspend our arrival at a conclusion about where those interests land. In this brief succession of sentences traversing history, memory, and ethics in "Notanda," I read Philip as modeling the relationship between ethics and uncertainty that the two novels I will discuss in this chapter confront. That is, in these questions as they inform other moments in "Notanda" and *Zong!* as a whole—such as the insistence that "the disorder, illogic, and irrationality of the *Zong!* poems can no more tell the story than the legal report of *Gregson v. Gilbert* masquerading as order, logic, and rationality"—Philip highlights that her poetry's project is one of uncertainty even as it does not waver in its belief in its own necessity.[15]

Readers will recognize that in "*Os,*" the first book of *Zong!,* African names appear as paratext at the bottom of each page, and most readers, including my students as well as numerous professional critics, read this as an attempt at providing names for those historical victims of the *Zong*'s voyage (*voyage* exceeds *massacre* as isolated juridical event because the voyage itself, like every Middle Passage voyage, was a disaster to the Africans on board, who were juridically conjured into objects of property). But when we read the names this way, we immediately confront the paradox that such an obvious reading immediately announces its own limitation, because as a matter of historical fact—a historical fact that the poetry cannot, for all its terrible beauty, change—we in the present do not have access to a knowable historical record of the names of the particular people on board that particular ship. Yet simultaneously, Philip shares in "Notanda," "the Africans on board the *Zong* must be named," unequivocally.[16] As Hartman articulates, "the loss of stories sharpens the hunger for them. So it is tempting to fill in the gaps and to provide closure where there is none. To create a space for mourning where it is prohibited. To fabricate a witness to a death not much noticed."[17] The fabrication of names born out of a hunger for persons to mourn in the face of an archive that has obliterated not only the lives of these people but their very mournability as lives at all is a creative task as necessary as it is impossible.

Recognizing the duality of necessity and impossibility, rather than reading the names at the bottom of *Zong!*'s pages as resuscitations of the dead, we can read them as indexing, through their own announced fabulation, the impossibility of recovering the lost lives after which they seek. Here impossibility becomes the condition under which ethics, understood not as axioms or axiology but as praxis in the face of ongoing harm, comes into being. The project inaugurated by *Zong!* and engaged by the reader of *Zong!*—and, I will argue, the project demanded by cultural production about slavery, regardless of the intentions of the artist—is a project of putting the impossible in motion.

Of course, "putting the impossible in motion" sounds like theoretical paradox. But this is where the current chapter of *Abolition Time* builds on the last. In theorizing *perforation* in chapter 2, I attempted to show that poetics of justice may at times need to *inhabit* grammars of law in order to do their extrajuridical work. Inhabitation helps us here in multiple ways. First, it establishes a framework for holding both the limits and possibilities of a poetic strategy simultaneously. In chapter 2, an example of this was how Harriet Jacobs's inhabitation of the grammar of *partus sequitur ventrem* both frames her arguments within the limits of liberal humanism and opens the possibility for undoing even perhaps her own most fundamental assumptions or understandings of gender itself. Here Philip's inhabitation of the grammar of the captain's lost logbook both traps her in the reality of the archive's absence and opens space for challenging the authority of that absence. Second, inhabitation helps us understand that a poetics of witnessing mobilizes a legal grammar of offering testimony before the law so that judgment can be made, thus limiting itself to law's appeal to the process of judgment; a poetics of witnessing goes beyond merely representing what happens when one looks at injustice and opens a space for considering the possibilities of intervention that risk the retribution of the law itself. Ultimately, like a poetics of perforation, a poetics of witnessing inhabits a grammar of law—witnessing in order to testify before the judge's bench—that seeks to limit the possibilities for justice's realization in order to move beyond that grammar into the very zone of action that the law seeks to deem impossible. In a poetics of witnessing, inhabitation continues to develop as a language for creating ethical possibility out of law's impossibility.

Like Philip's *Zong!*, D'Aguiar's *Feeding the Ghosts* revisits the Zong Massacre as a site for grappling with recovery's impossibility.[18] Deploying critical fabulation to imagine an entire novel out of a contested but by now well-circulated detail about the Zong Massacre that one of the Africans thrown overboard survived and climbed back on board, *Feeding the Ghosts* names this im/possible historical figure "Mintah." Part I of the novel takes place on board the *Zong* during the days of the massacre. A third person omniscient narrator follows Mintah as she recognizes the ship's first mate, Kelsel, from his time recovering from illness at a mission in which Mintah lived before being enslaved, and then as she is thrown into the Atlantic Ocean, where she does not drown. Instead, buoyed by the memory of her father, a wood carver, she makes her way back to the wood of the ship and climbs on board, where she is hidden by the cook's assistant, Simon, who falls in love with her. Mintah orchestrates a rebellion by visiting the slave quarters and recruiting men to follow her lead in taking the ship from the crew. The rebellion is squashed, and Mintah is sold in South Carolina at the end of the *Zong*'s voyage. Then the same narrator describes the *Gregson v. Gilbert* trial in part II, where the novel conjures a journal written by Mintah that records all of the events of the massacre and places it in Simon's hands. Simon brings it to the judge during the trial, but Mintah's account is ultimately dismissed. Finally, in part III, Mintah becomes the narrator, and we learn of her life as a self-emancipated person, first in Maryland, working to help enslaved people north on the Underground Railroad, and then as she moves south to Kingston, Jamaica, where she carves wooden statues for her fellow Africans on board the *Zong*, until finally she dies in a fire with visions of her past, of Simon, and of the celebration of her constant attempts to emancipate not only herself but all those she could touch resting on her mind.

Throughout the novel, Mintah is constantly thinking about how to help others out of slavery's grasp. She is decidedly, fundamentally oriented toward acting in solidarity with others rather than securing her own individual freedom. This begins when, upon surviving being jettisoned by the *Zong*'s crew, she climbs back on board and seeks out coconspirators to plan a rebellion rather than staying hidden in Simon's care to survive alone until landfall. After their rebellion is arrested by captain and crew, Mintah is kept shackled on deck as the massacre is resumed. She watches person after person being tossed overboard as Captain Cunningham (the stand-in for Collingwood) records their existence as a mark in his ledger. Here the novel represents the coming into existence of the legal archive that obliterates the subjectivity of the enslaved and that Philip will perforate in her poetry. As one particular woman is about to be thrown into the liquid graveyard of the Atlantic Ocean, Mintah calls out,

> "Your name! What is your name?" Mintah shouted in the three languages she knew and raised herself up on her knees.
>
> "Why? How will it save me?"
>
> The woman's grip was loosened by the struggle and by another man beating her arms with his club.
>
> "I will remember you! Others will remember you!"
>
> They lifted her above the side, but her passage into the sea was blocked by a sailor. There was a pause to allow him to duck from between the woman and the side.
>
> "I am Ama!"[19]

For me, this scene is a key moment in the novel's meta-interrogation of its own genre. As we learn in part II, Mintah will become the literal author of a slave narrative (the journal she gives to Simon) that will be lost to history, only to be "recovered" by the neo-slave narrative of *Feeding the Ghosts* itself. In seeking to recover that which not only was lost but needed to be imagined into existence in order to be identified as a lost object, *Feeding the Ghosts* is engaged in a poetics of witnessing circumscribed by the impossibility that necessitates invention. Similarly, in this scene with Ama, Mintah stands in as a figure not only for the neo-slave narrative genre but for contemporary readers of the genre. Mintah, "this one-hundred and thirty-second body," the novel tells us, "will have to be a witness again."[20] So if we understand the novel as directly confronting the problems and paradoxes of witnessing as a framework for comprehending the disaster of the Middle Passage as indexed by the *Zong* Massacre, then we need to take seriously what Mintah can and cannot do in this scene.

First, we need to notice the verbs and the details in the first lines of the passage, where we see Mintah "shout" and, while chained, "raise herself up on her knees." This is not a thin caricature of witnessing as passive reception. Mintah actively places herself in the scene of murder by throwing her voice, making the effort to speak three different languages to augment her *ability to respond* to the catastrophe before her. She is enacting her response-ability to Ama's suffering before she even knows her name.[21] In a novel deeply concerned with the gap between the intellectual comprehension of harm and taking action to stop, prevent, or alleviate that harm, it is significant that Mintah is a participant here rather than an observer. She has to risk harm to her own body (will a crew member's club strike her to silence her?) in order to bear witness to a stranger's suffering.

And yet, despite Mintah's best efforts to act with genuine responsibility on her obligation to a stranger, Ama, who is in her final moments before death, is not convinced of the value of Mintah's question: "Why? How will it save me?" In this moment, Ama is not worried about abstract questions of ethics or justice; she is concerned with what can be done to save her life from the fate determined by her oppressors. When my Neo–Slave Narratives students discussed this scene in class, both groups of students described the scene as an expression of the importance of their own reading. Mintah's answer, "I will remember you!" struck them as an instruction. One student even formulated it this way: "now that we've read these novels [students had read Morrison's *Beloved* and Colson Whitehead's *The Underground Railroad* before this], we have to also remember these stories so the dead aren't forgotten." After some silent nods, I responded to this student, "But what happens to Ama?"

Ama dies. The unspoken part of Mintah's answer to her life-or-death question is "it [telling me your name] *cannot* save you." She is therefore answering Ama's first question, "Why?" while leaving her second question, "How will it save me?" as unspeakable. Saving Ama is an impossible obligation, one that witnessing cannot fulfill. "Most scholars of slavery are drawn into the vortex of lives lost in the very moment in which they are found," writes Stephen Best, "out of a longing to bear witness to violent extermination and in the hope that such witness may occasion compassionate resuscitation."[22] While my arguments in this chapter certainly depart from Best's in some fundamental ways given my insistence on an ethical relation with the past (precisely because the past is not past), I cannot be any more sincere in my reception of the caution being levied here at scholars of slavery—and our students. Remembering is not resuscitation. Memory is not justice.

For me, this point is most crucial in teaching. For many of us who are professional literary scholars, it is in the classroom where reading most often (though not exclusively) shifts from being a solitary activity to being a collective one. And so every session, in my mind, is an opportunity to reflect on the stakes, possibilities, and limitations of reading itself, regardless of the particular text(s) on the table. I am therefore particularly sensitive to moments when students themselves articulate "lessons" or "takeaways" about what is at stake in their reading.

In my years of teaching the texts in this chapter, I have found that students consistently express the longing and hope articulated earlier by Best. Upon reading *Zong!*, students almost always believe they have "discovered" the "answer" as to why the text is so difficult to read: it is because the text is trying to disorient them so they can experience the kind of disorientation experienced by the enslaved on board the ship. Empathy, that "double-edged" sword, surfaces.[23] Or they confidently assert that Philip "gives voice to the dead" or "resurrects their ghosts" in the stories within the poetry or the names at the bottom of the pages in "*Os*." And upon reading the Ama scene in *Feeding the Ghosts*, students want to believe that if they do what Mintah says—if they *remember the dead*—then they have "done the work" to "do justice to the dead." These impulses are attempts at tying an ethical bow on an unruly, overwhelming injustice. They fit neatly into linear teleologies of moral progress. They put distance between the *then* of the atrocity and the *now* of the moment of reading. They place Philip and D'Aguiar as writers and us as readers in the position of *rescuer*, triumphantly righting the wrongs of history. They reparatively produce a narrative of triumph that feels better than the discomfort of confronting the impossible.

Justice for Ama would be a world wherein she did not die, where she would have never been captured and stuffed on a slave ship in the first place. Calling back to *Abolition Time*'s interlude, there is no lawsuit or jail sentence that can be justice for Eric Garner. Justice would be a world in which he was still alive, in which he would not need to sell loose cigarettes for extra cash to survive in the world in the first place. Historical recovery, cultural remembering, and discursive humanization of the juridically thingified all do certain forms of important work. As Philip writes about her own book,

> in its erasure and forgetting of the be-ing and humanity of the Africans on board the *Zong*, the legal text of *Gregson v. Gilbert* becomes a representation of the fugal state of amnesia, serving as a mechanism for erasure and alienation. Further, in my fragmenting the text and re-writing it through *Zong!*, or rather over it, thereby essentially erasing it, the original text becomes a fugal palimpsest through which *Zong!* is allowed to heal the original text of its fugal amnesia.[24]

Healing the amnesia inflicted by law's bludgeon is significant. But these forms of work do not and cannot bring justice because ultimately they all function through a framework of witnessing. That is, recovery, rememory, and humanization all function by way of positioning the subject as observer of the injured other (or of the event of injury if the other is disappeared) who in our observation *recognizes* the other as an unjustly injured party who fits into our existing schemas of injurable or mournable subjects. Witnessing, therefore, can open the door to justice, but it is not, in itself, justice.

RECOGNITION (FAILURE)

In his critique of recognition as a juridical paradigm for redressing political violence, Weheliye details how, "in western human rights discourse, for instance, the physical and psychic residues of political violence enable victims to be recognized as belonging to the 'brotherhood of Man.'" He writes, "Frequently, suffering becomes the defining feature of those subjects excluded from the law, the national community, humanity, and so on due to the political violence inflicted upon them even as it, paradoxically, grants them access to inclusion and equality."[25] That is, the very suffering produced through juridical exclusion becomes a mechanism for inclusion, allowing for absorption into law's field of recognition to be another iteration of the very suffering that caused the need for absorption altogether.

What this "inclusion" ultimately accomplishes, however, is the reification of the very categories of racialized, gendered Humanity from which the law's forces of obliteration are generated in the first place. I take Weheliye's critique for granted and understand recognition as a method of including the dispossessed within existing regimes of the Human.[26] This is recognition's success as a tool of liberal humanism and its failure as a means of ethical relation, because it reinscribes the political violence it ostensibly condemns.

As a piece of the formula for witnessing—when we witness injustice, we are asked to recognize the worthy suffering of the injured—recognition surfaces in my reading of two neo-slave narratives as the site of ethical failure *and also* the site of ethical potential. I elaborate this doubled failure/potential by examining, first, scenes in *Feeding the Ghosts* and Toni Morrison's *A Mercy* in which characters (mis)recognize the suffering induced by political violence and, second, the use of second person address to call upon the reader as witness in both texts. While they differ in their patterns and frequency of change, both *Feeding the Ghosts* and *A Mercy* deploy shifting focalization (including slipping into and out of free indirect discourse) and switching narrators to establish tension between the scales of individual psychology and historical atrocity. This tension, I extrapolate, is a *poetics of witnessing* that does not so much model how to ethically witness a history that hurts or simply critique witnessing as inevitable failure; rather, this tension as poetics invites a critical questioning of reading itself.

In addition to positioning Mintah as witness whose sincere attempt at ethical relation cannot save Ama's life, *Feeding the Ghosts* positions numerous white characters as witnesses to the violence of slavery in its deployment of metacritique as its particular mode of poetics of witnessing. Early in the novel, Mintah is beaten into unconsciousness by members of the crew for her disruption of their methodical jettisoning of sick Africans. At this point in the plot, the ship's surgeon is already dead, but when Mintah awakens, she draws on her experiences on board the *Zong* to imagine how he would have spoken to her if he were still alive:

She could hear his curmudgeonly barking of instructions as he shrugged his shoulders and shook his head as though he had already been disobeyed. He came to mind because she knew what he would have said if she had been brought before him. "The best cure, young woman, is prevention. Not to bring calamity on your head by sending out invitations of insolence." And he would have done nothing but have her returned to her slice of space below decks as if his reprimand were, in its own right, a prescription and remedy for her ailment.[27]

Mintah conjures the voice of the dead to imagine an external recognition of her suffering in the absence of an actual witness. However, the voice that comes to mind can only place blame on her, the object of violence, for inviting it upon herself, even as he rightly recognizes that what is happening on board the *Zong* is wrong. His recognition, however, ultimately fails to deliver remedy, let alone justice.

Importantly, the novel does not present the surgeon as unfeeling in his response to the suffering of Africans. He is not a caricature of a pathological villain, easily set aside as inhumane. Instead, the surgeon, as conjured by the omniscient narrator's focalization through Mintah's memories, understands the pain and suffering inflicted on Mintah and her racialized kin by the crew, and, importantly, he knows that the suffering of the Africans demands at least amelioration and perhaps intervention. While it is possible to read the sentence "He was old and had grown sick like the others and died shrugging his shoulders and shaking his head to the end without breath to power the vocal complaints that, doubtless, had been running through his head but had failed to connect with his disobedient tongue" as a literal description of his dying body's loss of its capacities, the novel uses repetition to invite another reading.

The surgeon's shrugging shoulders and shaking head are established patterns of movement, signifying in their first instance his uneasy acceptance of the infelicity of his speech. So when these bodily movements appear again on the same page, they may, of course, signify a dying body's aching jerks, but they may *also* resignify the ineffectual moral protest of a figure of author-ity. If we allow ourselves to hold this possibility for these repeated movements, then we might be able to read his loss of breath and his "disobedient tongue" not only as the failing organs of an ill body but also as the failure to act on internal beliefs. That is, the surgeon's recognition of the suffering of the enslaved high-lighted by his necessary position as witness on the ship because of his profession begins to consolidate in a sense of necessary intervention—"vocal complaints." However, the force of this in-tervention is arrested in the shoulders and neck before it can make its way to his tongue and vocal chords. It is not that he is unable to comprehend the suffering of the enslaved, nor that his moral or political imagination is incapable of comprehending Africans as human beings. Rather, it is that even as he recognizes human suffering, and even as he feels the injustice of it, this recognition and this professional witnessing fail to manifest in ethical action. While a feelings–actions binary may seem elementary for such a prolonged analysis, I believe it is essential to the novel's metacri-tique of its own genre and of reading and writing themselves as potential forms of witnessing.[28]

Among the crew, D'Aguiar invests the first mate, Kelsal, with the most extensive fabulation. And it is in Kelsal that the novel most strongly manifests its critique of "feeling right" as the ethical end of witnessing's recognition of the suffering of the dispossessed subject.[29] In numerous scenes, readers are given evidence of Kel-sal's inner humanity and complex emotional and psychological self. Even more so than the surgeon, he is not a caricature of evil. For example, while carrying out the captain's orders to oversee the jettisoning of Africans from the *Zong*, Kelsal is continuously uneasy about the work, both for the sake of his crew's morale and for the sake of the humanity of the Africans, among whom he had lived as he recovered his health at a mission on the West African coast after nearly drowning at sea years before the *Zong*'s voyage (in this novel's fictionalization). After throwing fifty-four bodies overboard, "the feeling he [Kelsal] had inside would not leave him. The female had brought it on by a mere calling of his name. And with each slave disposed of, the churning sensation in his stomach had intensified."[30] Like the ship's surgeon, Kelsal's body registers his disgust with the violent machinations of slavery. He literally cannot stomach the massacre in which he is participating. On one hand, this moment of feeling proves that Kelsal successfully witnesses the pain of the enslaved by recognizing the horror of suffering human beings. Yet, on the other hand, these feelings do nothing to ease, end, or somehow intervene in that suffering. It is not until the entire (white) crew can no longer stomach the work and Kelsal realizes morale would bottom out that he suggests to Captain Cunningham stopping the massacre. It is not the suffering of the enslaved, then, that persuades Kelsal but the suffering of his crew (and perhaps the fear of mutiny, i.e., the desire to maintain order, i.e., the fundamental grammar of law).

Standing in contrast to the surgeon and Kelsal is Simon, the cook's assistant, who purportedly falls in love with Mintah and contributes to her material survival after she climbs back on board the *Zong*. Importantly, his feelings alone do not allow him to intervene in the massacre on board the ship, nor do they allow him to change the course of the insurance trial so that the law acknowledges the humanity of the enslaved. Although he comes to the trial bearing the book written by the woman toward whom he feels such a strong connection, he cannot make the book matter to the court, because the writer is absent, and the word of an absent slave is simply no good against the word of a ship's captain. "Throughout the deliberations he was certain that Mintah's story and that of the other slaves would be told and some justice would come about," the narrator tells us. "After all, they were in an English court of law."[31] But Simon's expressions of feeling do not serve as effective paratext (as prefatory remarks that could be taken to verify the book's contents) to Mintah's literal slave narrative that is brought before the judge. Her testimony remains unheeded by the law, which, of course, calls back to Harriet Jacobs's plea to be heard and trusted in *Incidents in the Life of a Slave Girl*. The law's grammar is insufficient for responding to the suffering recognized by the witness who holds up the testimony of the suffering subject. Therefore, the novel argues, readers ought to pursue action that exceeds recognizing, remembering, or even amplifying the history told in the novel. Something else—something that neither the surgeon, nor Kelsal, nor Simon is able to do—has to come out of the insufficient-in-itself process of witnessing catastrophic suffering.

If our reading of literatures of slavery is attuned only to the mechanics of empathy and recognition, *Feeding the Ghosts* teaches us through its creation and dismissal of Mintah's journal-as-slave-narrative, then we miss the abolitionist call that may perhaps be moving through these texts' poetics of justice that exceed the grammar of the law. Even though a legal trial is the archival condition of possibility for literature about the *Zong* Massacre, and even though a representation of that trial is centered in *Feeding the Ghosts*, D'Aguiar's and Philip's texts cannot simply be read as only responding to, refuting, or resisting the force of law. If we follow Weheliye's argument that the law's grammar for interpreting the suffering subject is a grammar of recognition processed through a mode of witnessing, then we can see clearly where the poetics of these literary texts inhabit or move with this grammar as well as where they exceed such a grammar. In presenting readers with characters who literally stand in as witnesses to suffering and utilizing a third person omniscient narrator to unpack these characters' internal emotional lives while displaying the actions they take in the world around them, *Feeding the Ghosts*'s basic deployment of a tension between internal and external characterization becomes a poetics of justice through developing a critique of witnessing in the gap between the internal and the external. That is, as the focalization of the omniscient narrator in the first two parts of the novel narrows and widens, a tension is produced between the success of recognition at the scale of individual psychology and the failure of intervention at the scale of the massacre. That tension is itself a critique of witnessing and a calling into question of the ethics of reading itself, provoking a question for the reader to ask what good remembering this history does if the unnamed jettisoned body called "Ama" in the novel's fictionalization cannot be saved by any act of memory. When we relinquish our own grip on the grammar of law that makes the linear logic of recognition-begets-rights-begets-justice, we can attend to the poetics of narration that exceed this logic even in moves that seem familiar.

A second neo–slave narrative that deploys shifting focalization and narrative voice as a poetics of justice that traces the limits of recognition and recovery is Morrison's *A Mercy*. The chapters in this novel oscillate between first person and third person narration, with every other chapter narrated by the enslaved girl Florens. Each chapter alternating with the Florens chapters is narrated in third person focalized through another specific character—Jacob Vaark, who buys Florens at the beginning of the novel; Lina, an Indigenous woman bought by Jacob years before the novel's events; Rebekka, Jacob's wife, who outlives him and takes command of the farm when he dies of smallpox; Sorrow/Complete, a mixed-race girl traded to Jacob whom the other characters deem unintelligent and undesirable; and Willard, a white indentured servant who works on the Vaark farm to pay off a generational debt. The final chapter is narrated by Florens's unnamed mother in the first person, thus tying together the two strands of the novel's focal pattern (first person plus secondary character's perspective). I pair *A Mercy* with *Feeding the Ghosts* because both Morrison and D'Aguiar utilize shifting focalization and, to different degrees, narrative voice to develop tension between the familiar grammar of recognition and the poetics of witnessing that exceed recognition itself.

In Morrison's novel, Florens's chapters are structured by what Levy-Hussen calls "traumatic time": "a structure of narrative temporality prevalent in late twentieth-century and early twenty-first-century African American literature that defies chronological mapping and instead takes shape through repeated, affectively charged references to an original traumatic event."[32] For Florens, the traumatic event is when she perceives that her mother tells Jacob to buy Florens instead of herself and/or Florens's baby brother. This repeated scene of trauma, which is later revealed to be a scene of misreading as Florens's mother explains the logic of her choice to tell Jacob to buy Florens, structures the first person narrative voice in the Florens chapters, while readers are able to see different angles in the alternating chapters.

For example, the scene of Florens's sale is described in the greatest external detail in Jacob's chapter. This externalized look at a scene that Florens internalizes as a central trauma is not omnisciently narrated but is instead focalized through Jacob as a triangulation point between Florens's internal psychology and her mother's internal psychology, which remain opaque to one another. The scene becomes an occasion for examining the traumatic event from the perspective of one who witnesses the forces of violence that inflict trauma rather than from the perspective of the traumatized self. In other words, we can examine the role that Jacob plays in the scene and notice how the novel deploys the grammar of recognition precisely so that it may undo that grammar through Florens's narration.

In the novel's second chapter, we learn that a Spanish plantation owner named D'Ortega has lost the capital he was betting on being able to use to pay off a debt to Jacob when a ship holding enslaved Angolans that he owned sank, taking his human property with it and leaving him without means to pay. So he invites Jacob to his Maryland home in order to orchestrate a transaction that can settle his debt to the New York trader. As Jacob starts to perceive the purpose of his visit to Jublio (the name of D'Ortega's plantation), he thinks (the third person narrator tells us), "Flesh was not his commodity." Jacob does not think of himself as a slave trader, or as a participant in the slave trade in general (despite having bought a human being already before arriving at Jublio). But he finds himself being marketed fleshy commodities by his host: "The two men walked the row, inspecting. D'Ortega identifying talents, weaknesses and possibilities, but silent about the scars, the wounds like misplaced veins tracing their skin."[33] Because of the tension between the narrator's third person omniscience and its focalization through Jacob's perspective, it is ambiguous whether D'Ortega's silence is simply noted as objective fact or present in Jacob's experience of the scene. However, like Kelsal in *Feeding the Ghosts*, just down the page, "Jacob felt his stomach seize" when he noticed the glances exchanged by the enslaved Africans being presented to him, "judging the men who judged them." These details allow us to posit that Jacob not only recognizes what is right in front of him but is sophisticated enough in his moral reasoning to understand the violence of what he does not see in a place with "no sound, just the knowledge of a roar he could not hear."[34] In preparation for the ensuing scene of Florens's sale, we learn here that Jacob sees enslaved Africans as human beings suffering under a system he finds abhorrent. He recognizes not only the suffering of the dispossessed but also the injustice of the oppressor. Jacob is a morally competent witness.

But like in *Feeding the Ghosts,* the poetics of *A Mercy* trouble the efficacy of successful recognition. Following the previous scene, Jacob finally encounters Florens's mother, and the traumatic scene of Florens's sale resurfaces from the text's first chapter:

> "Please, Senhor. Not me. Take her. Take my daughter." . . .
>
> Suddenly the woman smelling of cloves knelt and closed her eyes.
>
> They wrote new papers. Agreeing that the girl was worth twenty pieces of eight, considering the number of years ahead of her and reducing the balance by three hogsheads of tobacco or fifteen English pounds, the latter preferred.[35]

The narrative voice of the chapter more than suggests Jacob's significant capacities for recognition. The smell of cloves on the enslaved woman's skin recalls Jacob's earlier thought when he "drew closer and, recognizing the clove-laced sweat, suspected there was more than cooking that D'Ortega stood to lose."[36] Readers of *Beloved* and students of the sexual economy of chattel slavery that Harriet Jacobs so meticulously delineates will quickly recognize, with Jacob, that D'Ortega rapes this enslaved woman, who is subject to his will in all things. There is no rape scene that definitively involves D'Ortega in *A Mercy,* but the novel makes this clear through accumulating details that erupt in Florens's mother's narration at the end: "To be female in this place is to be an open wound that cannot heal."[37] What Jacob recognizes is ultimately confirmed when the third person narrator completely disappears as the final Florens-narrated chapter is followed by her mother's first person narration. The novel thus figures witnessing through the accumulating repetitions of the scene of Florens's sale through shifting narrative focalizations that ultimately return to the voice of a woman stolen directly from Africa.

The paragraph break in Jacob's chapter between the image of the woman kneeling and the men writing transaction papers highlights the tension produced by the formal narrative technique of focalization as Morrison deploys it. In that break is the uncertainty of the extent of Jacob's capacity for recognition. In that break is both the limit and the potentiality of witnessing as a mode of ethics.

There is enough textual evidence for us to conclude that Jacob perceives D'Ortega's rape of the adult woman before them, and there is enough textual evidence for us to conclude that Jacob has a certain sentimental sympathy for "orphaned" subjects, though this latter evidence is most strongly secured through a cross-species analog of Florens with a trapped racoon in Jacob's matrix of moral perception. But there is not enough textual evidence for us to conclude that Jacob extrapolates that this woman's mode of subjection will be deployed against her daughter as well. Does Jacob take Florens to "save her" from rape by D'Ortega? There is enough in the text for us to say, *Perhaps.* What we can say is that Jacob successfully recognizes multiple forms of violence enacted by D'Ortega against those enslaved on Jublio, and perhaps this recognition influences his decision to accept Florens as payment for the debt owed to him, which drowned in the sea with the slave ship carrying the capital D'Ortega planned on utilizing for the purpose. Unlike D'Aguiar's surgeon, whose tongue is disobedient, and Kelsal, who is moved to act only out of fear of losing control, Morrison's Jacob *perhaps* turns his recognition-induced upset stomach into an intervention into slavery's machinations of violence. As Florens's mother says of Jacob, "He never looked at me the way Senhor [D'Ortega] does. He did not want."[38] He takes Florens away from Jublio, away from the only named rapist in the text.[39]

I want to follow two threads in the aftermath of Jacob's decision to buy Florens in order to extend this examination of *A Mercy*'s shifting focalization as a poetics of witnessing. First is Jacob's reflections, as refracted through our third person narrator, on his role within the slave trade, and second is Florens's narration as it is structured by "traumatic time" as defined by Levy-Hussen.

Throughout the last ten pages of *A Mercy*'s second chapter, in most of the moments when the narrator narrows focus to Jacob's internal thoughts, we observe him wrestling with his own moral culpability with the slave trade. This moral reasoning is entwined with Jacob's development of his class aspirations toward wealth accumulation, which refract his view of D'Ortega's property at Jublio. And although it happens quickly, the succession of sentences following the sale makes clear that Jacob's acquisition of Florens as enfleshed property propels him toward the vision of a future that brings the character of the Blacksmith to his farm and thus makes possible the novel's very text itself, because a major conceit of the novel is that Florens's chapters are written, not spoken, as a message for the Blacksmith. More clearly stated, I argue that it is precisely in the moment that flesh becomes his commodity when he buys Florens when Jacob formulates the vision of a future made possible by wealth accumulation and which therefore—linked with the death of the enslaved Angolans on board D'Ortega's sunken ship—sets in motion the very condition of possibility for the text's own narrative economy. Therefore, by linking Jacob's moral struggle over the question of slavery with the development of his vision for a future defined by securing private property through what Cheryl I. Harris identifies as the "conceptual nucleus of a right to exclude,"[40] A Mercy's narrowing, expanding, shifting, and disappearing narrative focalization demonstrates a very different though related pitfall of recognition from what we see in Feeding the Ghosts. Here the danger is in desire for cleansing or purifying via justified reasoning.

Directly following the moment when Jacob for the first time in his life realizes that what separates D'Ortega's class from his own is not character but property, Jacob's thoughts are conveyed through our third person narrator:

> Without a shipload of enslaved Angolans he would not merely be in debt; he would be eating from his palm instead of porcelain and sleeping in the bush of Africa rather than a four-post bed. Jacob sneered at wealth dependent on a captured workforce that required more force to maintain.[41]

Here we see Jacob's vision for a future begin to form into what by the end of the chapter will be "dreams . . . of a grand house with many rooms rising on a hill above the fog."[42] I am interested here in the work performed by the verb *sneered*, both for Jacob as a character and for the novel's poetics of witnessing, and the significance of attaching that verb to Jacob's proper name.

In the first quoted sentence, we see Jacob's recognition of the injustice of slavery as a violent condition of possibility for D'Ortega's comfort. The use of free indirect discourse allows the analysis in the sentence to stand both as Jacob's internal thought process and as a distanced, external evaluation of the economics of slavery as an early form of, rather than a premodern precursor to, capitalism.[43] In the space between the period and the beginning of the next sentence, before the narrative focalization widens out from Jacob's internal thought process to an external gaze upon Jacob, there is suspended the possibility for ethics—fleeting, ephemeral, liminal, in the break, uncertain, and, eventually, left behind as an unfulfilled possibility that haunts the text as its covered but not sutured perforation. In that space before Jacob-as-proper-name-as-subject stamps the page, there is the possibility that recognition of the necessary dependence on slavery's re/productive economies of extraction and thingification for the consolidation of private property as (white) self-actualization will lead to something different. In that space is the possibility that Jacob can make the choice not to build wealth that is dependent on a captured workforce that requires more force to maintain.

But the next sentence does come, and the first two words, "Jacob sneered," shift away from the free indirect discourse of the previous sentence, pulling the focalization of the narrator out of Jacob's internal thoughts to a vantage point from which to observe the enslaver's actions. In Jacob's *sneer* we see the failure of recognition. Rather than intervening or changing course—what is demanded by witnessing as a mode of ethics involving the recognition of suffering, domination, or other injustice—Jacob's sneer *distances* himself from the exceptionalized, individualized D'Ortega.[44] By closing himself off from identification with D'Ortega despite being a trader of flesh, Jacob attempts to purge the imagined dream house of his future of the clove-smelling, silent-screaming, violently enforced condition of possibility that he recognizes as tainting Jublio, his very model for that house on a hill, sitting above the fog of slavery. *Sneer* as a verb secures the individuation of its noun/subject, Jacob, through diametrically opposing Jacob as the other to D'Ortega. *Sneer* cleanses *Jacob* of the messiness of complicity. Here we see what one of my mentors in my undergraduate studies, Beth A. McCoy, called in her teaching the "danger of scorn as an epistemological position."[45] The scorn deployed in Jacob's sneer, in its very attempt at displacing his complicity with the object of his sneer, guarantees his implication in the systemic violence that is obscured by the logic of individuation and exceptionality at play.

While the verb *sneer* does the work of distancing and securitization for Jacob as a character, affixing the verb to Jacob's name, thus shifting the novel's focalization for the moment, it also shifts the figure of the witness at the scene of Florens's sale. While in free indirect discourse, the narrative voice can, like the narrator of *Feeding the Ghosts* does with the surgeon and Kelsal, figure Jacob as a literal witness to the suffering of the enslaved. But when the narrator pulls out to make Jacob the object of its gaze, the reader travels with the narrator, and Jacob comes into our gaze as the object of our witnessing. This narrational movement is itself the poetics of witnessing I am trying to extrapolate in Morrison's text. This poetics sets in motion the promise of ethics brought by the discourse of recognition that Weheliye and others critique, only to cut it off with the tension produced by repetition through different focalizations and narrators. Witnessing emerges not as a mode of ethics or as a formula for reading literatures of slavery correctly but rather as a set of questions about what it means to use our capacities for identifying injustice when the available grammars for restitution—the grammar of the law as characterized by individuation, exceptionalization, and punishment—return us to the scene of subjection.

In the classroom, when reading *A Mercy* with students, this looks like returning to this scene in chapter 2 when, while discussing the sexual violence of slavery at the end of the book, students slip into the scornful language of distancing—"we're not racist like people back then, anymore" being the most explicit comment to come up recently in my American Literature courses. It means asking ourselves if we, too, are *sneering* at these fictional characters, and if so, what is accomplished, what are we *securing*, and at the cost of whom, with our sneers? It means asking, What does it mean to refuse the sneer? What happens if we stew in the discomfiture of holding our own desire to sneer at Jacob as he sneers at D'Ortega?[46] What does it mean to start at complicity, messiness, and uncertainty—and to stay there longer than is comfortable?

Indeed, *A Mercy*'s first page utilizes direct address to position the reader in the discomfort of immediately being on the defensive (even if not all readers personally feel defensive). The very first sentence of the novel is "Don't be afraid." We are assured that the narrator's "telling can't hurt [us] in spite of what I have done." Immediately we are positioned to be thinking—again, whether we actually *are* does not override the *positioning of the reader* through the mode of direct address—of what we could possibly be afraid of, and how might the narrator, whom we don't yet know, hurt us? Before the end of this first page, the as-yet-unnamed narrator directly questions our hermeneutic capacities by linking ethical reasoning with literacy: "You know. I know you know. One question is who is responsible? Another is can you read?"[47] Simply by asking these questions, the text insists that we open ourselves to the possibility of being uncertain of the answers. *Can* I read? Can you? Who is responsible for answering that question? Can either of us answer for ourselves as individuals? Or does the individuation of responding to the "you" as if it is singular bring us too close to *sneering* at the question, to feeling too good about ourselves, too sure of what we know? This is a novel about reading itself, and reading is, on the first page, linked with ethics—not in a triumphant assertion but through the interrogative mode. Reading *A Mercy* is an exercise in questioning the ethics of reading. And in questioning the ethics of reading, what I mean is questioning the notion of the nature of the knowledge produced through reading, specifically reading literatures of slavery, in this case, though my hope is that readers of *Abolition Time* will take these sets of questions to their own literary archives and historical contexts.

Conversely from *A Mercy* opening with first person narration and direct address, *Feeding the Ghosts* maintains third person narration throughout the bulk of its narrative, until Mintah emerges as first person narrator for the first two chapters of part III. Then the third and final chapter of part III maintains focalization through Mintah, but because it narrates her death, it does so through the third person. Then there is one final chapter, an epilogue, narrated in first person by an unlocatable voice. This final narrator states, "I have a list of names. I know who did what to whom. But my detailed knowledge has not made an iota of difference to history or to the sea. All the knowledge has done is burden me."[48] If *A Mercy* opens by asking us if we can even read at all, *Feeding the Ghosts* thus closes by admitting that even if we can read so well that we can compile a list of names so well ordered by the grammar of the law that we know who did what to whom and therefore who is responsible for which harms and in which direction to levy punishment in the aftermath of atrocity, this still makes no difference to history or to the sea.

Ama is still drowned.

And Eric and Erica Garner are still dead.

And.

And.

And.

All of *Abolition Time* is motivated by the concerns of the short interlude at its center, and as I opened this chapter by saying, my interrogation of a poetics of witnessing in literatures of slavery is directly motivated by the search to find a way to think the problem of witnessing as an insufficient means for practicing justice in the afterlife of slavery, which is to say, slavery's ongoingness as the continuing disaster of the Western Civilization project of colonial conquest and extraction. Resisting the desires we and/or our students may bring to these texts about the past that is not past to deploy scorn as a means of distancing ourselves from the objects of our critical gaze, as the poetics of witnessing deployed by D'Aguiar's and Morrison's novels encourages us to do, allows us to think in the discomfort produced by such insistent close reading. When we read literatures of slavery—and perhaps any literatures of catastrophe, atrocity, or injustice—we cannot do justice to the dead. Our saying of their names—fictional or real—cannot recover what is lost. Rather, our calling of the names of the dead—both those we know and those we cannot know—must be a call for a different future, right now, in the moment of the call itself. Our present ought to be the future that the dead were and are owed and which it is impossible for them to see.

Naming the dead is a demand for a future when the naming ceases.

RISK (OBLIGATION)

At one point in Octavia Butler's 1979 time-travel (neo-)slave narrative *Kindred*, the protagonist Dana returns to her contemporary moment after teaching enslaved people to read. Upon her return, she remarks to her partner, "It's nineteen seventy-six shielding and cushioning eighteen nineteen for me. But now and then, like with the kids' game, I can't maintain the distance. I'm drawn all the way into eighteen nineteen, and I don't know what to do. I ought to be doing something though. I know that."[49] I leave a full analysis of *Kindred* to other writers, but I highlight this moment because Dana's invocation of certainty and uncertainty as simultaneous ethical convictions reflects the spirit with which I close the third chapter of *Abolition Time*.

I want to take Philip at her word in "Notanda" that we all—she as writer and we as readers—are "implicated in, if not contaminated by," the very project of trying to understand, of trying to make or find meaning in, and of building a body of knowledge about the catastrophe of slavery as it is distilled in the *Zong* Massacre and its literary afterlife.[50] (I pause to parenthetically ask, If the *Zong* stands in for so many massacres of drowned slaves, does D'Ortega's "lost cargo" of Angolans index the massacre? If the deaths of those slaves set in motion the entire plot of the book insofar as it is their deaths that make D'Ortega unable to pay Jacob in cash and that therefore make possible the sale of Florens, which brings her to the Vaark farm, where she meets the Blacksmith, to whom half the book is written, then is *A Mercy* also a *Zong* novel?) If we are all implicated, we can neither sneer at nor cheer for our positions as witnesses that can re-member dis-membered histories. Reading while conscious of our implication/contamination may produce more questions than clarity, but as John D. Caputo argues, "undecidability is not the opposite of decision but a condition of its possibility."[51] For me, I take *decision* to be the territory of ethics. Knowledge or ignorance can be neither ethical nor unethical. It is the decision that is made and the action that is taken in the context of knowledge/ignorance that open the realm of ethics.

And one step further, for me, the moment of decision is inseparable from *risk*. So far in this third chapter's consideration of poetics of witnessing, I have examined the impossibility of recovery as a project of critical fabulation aimed at witnessing a dis-membered history, and I have analyzed the failure of recognition to be in itself a viable grammar of justice insofar as it is demarcated by law's grammar of individuation. Here I look at two final textual moments in *A Mercy* and *Feeding the Ghosts* that outline the obligation of risk as a necessary component for witnessing not to be arrested at the stage of recognition. Ultimately, I conclude, the condition of possibility for ethics is risk.

At one point in her journey to find the Blacksmith so he can cure Rebekka of smallpox, Florens winds up on a farm in a small village inhabited by strictly religious white folks. She does not know this when she approaches the door of one house to knock and is greeted by Widow Ealing. Widow, as Florens calls her, welcomes Florens into her home and feeds her. Florens meets Widow's daughter Jane, who has one eye that focuses "normally" and one that crosses. As the chapter unfolds, we learn that Jane's strabismus is interpreted by her community as a sign that she may be a demon in human form. Similarly, Florens's dark skin may signal to the village's authority figures that she is the "Black Man's minion," where it is clear that the Black Man is super/sub/nonhuman. Florens is examined by some of the adults of the village, whom she describes as "looking at me my body across distances without recognition."[52] She explains that she is nobody's minion and produces a letter of authentication that Rebekka had written, which she had been carrying in her shoe. The letter is her authenticating document, the paratext to her body's disruptive sign of Blackness.[53] So when the village leader leaves the house with the letter, Florens is left without (the illusion of) legal protection. Widow follows the rest of the villagers out of her home to find someone to help with the situation, and Florens is left alone with Jane, the suspected demon.

And in this moment of shared vulnerability, the novel shows us a fictional representation of fully realized witnessing: Jane boils eggs for Florens and leads the enslaved girl away from the house, showing her how to get to the hamlet where the Blacksmith is supposed to be. Florens narrates: "I say thank you and lift her hand to kiss it. She says no, I thank you. They look at you and forget about me."[54] Right before Florens arrived at the house, Widow had been wounding Jane's legs, cutting them so that she bled in order to prove to the village authorities that she is not a demon, because, they believe, demons do not bleed. With Florens around, the village's attention is off of Jane, and her suffering is alleviated. And yet, rather than hide in the security she is afforded by Florens's presence, Jane decides to help Florens get away without knowing whether the fact that she bleeds will put an end to her persecution or if she will be designated an exception to this demon rule.

Florens reflects on this moment later in the novel. During an argument with the Blacksmith in which he tosses her out of his life, she recalls:

> You say you see slaves freer than free men. One is a lion in the skin of an ass. The other is an ass in the skin of a lion. . . . Still, there is another thing. A lion who thinks his mane is all. A she-lion who does not. I learn this from Daughter Jane. Her bloody legs do not stop her. She risks. Risks all to save the slave you throw out.[55]

Here, as she again relives her trauma of abandonment, Florens understands the extent of what Jane has done. By helping Florens flee whatever potential harm might have come from the authorities of the village, Jane risked the possibility of abuse being redirected toward herself. The undecidability of Jane's moment of decision—will her bloody legs stop the abuse, or will Florens's absence open another wave of violence?—is precisely what underlines the ethics of her decision. Jane's witnessing is not arrested at the moment of recognition; instead, she intervenes in the violence that may be coming for Florens. And she does so at the risk of her own safety.

I have argued at length elsewhere that "Florens's *you* is not addressed to either the reader or to the blacksmith, but to both of them."[56] And so in the sentence "Risks all to save the slave you throw out," I would argue that whereas Florens is, of course, addressing the Blacksmith, the novel is addressing the reader. At this point in the text, a metacritique of reading has been developed through explicit questions about multiple forms of literacy, and reading has been conceptually attached to the framework of moral responsibility, so the *you* who throws out (jettisons) "the slave" can be read as accusatory toward the reader. This returns us to the first page: Who is responsible? Can I read? These questions position the reader as defensive. In what she teaches Florens, Jane teaches us that it is possible to choose our own vulnerability. We can risk the discomfort of culpability that is indexed by the discomfort of defensiveness.

A poetics of witnessing, then, is the use of narrative voice to interpellate the reader into the role of witnessing subject while also putting the act of reading itself under question through producing tension between the knowledge produced in and by the text and the limits of knowledge as a discernable force in the narrative economy. To be as clear as possible, a poetics of witnessing is not merely a matter of representation; including a scene in which one character witnesses the suffering of another is not sufficient. The poetics activates in the text's manipulation of narrative voice and focalization. From the position of witnessing produced by this poetics, recovery of a lost object is the impossible and necessary task of fabulation, which cannot be pursued through the grammar of recognition and which calls upon our obligation to risk vulnerability at the site of undecidability.

Feeding the Ghosts finishes with a two-paragraph epilogue that extrapolates the weight of Florens's *you* in more explicit and yet still confounding ways. The epilogue begins by placing the *Zong* in the past: "the ship *was* full of ghosts."[57] But by the end of the first paragraph, the past tense has become the present, and the speaker declares, "I *have* a list of names. I *know* who did what to whom. But my detailed knowledge has not made an iota of difference to history or to the sea. All the knowledge has done is burden me" (my emphasis). This speaker is not asking to be believed, like Jacobs is in her nineteenth-century text, nor do they see their knowledge as having any effect on the world around them, heeding the warning of Best. The knowledge itself, gained by witnessing, is ineffectual.

Then, in the next and final paragraph, this speaker slips fully from the past into the present:

> I am in your community. . . . The *Zong* is on the high seas. . . . Men, women, and children are thrown overboard by the captain and his crew. One of them is me. One of them is you. One of them is doing the throwing, the other is being thrown. I'm not sure who is who, you or I.[58]

Here the uncertainty of the unnamed speaker pulsates out through the interpellation of direct address to destabilize the singularity of the reader in the very same moment it makes itself unlocatable within the matrix of violence that is the *Zong* Massacre. Like the accumulating *you* destabilizing the singularity of the lyric *I* of Claudia Rankine's *Citizen* that we observed in chapter 1, here the destabilization of individuation has ethical and political implications. In the very same moment that the reader is called on to intervene and cease the jettisoning of enslaved Africans from the ship, we are split across the subjectivity of the thrower and the jettisoned.[59] We are, as Philip tells us in *Zong!*, implicated and contaminated. This is the "irreducible complexity" that, Derrida asserts, demands an accounting "if only to avoid the arrogance of so many 'clean consciences.'"[60]

Staying with the irreducible complexity of dispersed and uncertain subjectivity, the narrator of *Feeding the Ghosts* tells us,

> There is no fear, nor shame in this piece of information. There is only the fact of the *Zong* and its unending voyage and those deaths that cannot be undone. Where death has begun but remains unfinished because it recurs. Where there is only the record of the sea.[61]

Neither fear nor shame but only the facts of brutality that constitute the disaster of our present consolidate in recognition of the linked potentialities of our complicity and our intervention. If we do nothing, the record of the sea as it is written by law's grammar continues the recurring deaths that cannot be undone. Undecidability—thrower or thrown?—demands decision. Of course, there is risk, because we may become the thrower even as we attempt to stop the throwing. "We inevitably produce new evils in trying to solve existing ones," Caputo writes. "But that is no excuse not to act, not to do whatever we can. The imperative to act, the power of obligation, is urgent, incessant."[62] In helping Florens escape the potential harm that may come from the white folks in her village, Jane unwittingly sends her on the path to one of the most traumatic moments of her life—her conflict with the Blacksmith. We ought not be too quick to praise. No sneers, but also no cheers. D'Aguiar's novel concludes, "Those spirits are fled into wood. The ghosts feed on the story of themselves. The past is laid to rest when it is told."[63] To tell the story is to lay the past to rest. The telling cannot hurt us; we need not be afraid. But questions remain: How can we be responsible to the past that we read? If the death of the massacre "remains unfinished because it recurs," then stopping the recursion is necessary for laying the past to rest. Our telling of the past cannot be arrested in its tracks by grammars of law. We must seek poetics of justice that can release witnessing from the secure position of individuated observer into the risky terrain of shared vulnerability. We have to move from witnessing to beholding.

BEHOLDING (UNCERTAINTY)

When I teach *Zong!,* I begin the unit with a class session in which we collectively read aloud one of the poems in "*Os.*" Every time we do this activity, there comes a moment when I decide to read the poem "out of order"; that is, instead of reading left to right and top to bottom, I read groupings of words and letters as phrases or sounds that differ from my students' standard reading practices. Our first class session becomes a meditation on the desire for order and discernable grammar for making sense of profoundly difficult poetry. In the second class, I read aloud from *Ventus* in such a way that highlights specific lines of "plot" before closing my book and telling students that I will not speak for the rest of the class and that it is their responsibility to come up with "presentations" on the text. Following this, I usually observe an upsurge in student confidence in making claims about the poetry, resulting in some of the remarks that I paraphrased and quoted in the opening section of this chapter. But then we get to "Notanda." I reinvoke here the three passages with which I closed *Abolition Time*'s second chapter:

> And since we have to work to complete the events, we all become implicated in, if not contaminated by, this activity. . . .
>
> The half-tellings, and un-tellings force me to enter the zone of contamination to complete it; in so doing I risk being contaminated by the prescribed language of the law—by language in fact. . . .
>
> And, by refusing the risk of allowing ourselves to be absolved of authorial intention, we escape an understanding that we are at least one and the Other.[64]

This final day of discussing *Zong!* inevitably brings us back to confusion as we settle into Philip's insistence of contamination and complicity, of the risk of refusing risk. Just as students begin to feel confident making declarative statements about the poetry, Philip's critical self-reflection throws comfort out of the classroom, and we can no longer take refuge in the interpretation that by writing *Zong!*, Philip has somehow recovered the past or done justice to the dead, or that by reading *Zong!*, we have made some kind of moral accomplishment in recognizing the need to right a wrong. One semester, when I asked students what they felt they were left with having completed reading *Zong!*, one student said, "I know about this terrible history but I don't know what to do about it." After waiting for another student to respond and sitting for a moment in silence, I simply commented, admittedly without much thought, "It is certainly heavy." And a different student followed up: "Maybe we can help each other hold it."

My student's articulation of holding as a collective effort, rather than an individual action, makes me think of Christina Sharpe's emphasis on beholding:

> Across time and space the languages and apparatus of the hold [of the slave ship] and its violences multiply; so, too, the languages of beholding. In what ways might we enact a beholden-ness to each

other, laterally? "Beholden: to hold by some tie of duty or obligation, to retain as a client or a person in duty bound" (OED Online). This is what [Hortense] Spillers calls the intramural. How are we beholden to and beholders of each other in ways that change across time and place and space and yet remain.[65]

Maybe we can help each other hold the knowledge of the disaster that is too excessive to be contained in the past, too heavy to be borne by an individuated subject, and too complex to be sneered away or triumphantly repaired. (Ships also hold. As do prisons. But also, so do we. We hold each other. I promised.) Maybe holding that which we cannot grasp means beholding each other. And maybe beholding is the point. For now.

What might constitute this beholding? What might grant us the collective capacity to answer the imperative to bring into being a future in the present in which the naming of the dead need not continue? How do we hold on to each other without knowing whether we will grip too tightly, hurting in our very attempt to help? These are questions that cannot be answered within the disciplinary bounds of literary studies or the temporal bounds of the time of reading. These questions come alive in reading's afterlife. They extend to further questions and uncomfortable conclusions. For example, what if asking the legal apparatus of a settler-colonial nation-state to recognize the Humanity of racialized peoples is too easily absorbed by the grammars of state violence in the first place? That is, if we return to the crisis of witnessing that opens this chapter, what if bearing witness to the state-sanctioned murder of Black and Indigenous and trans and disabled and colonized people—what if saying their names—cannot bring justice? What must we do?

It is impossible to know in advance the full form that abolition will take. All we have are tiny perforations through which to catch a glimpse of the future that we make as we behold the disaster that conjures our obligation, can we but read it, to pursue that which is impossible within grammars of law. All we have is the imperative to improvise and experiment, to discover what a poetics of justice looks like when it exceeds the edges of the page.

FOUR

Breath

ASPIRATION, UNGENDERED MOTHERING, AND IM/POSSIBLE FUTURES

I've been thinking about what it takes, in the midst of the singularity, the virulent antiblackness everywhere and always remotivated, to keep breath in the Black body. . . . In the weather of the wake, one cannot trust, support, or condone the state's application of something called justice, but one can only hold one's breath for so long.

—Christina Sharpe, *In the Wake: On Blackness and Being*

The queer futurity that I am describing is not an end but an opening or horizon. Queer utopia is a modality of critique that speaks to quotidian gestures as laden with potentiality. The queerness of queer futurity, like the blackness of a black radical tradition, is a relational and collective modality of endurance and support. The gesture of cradling the head of one's lover, a lover one has betrayed, is therefore not an act of redemption that mitigates violence; it is instead a future being within the present that is both a utopian kernel and an anticipatory illumination. It is a being in, toward, and for futurity.

—José Esteban Muñoz, *Cruising Utopia: The Then and There of Queer Futurity*

Up until this point, the chapters of *Abolition Time* have traced a theorization of justice against the law in roughly the following manner: poetics of accumulation rupture the framing device of the juridical event underpinning legal conceptions of justice and freedom, opening thought from the ordered grammar of the law toward the excessive present terrain of ethics unbound by event-time. Poetics of perforation index that the law's force is constituted by its very own vulnerability, and so ethics in the register of the flesh that is both violated by and exceeds law's violence stretches the horizon of justice beyond law's reach. Poetics of witnessing register that although it is tempting to take up the call to recognize the law's violence as means toward redress, witnessing remains an insufficient mode of ethics when it crashes against the enormity of unredressable catastrophe and the impossibility of resurrection. This final chapter, then, continues chapter 3's meditation on the inability of witnessing Eric Garner's murder to bring justice in order to examine how a poetics of breath might break through the ordering grammar of the law that renders justice impossible.

Temporality is the overarching concept tying together these four poetics of justice that are so squarely grounded in formalist close reading with the radical politics of abolitionist thought that exceeds the narrow framework of literary studies and its specific jargon. Abolition time is the ethical-political imperative of the excessive present that coheres into view through poetics of justice. Against an impulse to overemphasize either a backward gaze at the past via memory studies or historical recovery (that some, though not I, would call melancholic or pessimistic), or a forward gaze at the future vis-à-vis radical breaks and fantastic flights of futurism (that some, though not I, would call idealistic or optimistic), I have tried to emphasize in this book that past and future are coeval in the excessive present such that "backward" and "forward" fall away.

Accumulation shows us how to read the past that is not past as constituting the very infrastructure of our present. Perforation shows us how to read the radical contingency of the present in which we find ourselves such that no future is ever quite out of reach even as we may reinforce conditions of captivity in reaching for it. And witnessing shows us that the calls of the dead whom we can never recover still elicit in us an obligation to behold the ruins of our present and, in our be-holding, risk something of ourselves in order to put together something different, making a future in the present, now. I write in the spirit of these three poetics as I bring *Abolition Time* to a close on an unapologetically critical utopian impulse (that's unapologetically critical *and* unapologetically utopian). With José Muñoz, I locate the utopianism of abolition time in "quotidian gestures . . . laden with possibility." Like Muñoz's discussion of the gesture that closes Leroi Jones's *The Toilet*, and in keeping the cautionary notes of perforation and witnessing in mind for my own project, the utopianism of this final chapter is neither redemptive nor a break from the past that is not past. It is "a future being within the present."[1] It is a conviction that futures that are precluded by the ordering grammar of the law can be manifested in the here and now of what moves through law's perforations.

In other words, this chapter examines how abolitionist close reading can be a means of thinking the impossible that abolitionist ethics demands: how to bring into being the future where those blank spaces in Claudia Rankine's catalog of Black people killed by police and vigilantes at the end of *Citizen* are never filled with any more names. Or, to return to the *Zong* Massacre, how to undrown the lives recorded as property in law's archive. To do either of these things is as impossible and as necessary as to be free of air while admitting that there is no other source of breath, as Frank Wilderson III puts it.[2] It is as impossible as keeping breath in the Black body—the task on which Christina Sharpe meditates as she theorizes *aspiration*.[3] Which is to say, it is possible precisely because it is necessary.

This final chapter, then, is about im/possibility. The grammar of the law renders Black freedom—which the Combahee River Collective recognizes is *freedom itself*—impossible.[4] But the wake work of ethics lived in excess of law's grammar insists Black being into the future. With breathing in mind as simultaneously that which the law renders impossible and that which is made possible by everyday praxis, this chapter elaborates a poetics of breath in the form of literary representations of ungendered mothering in two texts that explicitly confront the impossibility of Black futurity imposed by the law: David Dabydeen's poem "Turner" and Angelina Weld Grimké's play *Rachel*.

What draws me to these two texts in conjunction for this chapter is the way in which each one asks seemingly unanswerable questions about birthing and mothering Black children explicitly in the wake of death by suffocation or strangulation—in the wake of stolen breath. They ask how to nourish a newly breathing body in the face of breath destroyed by drowning or hanging. In so asking, I believe these texts queer futurity beyond reproductivity through their nonnormative mother and child figures. While the Middle Passage un/genders the Black subject, "Turner" ungenders motherhood and *Rachel* unmothers gender. This reworking of motherhood through characters who are not biological mothers is grounded in the queerness of Blackness and the Blackness of queerness. To ground that abstract theoretical phrasing, in "Turner," Black families are literally torn apart, Black boys are sexually abused, and a speaker who is both nongendered and gendered male strives to mother a stillborn child, while in *Rachel*, a Black family is fractured by the lynching of the husband/father and his son/brother, and the protagonist refuses to allow her body to reproduce while still insisting on acting as a mother to Black children. Heteronormativity—especially the figure of the heteronormative family—is forestalled by the violences of colonialism, slavery, and slavery's aftermath, and thus so is reproductive futurity. In the absence of normative family structures, queer kinship and Black sociality become sites for enacting futurity in the figures of children whom white supremacy would ostensibly designate as futureless. In both texts, breath that is stopped in the past foreshadows the characters' struggle to find a way to breathe while being denied air. Dabydeen's fractured speaker and Grimké's Rachel both create futurity where it is deemed impossible precisely because it is necessary.

As two texts that both literally address the enforced precarity of breathing for Black subjects, "Turner" and *Rachel* offer, for me, the language of *breath* to describe not only the concerns of their representation but also their poetics of justice. As I have been emphasizing throughout *Abolition Time,* one of the primary functions of grammars of law is the locking in place of borders around what is possible within existing regimes of the social. Examples of these delimiting grammars are justice-as-event, citizenship-as-singularity, colonial Western Gender, and the recognition-rights-witnessing nexus. Respectively, my readings thus far attempted to show how the poetics of Claudia Rankine's *Citizen: An American Lyric,* Suzan-Lori Parks's *Imperceptible Mutabilities in the Third Kingdom,* Harriet Jacobs's *Incidents in the Life of a Slave Girl,* M. NourbeSe Philip's *Zong!,* Fred D'Aguiar's *Feeding the Ghosts,* and Toni Morrison's *A Mercy* deconstruct, often while inhabiting, those grammars through their various poetics of accumulation, perforation, and witnessing. In deconstructing their respective grammars of law, the poetics of justice I delineate seek to abolish the borders demarcating the territory of the ethically possible drawn by the force of law's grammar. On a terrain without borders, what was previously impossible becomes possibility. Breath, in this chapter, signals the impossibility imposed by grammars of law that extinguish Black breathing as well as the possibility for Black futurity enacted through the quotidian utopian gesture of sustaining breath. "Turner" and *Rachel* represent this paradox not only in their plots' literal narrativization of drowning and lynching but in their modes of address, shifting pronouns and antecedents, and in their figurations of Black mothers as forces of fabulation and Black children as ghostly flesh. *Poetics of breath is the literary conjuring of impossible figures with realist fidelity to the forces that make those figures impossible in the first place.*

REFERENTIAL FLUIDITY (REPRISE):
RACIAL-SEXUAL VIOLENCE AND THE
IMPOSSIBLE CHILD IN "TURNER"

Reflecting on her landmark essay "Punks, Bulldaggers, and Welfare Queens: The Radical Potential of Queer Politics?" twenty years after its publication, Cathy Cohen argues that "Michael Brown and Rekia Boyd are important queer subjects not because of their sexual practice, identity, or performance but because

they . . . operate in the world as queer subjects: the targets of racial normalizing projects intent on pathologizing them across the
dimensions of race, class, gender, and sexuality."[5] Cohen, who has
spent decades theorizing *queer* as an index of and potential for a
political posture against normativity in opposition to its common
usage as an identity marker to describe an individual person's
gender or sexuality, in that sentence recognizes that Black subjects are jettisoned from normativity itself such that Black death
becomes constitutive of the normal. This is why Jeffrey McCune,
writing in the aftermath of Michael Brown's death, riffs on Abdul
JanMohamed's "death-bound subject" to identify the "queerness
of blackness."[6] Not simply a flattening into synonyms, where *Black*
and *queer* become interchangeable terms, the analysis offered by
Cohen, McCune, and others working in Black feminist, queer, and
trans studies asks us to sit with, rather than too quickly or confidently untangle—or, worse, quantify—what Eric A. Stanley calls
the "knot of power's localization we misname identity."[7] When we
sit with the history of Blackness as a legal construction and sociopolitical projection of the Western Enlightenment's colonization
projects—with how, in C. Riley Snorton's words, "in apposition
with transness, blackness . . . structure[s] modes of valuation
through various forms . . . giv[ing] meaning to how gender is conceptualized, traversed, and lived"—we might start to see gender as
an ordering grammar constituted by its negation of/in Blackness.[8]

Building on the work of Hortense Spillers and Saidiya Hartman,
whose scholarship meticulously traces Blackness and gender as
historically produced grammars of discipline and control manifest in differentially experienced forms of sexual violence, Patrice
Douglass theorizes "Black gender" as an analytical matrix for understanding the *productive capacities of racial-sexual violence*. In
most scholarship and political discourse, race and gender are invoked as explanatory terms for identifying targets of violence.
In these formulations, raced and gendered subjects are taken for
granted as existing targets for violence directed at their preemp-
tively constituted object-status. However, Douglass argues that the
"structural positioning of Blackness blurs the lines of difference
demonstrating an intimate proximity to violence that troubles

the water of gender as an explanatory category."[9] That is, as Sarah Haley's work on "gendered racial terror" demonstrates, gender cannot explain the violence meted out against Black subjects.[10] Instead, gender winds up being *produced by* the sexually differentiated violence of anti-Blackness, rendering gender itself an ordering grammar from which Black subjects are jettisoned as the constitutive, excluded term.[11]

It is essential to frame my analysis of "Turner" with these analytical concepts in order to take seriously all that the poem does with gender and reproduction as figures of what Sharpe theorizes as aspiration, or the wake work of "imagining and keeping and putting breath back in the Black body in hostile weather . . . (aspiration is violent and life-saving)."[12] While Dabydeen's poem explicitly foregrounds birthing and nurturing, it also "allows its characters to slide between genders and races, destabilizing the authorial voice and flagging the flexibility and uncertainty of individual identity."[13] Like *Citizen* and *Zong!*, then, "Turner" works against forces of coherence in order to fracture individuation. In its unique deployment of such fracturing poetics, Dabydeen's poem clears space for futurity delinked from grammars of gendered economies of reproduction while refusing to erase the violent histories of the ungendering of Blackness through the terrors of slavery. The poem dis- and re-articulates new grammars of gender—what Marquis Bey would call "genders that might have arisen but for Gender"—through figurations of impossible motherhood as a utopian impulse that resides in, rather than erases, the impossibility of resurrection.[14] The poem undrowns the dead without regard for redemption or recovery. The future is not a break from but emerges in the presence of the past.

The final line of "Turner" is "No mother."[15] This ending has been read variously as a failure to recuperate the past of slavery or pessimism about wresting a future out of slavery's past. This line certainly does have those resonances, but I believe there is more there by the end of the poem than the absence or absent presence of mothers.[16] The poem both posits the mother-figure as one of the conditions of possibility of futurity and suggests that the figure of the mother is cut and queered by race in a way that cuts and queers the futurity that such a figure ostensibly nurtures. At the same time, the poem conjures the child-figure as the impossibility of the future that the mother-figure nurtures. As such, the poem's conjuration of spectral literary figures in the realist setting of enslaved Africans being drowned in the Atlantic positions the condition of possibility for futurity as tasked with nurturing futurity's impossibility. This paradoxical figuration is a poetics of breath.

In his preface, Dabydeen positions his poem as a response to J. M. W. Turner's painting *The Slave Ship* as well as to John Ruskin's (in)famous review in *Modern Painters*. Dabydeen is drawn to what Turner's painting and Ruskin's writing obscure. Not only is he writing from the position of one of the figures in *The Slave Ship*—a drowning enslaved African—but he is also responding to the rhetorical violence of Ruskin's essay: "[The painting's] subject, the shackling and drowning of Africans, was relegated to a brief footnote in Ruskin's essay. The footnote reads like an afterthought, something tossed overboard."[17] It is thus into the sea, to the sunken place of the drowned, to Édouard Glissant's "abyss," that Dabydeen goes to poeticize his meditation on slavery and its afterlife.[18] "Turner" does not explicitly refer to but, by way of lineage, is haunted by the historical event of the *Zong* Massacre, which partially inspired Turner's painting. The 132 human beings Luke Collingwood ordered jettisoned from the *Zong*, the obscured figure plunged into the sea by Turner's painting, the history of slavery that Ruskin buries in a footnote—Dabydeen wrests poetry from what Ian Baucom calls "this repeating moment in the history of trans-Atlantic slavery, this moment of drowning, and drowning, and drowning."[19] In the response he pens, Dabydeen is ardent in his conviction that he is no savior, diving into the sea of history to save the lives of the drowned. "Neither [the poem's speaker nor the stillborn child he yearns to mother] can escape Turner's representation of them as exotic and sublime victims," Dabydeen himself writes. "Neither can describe themselves anew but are indelibly stained by Turner's language and imagery."[20] The poem is neither mourning nor melancholia, as Stef Craps argues, but rather hauntology.[21] Remembering Jacques Derrida's thesis that hauntology is as much about the justice to be done as it is about the

catastrophe that has already occurred and does not cease occurring, I argue that Dabydeen's poem articulates futurity as a queer
temporality running through the afterlife of slavery, and it does so
through the tropes of mothers/mothering and kinship as well as
the figure of the stillborn child.

"Turner" is a narrative poem focalized through a single, if fractured and variously displaced, speaker—the submerged enslaved
African in the foreground of *The Slave Ship*. Dabydeen specifies
that it is the African's "submerged head" that is the focus, underlining the doubly synecdochical way in which slavery appears in
the painting: whereas in the *Zong* Massacre, a historical antecedent to the painting, more than one hundred enslaved people were
thrown overboard, and whereas millions of people were taken
from the African continent, only a few bodies float in Turner's
sea. Of these few bodies, none of them appears as a full body, but
each is only visible as parts. Turner thus performs a kind of dismembering of the figure of the slave that Dabydeen seeks to
re-member through his own figurative language. In the poem's
narrative, the drowned speaker awakens in the sea to the sight
of a stillborn child floating through the water toward it/him
(Dabydeen at first calls the speaker "it" but later shifts to "him").
He recalls some of his life on board a slave ship as a young boy,
sexually abused and eventually thrown overboard by a captain he
calls Turner. He also names the stillborn child "Turner," and as
he contemplates the child and his own desire to mother it, he partially remembers and partially invents memories of his life before
his capture.

Dabydeen's preface positions the poem's speaker as at first
ungendered—"When *it* awakens *it* can only partially recall the
sources of its life"—and then male—"*His* real desire is to begin
anew in the sea." This unnamed, drowned African has had its/his
lungs emptied of air and filled with water, but not only that. "Although the sea has transformed him—bleached him of color and
complicated his sense of gender—he still recognizes himself as
'n——r.'"[22] So when he awakens, he recognizes his subjectivity as
marked by the political ontology of Blackness packed into the racist epithet but also recognizes that as he is marked by the violence

of that word, he is also a differently gendered subject. Reading into Dabydeen's own use of the verb "complicates," we can see the speaker understand it/himself as ungendered by the experience of the Middle Passage that has plunged him into this "ocean of violence," as Douglass describes the meeting point "when gender and Blackness converge" to produce "Black gender as a theorem, not a thing, [which] dismantles the predicate of gender."[23] This un/gendering of the speaker does not deny the ways in which gender and sex are weaponized by enslavers under white supremacy, as the speaker repeatedly recounts sexual violence and the weaponization of gender in the service of white supremacy.[24]

In section XII of the poem, the speaker's stream of consciousness moves from the stillborn child floating toward him to the voice of his mother panicking after he hurt himself diving into a shallow pond before being interrupted by a parenthetical memory of Turner parceling the speaker and their fellow captives aboard the ship.

Turner's grasp (he sketches endless numbers
. . . .
                He checks that we are parceled
In equal lots, men divided from women,
Chained in fours and children subtracted
From mothers. When all things tally
He snaps the book shut, his creased mouth
Unfolding in a smile, as when, entering
His cabin, mind heavy with care, breeding
And multiplying percentages, he beholds
A boy disheveled on his bed.)[25]

The mathematical precision in these lines registers the calculated balance of material and discursive violence happening in the scenes: parceling enslaved people in equal lots, dividing men from women, being held captive in equal groups of a square number, children being subtracted from mothers to perhaps become remainders (are children not the remainder of the phrase "men, women, and children" when "men [are] divided from women"?), the tallying of human persons as "goods" in a logbook, and the multiplication of percentages of profit all illustrate the systemic, pervasive reach of slavery. Stephanie Smallwood and Jennifer L. Morgan demonstrate that the abstract mathematics of enslaver's logbooks and merchant bills mark where the historical archive registers the thingifying power and reach of slave law as it transforms the enslaved body into a commodity and the womb of the enslaved body into a factory for both capital and labor re/production.[26] But here in Dabydeen's poetry, that murderous mathematics uncovers the libidinal violence covered over by the grammar of economics in the so-called slave trade's archive.

The pervasive reach of slavery's mathematical violence is grounded in the details of the violent blending of white supremacy and heteronormativity, of racial violence and sexual violence. If we trace the enjambment of these lines, we might see a building emphasis through *mouth, entering, breeding,* and be*holds* that culminates in the final image of the parenthetical "A boy disheveled on [the captain's] bed." The suggestion of penetrative violence and the obliteration of consent that accumulates through the enjambment of the four preceding lines insist that we read "disheveled" not solely as an adjective but also as an attributive verb. That is, there is a subject, Turner, who did the disheveling of which the boy is the object. We might then read the interruptive quality of the parentheses enclosing these lines as signaling the temporal rupture of trauma, where the "boy" disheveled by Turner is the memory of the speaker's self, set off in parentheses. It is then important to notice how the individual trauma of sexual assault erupts in concert with an account of an "instance of vestibular cultural formation where 'kinship' loses meaning, *since it can be invaded at any given and arbitrary moment by the property relations.*"[27] That is, the image of sexual invasion of an individual enslaved subject is grafted to an image of the racializing invasion of kinship, linking sexual violence to the overarching project of domination that produces and is produced by that violence.

The process of enslavement uses binary sex categories to fracture familial relations, breaking up kinship networks and introducing natal alienation to the imagination of the Black subject as ontological Slave. Like Spillers in "Mama's Baby, Papa's Maybe," Dabydeen asserts in his poem the centuries of history that predate Daniel Patrick Moynihan's railing against the ostensible "failure" of Black people to form or sustain traditional family units. The racist violence of slavery intentionally (and unintentionally) tore Black people from their biological families and extrabiological networks of relation and kin, and the sexual violence of slavery multiplied percentages of profits through rape as a weapon of domination.[28] "Turner" figures these multiple forms of violence through a scene of an assault on a boy. This scene is doubly removed from the literal economics of biological reproduction that can sometimes be too quickly and easily explained in discussion of the rape of enslaved childbearers, who are quickly called "women" in a shorthand that betrays their exclusion from the dominant grammar of gender that disallows "Black woman" from cohering without definitional problems.

The boy is *doubly* removed in his designation as a male and a child; he is both too young and, presumably, has the wrong bodily capacities for his rape to be explained as the re/production of capital in the form of thingified human bodies made property. This scene marks a nonreproductive thread within the matrix of what Sarah Clarke Kaplan calls the "black reproductive."[29] That is, although the assault on this boy will not reproduce capital, it *will* re/produce the futurity of white supremacy held together by racial-sexual domination. "Turner" makes us take seriously that nonreproductive futurity, often figured in queer theory as oppositional to the reproductive futurity of heteronormativity and thus as a site of alternative possibilities beyond normativity's grasp, is and has been also a tool of white supremacy. Turner cannot reproduce a literal child by raping the boy on his bed, but he can insist his domination into the future as it erupts in the traumatic parenthetical of the speaker.

Coming near the end of the poem, section XXIV of "Turner" is a disturbingly graphic account of child rape without using literal description. Rather, Dabydeen's figurative language portrays the rape as a discursive act, one in which the young boys' language is disfigured by the imposition of Turner's words:

> Each night
> Aboard ship he gave selflessly the nipple
> Of his tongue until we learnt to say profitably
> In his own language, *we desire you, we love*
> *You, we forgive you.* He whispered eloquently
> Into our ears even as we wriggled beneath him,
> Breathless with pain, wanting to remove his hook
> Implanted in our flesh.[30]

Dabydeen's text both refuses and cannot refuse representing the bodily harm of rape. Coercion and the obliteration of consent are present throughout these lines in the words Dabydeen italicizes, which the children are made to repeat back to the captain after he whispers them into their ears from on top of them. The phallic imagery of the "hook / Implanted in our flesh" is only exacerbated by the explicit nonconsent compounded by the inability of refusal. In her insightful analysis of "Turner," Veronica Austen reads this section of the poem through the lens of consumption and nourishment to contrast it with the speaker's childhood memories of a man he calls Manu.[31] I follow Austen's comparative move to shift my reading here from these scenes of sexual-racial violence to scenes of mothering in the poem before taking up again nonreproductive futurity.

Two mother-figures are introduced in the speaker's memory of his childhood on the continent of Africa: his unnamed familial mother and a man named Manu, who plays the role of teacher and village elder in his community. The woman mothering the speaker is portrayed as his nourisher and protector; she cares for him when he has a fever (18), panics but remains steadfast in caring for him when he hurts himself playing (22), screams out for him when he is separated from her by Turner (14), protects him from the heat of the sun while gathering crops in the field (26), catches him when he falls before he actually hits the ground (23), and is represented throughout the poem as a disappeared or disappearing figure (22, 23, 26). Through her presence, the poem establishes *nourishment,* or the practice of keeping the child's body healthy and satisfied, as the future-oriented practice of mothering.

It is through this framing of *mothering* as a role characterized by the kind of work one does rather than by the kind of body one possesses that Manu emerges as a male mother-figure. My disarticulation of "mother" from the fixed gender identity of "woman" is enabled both by Dabydeen's poem and by Oyèrónkẹ́ Oyěwùmí's argument that "the emergence of women as an identifiable category, defined by their anatomy and subordinated to men in all situations, resulted, in part, from the imposition of a patriarchal colonial state."[32] Oyěwùmí's analysis of Yoruban culture helps us to understand that for some peoples, at least, the roles that a person performs in relation to other members of a community can be a way of defining the person by a grammar that is not merely oppositional to but outside of the ordering grammar of colonial Gender. Though Turner identifies his speaker only as "African," without more particular markers to tell readers that the speaker, his mother, and Manu definitively belong to a social world in which *mothering* is not defined by *womanhood*—which means we cannot simply universalize Oyěwùmí's argument about a particular group of people to represent all social relations on the African continent to confidently assert claims about Dabydeen's character's cultural understandings of non/gender—I believe that the poem does enough work to displace and question normative gender frameworks to invite an expansive, ungendered reading of motherhood.

As teacher, it is Manu's job to synthesize and distill generational wisdom for the children of his community, teaching them how to live fully. In section xx, his teaching is most obviously represented as nourishment:

> [...]The first word
> Shot from his mouth, he stretched out his lizard's
> Tongue after it, retrieved it instantly
> On the curled tip, closed his mouth, chewed. When he
> Grinded the word into bits he began his tale,
> One grain at a time fed to our lips
> Endlessly, the sack of his mouth bulging
> With wheat, until we grew sluggish and tame

With overeating, and fell asleep, his life-
Long tale to be continued in dreams.[33]

These lines display Manu as a mother bird premasticating a meal for her/his/their babies. For the children of the community, Manu's stories are nourishment for the body and the mind, and he is careful to share them only through careful consideration of how the children can most readily handle them. There is a power difference between mother-figure and child-figure here, but that difference is an occasion for compassion rather than domination. As Austen writes, "through storytelling, Manu is shown to be nourishing the future generations, thus enabling the persistence of cultural practices and histories."[34] These two figures, one called male and one called female within the grammatical schema of Western Gender, thus orient the poem's understanding of motherhood toward futurity, where *to mother* is *to nourish children into the future,* regardless of one's ability to physically birth a child in the first place.[35] This break between the physical capacity to reproduce biological children and the social capacity to nourish is also the delinking of futurity from reproduction mobilized by the poem which I read as a queer futurity of abolition time opened by the poem's poetics of breath.

It is in this context that Turner (the ship captain) is figured as a kind of perverse (anti)mother. The phrase "[Turner] gave selflessly the nipple / Of his tongue" contrasts sharply with the safety of the speaker's mother's bosom and the care with which Manu feeds him stories of wisdom. While the speaker's mother and Manu provide nourishment for the future, Turner delivers malnourishment and violence—indeed, the guarantee of the speaker having "no future" at all, as a child jettisoned from the floating ship of the Human. Turner's figuration through (mal)nourishment not only ungenders but also deromanticizes motherhood, then, by offering a disturbing mother-figure who makes free use of phallic sexual violence in the service of racial domination. Austen focuses on the final word of the section, "Endlessly," and its repetition: "Not only do Turner's words 'flow endlessly' but the words fill the children endlessly; they cannot escape this unwanted ingestion, an ingestion that leaves no room for other forms of nourishment."[36] The poem as a whole thus viscerally rejects a utopian vision of mothering as guarantor of the future, because it is through his perverse performances of pseudo-mothering that Turner wounds Black kinship.

The uneasy juxtaposition between the speaker's two nurturing mother-figures and Turner himself makes clear that "Turner" is not only a poem about violence. It is also a poem about the possibilities seized and/or insisted within and in the wake of violence. In section XXI, Manu has a glimpse of the future, and seeing the colonial violence about to be visited upon his people, he tears away the necklace of beads he wears around his neck and scatters the beads over the ground in front of the children.

> The beads rolled from the thread, scattered like coloured
> Marbles and we scrambled to gather them,
> Each child clutching an accidental handful
> Where before they hung in a sequence of hues
> Around his neck, the pattern of which only he
> Knew—from his father and those before—to preserve.
> The jouti lay in different hands, in different
> Colours. We stared bleakly at them and looked
> To Manu for guidance, but he gave no instruction
> Except—and his voice gathered rage and unhappiness—
> That in the future time each must learn to live
> Beadless in a foreign land; or perish.
> Or each must learn to make new jouti,
> Arrange them by instinct, imagination, study
> And arbitrary choice into a pattern
> Pleasing to the self and to others
> Of the scattered tribe; or perish.[37]

In these lines, readers see Manu struggle to balance the compassion of his normal method of feeding his pupils knowledge expressed through the bird-feeding analogy with the enormity of the violence he sees on the horizon. In an explosive gesture, he throws away a symbol of generational wisdom passed to him "from his father and those before him," which causes the children to scramble to collect the beads before staring bleakly at Manu, craving explanation. The only nourishment the elder can offer is the knowledge that death approaches and that survival will depend on learning to live differently, to make life anew in the wake of catastrophe, "or perish." Tellingly, Manu does not offer a deterministic apocalypse. There will be death, but there will be ways to make life. I read the poem's speaker's desire to mother the stillborn child he encounters to be a form of figuratively "mak[ing] new jouti" through queer (in the double sense of being outside normative conceptions of gender and also resisting normative political formations, in this case by imagining nonreproductive futurity) kinship.

The first word of Dabydeen's poem is "stillborn," thus inaugurating the poetic narrative with the contradiction of being born dead. The speaker, who himself has apparently awakened from drowning to death, sees a dead infant floating in the sea toward him and feels a deep desire to form a bond with the child, anticipating "this longed-for gift of motherhood."[38] Section XI elaborates:

> It broke the waters and made the years
> Stir, not in faint murmurs but a whirlpool
> That sucks me under with lust for the smell
> Of earth and root and freshly burst fruit,
> My breasts a woman's which I surrender
> To my child-mouth, feeding my own hurt
> For the taste of sugared milk, mantee seeds
> Crushed, my mother dipping them in sweet paste,
> Letting me lick her fingers afterwards.[39]

These lines demonstrate a recurring trope in the poem, whereby the speaker shifts to remembering his own mother's care whenever he considers the stillborn child before him. In this section, he describes how the very presence of the infant "made the years stir" in a "whirlpool," and we see a literal swirling together of past, present, and future in his stream of consciousness. The prospect of (bringing to life and) nurturing the child before him—this present task of creating futurity—conjures his longing for the mother he himself has lost, and so he moves in a whirlpool where the loss caused by the violence of a past catastrophe refuses to remain in the past even as he refuses the prognosis of "no future" that is supposed, by definition, to be marked on a stillborn child by yearning to do the work of mothering.

The whirlpool, in my reading, is a figure of the dynamic—and dangerous—excessive present. In this whirlpool, not only does the speaker fail to maintain separation between past, present, and future but his sense of gender begins to exceed normative binaries. He sees himself with "a woman's" breasts, and he feeds "my child-mouth"—an ambiguous reference; is he feeding the mouth of his child, the stillborn infant he has claimed, or is he feeding his own mouth with his own breast? In either case, the act of nurturing—whether given to himself as future-child of the past signified by his mother or to the infant as stilled future-in-the-present floating before him—engenders him "feeding [his] own hurt" by invoking the loss of his mother specifically through the memory of feeding. The section of the poem continues,

> This creature kicks alive in my stomach
> Such dreams of family, this thing which I cannot
> Fathom, resembling a piece of ragged flesh,
> Though human from the shape of its head,
> Its half-formed eyes, seeming jaw and as yet
> Sealed lips.[40]

Though only barely recognizable as human, the speaker sees the child as kin, as potential fulfillment of "such dreams of family" that remain in the wake of his irrevocable loss. We can also read the double meaning of the infant kicking in the speaker's stomach as another reference to mothering, though this time to the experience of carrying a child in one's body. We are left again to consider the gendering of this speaker whom Dabydeen calls "it" and "he." The possibility of trans subjectivity manifests in these passages in the figure of the pregnant man. At the very least, these lines gesture toward the possibility of crafting queer kinship between indefinite, slippery, liminal subjects.

The final section of the poem wrestles with the im/possibility of futurity for such liminal subjects floating in the sea as living dead remainders of the transatlantic slave trade. For the last time, the speaker recounts how the child has called him "n——r" as it floats away from him, leaving him to ponder his conjuration of memory and imagination. "I wanted to begin anew in the sea," he recalls, "but the child would not bear the future nor its inventions."[41] It seems as if the speaker's pursuit of mothering is doomed. Austen observes, "The cyclical pursuit of nourishment whereby the speaker sees himself both as nourishing the baby and being nourished by it, ultimately speaks to the impossibility of their food chain. . . . The baby's existence is thus impossible."[42] She concludes her reading of Dabydeen's poem with the assertion, "The speaker can turn neither backward to the past nor forward to the future for comfort: he can neither have a mother, nor be a mother; neither achieve nourishment, nor offer it."[43] And yet.

How might we think the figure of the impossible child? The stillborn? What might be left for a speaker who can turn neither to the past nor to the future? Drawing on the poem's own figure of the whirlpool in which past and future swirl together, I read the poem's final words, "No mother," not as a teleological *ending* of the narrative poetry but as a point in the field of the poem's temporality. This point occurs appositionally with the speaker's mother protecting him from tumbling off of her lap to the ground and alongside Manu's prophetic wisdom that in the future the children must learn to live beadless and make new necklaces — new kinship networks — or else perish. History of course tells us that those thrown overboard slave ships like the *Zong* died. There is no saving them. The poem's solemn final image makes that clear, and my insistence on the excessive present does not deny that. Rather, I want to look at the history of defeat painted with such vibrancy in Turner's *The Slave Ship* and interrogated with such wonder and pain in Dabydeen's poem in order to encounter radical imaginations of freedom in excess of violence. We might find livable practices of enacting futurity in the present that is inseparable from the past catastrophe, this moment of drowning, and drowning, and drowning. A poetics of breath, then, when we consider

Dabydeen's "Turner," is a fabulation of a future conjured through impossible figures, where, for example, a stillborn child fed by the breast of a male speaker is precisely the literary invocation of futurity that normative grammars of gender render impossible and yet cannot erase.

BLACK ASPIRATION AND NONREPRODUCTIVE FUTURITY IN *RACHEL*

Written in 1916, Angelina Weld Grimké's play *Rachel* stands as the inauguration of Harlem Renaissance drama, an origin point of antilynching drama, and, I believe, a Black queer theorization that prefigures twenty-first-century debates over queer futurity and Afropessimism.[44] More complex than merely a play that advocates "race suicide," as some contemporary reviewers charged, and more layered than an appeal to white women to forge cross-racial sympathy through the common experience of motherhood, as Grimké herself claimed, *Rachel* asks audiences to witness the psychological assault on Black life that the violence of Black death inflicts as well as the living and the insistence of living that produce a future amid so much destruction. Like the children whom Manu charges with the task of building alternative methods of organizing sociality in "Turner," Grimké's titular character, Rachel, exceeds the bounds of blood kin in her cultivation of nurturing relationships with those both within and beyond her biological family. While being marked by a heavy-handed name that she queers through these relationships which exceed heteronormativity, Rachel "insist[s] black being into the wake" of slavery's aftermath, though she does so without bearing any children of her own.[45] In this section, I read *Rachel* as a meditation on a set of questions posed by Sharpe:

> In the afterlives of *partus sequitur ventrem* what does, what can, mothering mean for Black women, for Black people? What kind of mother/ing is it if one must always be prepared with the knowledge of the possibility of the violent and quotidian death of one's child? Is it mothering if one knows that one's child might be killed at any time in the hold, in the wake by the state no matter who wields the gun?[46]

In grappling with these questions, Grimké's play, like Dabydeen's poem, offers impossible children. But instead of being stillborn—instead of coming into the world dead—Rachel's impossible children are never born, and bodying forth in the absence of these never-born children are the children of her community whom Rachel cares for and nurtures, displacing her motherhood from her womb and displacing futurity from the scene of birthing.

The beginning of the play sees its titular character, Rachel Loving, coming home late because she paused to play with a little Black boy named Jimmy in the stairway of her family's apartment building. She declares to her mother that "if I believed that I should grow up and not be a mother, I'd pray to die now."[47] The play goes to melodramatic lengths to establish that Rachel in these early moments of the first act is determined to become a mother to the point where it is an essentially defining trait of her character, not merely because she is a girl and girls grow up to be women who must be mothers in a crudely essentializing way—though gendered socialization can never be swept away—but rather because she bears a particular desire to perform care work for children. The desire takes on a racial inflection, because Rachel declares that she loves "little black and brown babies best of all" because they seem to need "protection," though from what she does not know.[48] Echoing Florens's mother's declaration at the end of A Mercy that "there is no protection, but there is difference," it is the notion of "protection" that the play most viciously destroys in its critique of the violence of white supremacy enacted through lynching and its aftereffects.[49]

In the climactic moment of the first act, Mrs. Loving breaks her ten-year silence about the deaths of her husband and eldest son—Rachel and her brother Tom's father and half brother—and shares with her nearly adult children the story of how the two were lynched "by church members in good standing."[50] Mr. Loving was the editor of a Black newspaper and a respected member of his community; the audience can infer the proxy-middle-class status that the Loving family may have enjoyed through Mrs. Loving's recollections of her husband's standing in their town, his ownership of a newspaper, and the family's place in their own house.[51]

After a lifetime of enduring racism, Mr. Loving published a condemnation of a lynch mob that killed an innocent Black man, and he received an anonymous letter threatening him if he did not retract his remarks. He, of course, would not do so, and one night, a dozen masked men broke into the Lovings' house, dragged Mr. Loving and his seventeen-year-old son George out into the street, and hanged them.

Importantly, then, lynching does not actually happen during the time line of the play's action—which would become an important aspect of early lynching plays as a genre. Rather, it is the specter that haunts the action, the unspeakable thing unspoken by Mrs. Loving until she is forced to give utterance to the pain conjured up by seeing Jimmy, the little boy with whom Rachel was playing, because the boy looks so much like George in Mrs. Loving's eyes. Jimmy stands in as a substitute, a revised repetition of Mrs. Loving's dead child that calls forward to our own time in the forms of Tamir Rice and Ma'Khia Bryant, while in the play calling forth the revenant of George, who demands an articulation from his mother.[52] To break that down, Jimmy in the present appears as *pre-sent* to Mrs. Loving. She sees in the living child the figure of her dead child George. For her, Jimmy is both real flesh and embodied ghost. For us as twenty-first-century viewers or readers of the play, George's lynching may conjure images of Black children killed by police like Tamir Rice or Ma'Khia Bryant.[53] In that sense, Jimmy gathers that past of George's lynching with the future of more Black children killed by anti-Black violence.[54] Jimmy, therefore, is a character who cannot escape multiple forms of spectrality. At the end of act 1, Rachel begins to grasp part of the responsibility called forth by the specter of lynching as Mrs. Loving recalls it. She declares, "Everywhere throughout the South, there are hundreds of dark mothers who live in . . . suffocating fear. . . . It would be more merciful—to strangle the little [babies] at birth. . . . So, this is what [motherhood] means."[55] The overwhelming threat of lynching—of lynching that can happen to any Black person in any space, because the home is not a sanctuary, is indeed no protection against the lynch mob—marks this evaluation of motherhood as a raced consequence.

Rachel has not declared anything about motherhood in the abstract but has articulated a specifically Black condition of the universalized and (hetero)normalized notion of motherhood that is produced by white supremacy's racial-sexual violence as theorized by Douglass, Spillers, Hartman, and Sharpe and as rethought in Dabydeen's "Turner." The condition under which Black women like Rachel might become mothers is what Sharpe describes as "disfigure[d] black maternity" which "turn[s] the womb into a factory (producing blackness as abjection much like the slave ship's hold and the prison), and turning the birth canal into another domestic middle passage with black mothers, after the end of legal hypodescent, still ushering their children into her condition; her non-status, her non-being-ness."[56] Bringing a Black child into the world as a Black mother in the era of lynching is an act of bringing Black being into the wake of slavery, insofar as lynching is one more fold in the continuous unfolding of slavery's afterlife.

This is where the play seems to be doing more than Grimké might be intending, according to her written response to the "race suicide" charges. In an essay in a 1920 edition of *Competitor*, Grimké states that the play is primarily for white audiences and that rather than advocating race suicide to Black people, it is attempting an appeal for cross-racial empathy.[57] This may be true, and still even so, the fact that the play ends with its protagonist swearing an oath not to bring Black children into this world not merely as a personal preference but as an ethical mandate suggests that there might be something going on here beyond the familiar trope in African American literary studies of appealing to white people's imagined sympathies by passing Black characters through the universal category of the Human via ostensibly nonracialized sets of experiences.[58]

It might be important to linger with the suggestion to discontinue the race at *Rachel*'s conclusion. Such a suggestion seems to indicate that Black people ought to meet the force of white supremacy by turning away from its demands, by turning away from futurity itself in a way that does not sound unlike Lee Edelman's argument in *No Future: Queer Theory and the Death Drive*. In that book, Edelman argues that because "the Child has come to embody for us the telos of the social order and come to be seen as the one for whom that order is held in perpetual trust," the ultimate act of resistance is to refuse the terms of heteronormative society and turn away from futurity itself, to "insist that the future stop here."[59] In a certain sense, this is persuasive as an ultimate act against the oppressive politics of heteronormativity, but the more one listens, the more one hears questions come up, like which children get to be figured by Edelman's capital-C Child and who is the "us" who decide upon the telos of the social order? Indeed, to advocate to Black people that they ought to embrace a sense of "no future" requires an erasure of the fact that normative society does not in fact bend itself toward Black children's futures at all. So when some Black audience members witnessed the end of *Rachel* and heard in its final moments a call to refuse reproductive futurity, it is understandable why they were perhaps not as excited about the prospect of foreclosing futures as, in the realm of queer theory, Edelman might be.[60]

Like Edelman's argument, this critique of antifuturity or antirelationality has also become familiar, and Muñoz makes it when he writes, "In the same way all queers are not the stealth-universal-white-gay-man invoked in queer anti-relational formulation, all children are not the privileged white babies to whom contemporary society caters."[61] Clearly. One need only utter the name Tamir Rice or Aiyana Stanley-Jones or Trayvon Martin or Ma'Khia Bryant or Emmett Till or Addie Mae Collins or Carol Denise McNair or Carole Rosamond Robertson or Cynthia Dionne Wesley to see this. Or in the case of *Rachel*, one need only look to the minor character Ethel, who has been traumatized by racism to the point where she will only trust and communicate with her own parents, much to Rachel's dismay.

Rachel meets Ethel in the second act of the play, which, as a whole, serves to demonstrate to her the futility of believing she can protect Black children from racism. After meeting the traumatized Ethel, Rachel learns that her adopted son Jimmy has been verbally and physically attacked at his school, though he says that being pelted by rocks hurts far less than being called the n-word. This act ends with Rachel throwing to the floor a bunch of rosebuds that her suiter John Strong has sent her. The dramatic moment resonates with her own adopted son's observation that it would be kinder to kill the rosebuds immediately than to let them wither and die a slow, agonizing death. The obvious and yet still shocking metaphor represented in the rosebuds is voiced by Rachel when she declares that she will kill the flowers/her children immediately rather than prolong a slow death: "no child of mine shall ever lie upon my breast . . . if I kill, You Mighty God, I kill at once—I do not torture."[62] Then, in the third and final act of the play, Rachel puts her moral decision into practice. John Strong proposes to marry her and for the two of them to live together as a Strong-Loving family.

Rachel refuses John's proposal on the grounds that she cannot bring herself to bear Black children into the world, and if she were to marry and live with him, there would inevitably, within the context of the scripts for a heterosexual marriage in the early decades of the twentieth century, arise the moment when she would be expected to take up the task of childbearing. Within the context of white supremacy, though, bringing Black children into an anti-Black world is, according to Rachel's logic, to initiate a path of suffering. Rachel negotiates the question of parenting in the wake of her own father's extralegal murder by upstanding white citizens *who came in her parents' ~~yard~~house*, and, like Dabydeen's speaker looking for a way to grasp life while still in the sea in which he drowned, Rachel seeks ways of living squarely within this condition, rather than outside of it.

It is noteworthy that Grimké, herself a Black lesbian whose romantic and sexual desires moved against reproductive domesticity and ultimately went unfulfilled during her lifetime, writes a protagonist who so decisively refuses both birthing and heterosexual marriage. When I teach *Rachel*, I wait until we have finished reading the play before delving into Grimké's biography in order to stave off the temptation of seeing Rachel as an autobiographical character as the "correct" reading of the play, but any queer reading of the play, even one that resists the autobiographical, cannot neglect embodied sexuality as a thread of analysis.[63] K. Allison Hammer demonstrates that

> *Rachel*'s queer content becomes particularly evident when the plays
> are read alongside Grimké's erotic poetry. While most critics view
> her poetry and lynching plays as separate bodies of work, Grimké
> must be approached through her total writing. . . . Her poems may
> seem overly formal. . . . However, her use of genre, such as the
> gothic in the lynching stories and the sonnet in her poetry, confirm
> Grimké's strategic use of formal structure to call attention to the an-
> timodern impulses of lynching.[64]

Hammer goes on to read *Rachel* in conjunction with Grimké's poetry to demonstrate "two potential queer readings of Rachel: first,
the view that Rachel resembles Grimké and is therefore autobiographical, and second, that Rachel represents the kind of woman
Grimké desired, a hypothesis supported through close readings of
the poems."[65] While I find both of these readings of Rachel, which
trace her as a character back to Grimké's autobiography, compelling, I want to read in a different direction. I want to ask, If Rachel
as a mother is barred from the gender position of "womanhood"
(following Douglass's theorization of "Black gender" as it extends
the work of Spillers and Hartman as well as Cohen, McCune,
Snorton, and Bey's compelling arguments against the ability of
Blackness to cohere within gender normativity), and if normative
sexuality and all of its trappings are built upon stable gender categories from which she, as Black, is expelled, then is there a way
in which Rachel's refusal of heterosexual reproduction is actually
a turn toward the queerness of her own figuration? And if we can
read her that way, then how does that help us read *Rachel*'s advocacy against birthing Black children as, without qualification, a
vision of Black futurity?

   In refusing to play the game of domesticity, I argue, Rachel does
not refuse futurity itself, and the play does not, in fact, advocate
race suicide, but not only for the reasons Grimké herself articulated in 1920. I will close-read Rachel's two monologues at the
ends of acts 2 and 3, dialogue from John and Rachel's brother Tom,
and key stage directions to illuminate that Grimké's play is a critique of antirelational queer politics. It manifests such a critique

by taking our imaginations to places where antirelationality cannot go. That is, in order to imagine the futurity wrested out of an imposed "no future," we must understand that, as Sharpe puts it, Black life is lived in the *nos*, one of which manifests in the "no future" slogan.[66] We must think the impossible that is demanded by Black Aspiration, or the capacity, again, to live *in the* nos. When we orient ourselves as critics toward thinking nonnormative familial bonds as sites of "nonreproductive futurity," which of course requires that we take seriously natal alienation and social death, we are able to consider *Rachel* as a play that queerly resists white supremacy by attempting the impossible task of mothering without giving birth.

In an essay synthesizing queer theory, Black feminism, and Afropessimism, James Bliss writes, "There are many ways of accessing and inhabiting the future, and the problem is not that young Black queers have *no* access to the future but that the future is, itself, structured by an antiblackness that shapes access to future(s) for *all* subjects."[67] This emphasis on "all" subjects is absolutely not the facile universal *we all suffer equally because of racism* platitude but rather the point made by Wilderson, Hartman, and others that in what we think we know as Western modernity, the World, both discursively and materially, is predicated on the violent subjugation of Black peoples, and the ostensibly universal category of the capital-*H* Human is made possible by the genocidally violent exclusion of Black human bodies from its purview, as Sylvia Wynter teaches us.[68] What this means is that anti-Black violence, as that force that blocks individual Black subjects from accessing the future as such, is also the force that creates the viability of white futures.

Leading up to Rachel's dramatic rosebuds monologue in act 2, her brother Tom forcefully and poetically articulates the problem of Black futurity identified in this schema. In dialogue with his sister and mother, John contrasts the condition of being foreclosed from discursive Humanity with the existence of white murderers in a moment that seems infused with the critical insight that access to modernity for white people is both *en*sured and *in*sured by anti-Blackness when he says, "*Their* children shall grow up in *hope*; ours, in despair. Our hands are clean;—*theirs* are red with blood— red with the blood of a noble man—and a boy."[69] These lines employ multiple layers of chiasmus to illuminate the inextricability of anti-Blackness and white futurity.

At the first level of the chiasmus, "theirs" and "ours" switch places from the first sentence to the second, crisscrossing a net of entanglement as opposed to creating an uncrossable divide that would emerge between the never-crossing lines of a parallel structure (that is, if the sentences both had an "our/theirs" parallel structure rather than what Grimké wrote, which flips "their/ ours" to "our/theirs" in the second sentence). At the second level of the chiasmus, the hope-despair dichotomy is paired with an innocence-guilt dichotomy in parallel structure that is *interrupted* or *ruptured* by the first level of the chiasmus. That is, the parallel structure keeps intact the conceptual pairing of *hope* with *innocence* and *despair* with *guilt* (being "red with blood"), but those parallel lines are cut by the inversion of "us" and "them" at the first level of the chiasmus.

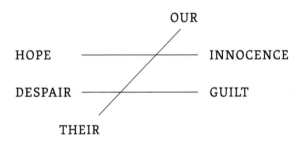

We now have what looks like the "not equivalent" symbol in mathematics, with two parallel lines representing normative conceptual pairings being cut, slashed, bisected by the linguistic crisscrossing of pronouns. Here the parallel lines are legal justice (those who are innocent have hope and those who commit murder shall have despair), where the chiasmus's cut (swapping pronouns so that the same subjects who commit murder have hope and the ones who are innocent have despair) is the entanglement of white life with Black suffering that produces the law as unjust.

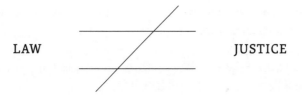

LAW   JUSTICE

Those whose hands are red with blood have access to a future structured by the very violence which that blood signifies, and those children who grow up in despair will also grow up into that very same future. And it is precisely this prospect of growing into the future that so worries Rachel. It is *not* that Black children are guaranteed to have *no future* but rather that the future that they *will* experience is predicated upon the possibility that at any time they may be destroyed.

Although Rachel understands that Black children may indeed have access to futurity—a futurity predicated upon their subjection, where, in Kara Keeling's words, "from within the logics of existing possible worlds and the range of possible trajectories into the future that they currently make perceptible, a Black future looks like no future at all"—she does not reject futurity outright.[70] To understand this, we need to attend closely to both the words of her monologues and the stage directions closing the second and third acts of the play.

When we look at Rachel's rosebuds speech, we see that it begins as soliloquy, with her reflecting, "First, it's little, black Ethel—and then it's Jimmy. Tomorrow, it will be some other little child." Yesterday Ethel, today Jimmy, tomorrow the unnamed—past, present, and future consolidated into what Jared Sexton calls anti-Blackness "without punctuation."[71] It may seem like George goes forgotten here, but again, he is the unspoken presence perceived by Rachel's mother in Jimmy's body. Jimmy is himself ghosted by death even as he breathes life, his body bearing past, present, and future as an excessive burden no small child should bear.

Rachel holds this in her own psyche as she laments that her dream of being a mother is dead now that she knows what mothering Black children entails. But then the monologue pivots from soliloquy to apostrophe at the moment the stage directions state,

"*Pauses, then slowly and with dawning surprise.*" Following this, Rachel directly addresses God:

> Why, God, you were making a mock of me; you were laughing at me. . . . You can laugh, Oh God! Well, so can I. . . . But I can be kinder than You. . . . If I kill, You Mighty God, I kill at once—I do not torture.[72]

This pivot from one form of monologue, soliloquy, to another, apostrophe, is essential to understanding the complexity of the play's formulations of futurity by its end. Rachel pivots from addressing herself and her own hurt, the imprisonment she feels within the pain of even the potential of Black motherhood, to addressing an external force. If we can follow the move from soliloquy to apostrophe as a move from internalization to projection, we can see Rachel recognizing an external force that is imposing the terms of reality on her.[73] At this moment she sees only two choices: either (1) raise children and watch them suffer and be destroyed by a world that hates them or (2) kill her own children at birth so that they might never experience the suffering of the anti-Black world. At the end of act 2, this apostrophe to God, who stands in as Law itself, marks Black futures as impossible, rendering Rachel's only choices as being over *how early* a Black child's life will end.

But then at the end of act 3, this impossibility shifts as Rachel switches targets for her final apostrophe of the play. After dismissing John upon rejecting his proposal, she declares,

> And my little children! I shall never see you now. . . . But you are somewhere and wherever you are you are mine! . . . Even God can't take you away. . . . You may be happy now you are safe.[74]

Here she no longer speaks to power in an act of defiance; rather, she speaks to her unborn children, telling them that they are safe where they are in the then and there of a different plane of reality. This marks a shift *from* direct opposition *to* care, which itself is a shift into the *insistence* that marks Black Aspiration as a mode of crafting queer futurity in the now.

To emphasize this shift in Rachel's assessment of futurity that is figured by the rhetorical mode of her monologues, the play ends *not* with Rachel's declaration of her unborn children's nonlife (as opposed to *death*) but with her running to Jimmy:

> (*The weeping begins again. To Jimmy, her whole soul in her voice*) Jimmy! My little Jimmy! Honey! I'm coming. Ma Rachel loves you so. (*Sobs and goes blindly, unsteadily to the rear doorway; she leans her head there one second against the door; and then stumbles through and disappears. The light in the lamp flickers and goes out . . . It is black. The terrible, heart-breaking weeping continues*). THE END.[75]

It is with this lingering gesture that the play comes to a close, leaving no actors onstage but letting the audience stew in the discomfiture created by Jimmy's "terrible, heart-breaking weeping." This matters because it is not dead or nonliving children with which the play leaves audience members but living children who have futures and who demand a different kind of ethics than either Edelman's antifuture or standard reproductive futurity. They demand an ethics of im/possible responsibility and a nonreproductive futurity. Rachel rejects reproduction—she declares that her bio-children shall remain in heaven, never to be birthed by her—but flies offstage to nurture Black futures as an ungendered mother for Jimmy and the rest of the children of her apartment complex. At the end of act 2, in addressing God, Rachel sees motherhood as an impossibility for her imposed by a power too great to overcome. But at the play's end, Jimmy's crying *necessitates* Rachel's care work, and so Black motherhood is transformed from impossibility into possibility by its very necessity in the moment of the now. The impossible is made possible, and the future is outside the regime of (racial capitalist) reproduction.

All of the characters in *Rachel* live in the space of death, always already susceptible to violence and beyond the protection of the law. At the same time, the anti-Blackness of the world fails to stop them from building kinship networks and living beyond mere survival. Rachel herself is the best example of this. From the beginning of the play, the audience hears her call her mother "ma dear," and so that "ma" becomes, through repetition, encoded with the relationship of child to mother. Then the very first line of the second act is spoken by Jimmy, and it is, "Ma Rachel!" The point is obvious but significant: Rachel is not, in fact, Jimmy's biological mother, but rather she is a kind of found mother or, in sociological terms, an "othermother."[76] This moment also signals the pervasive logic of substitution underlying the play's poetics. Jimmy, as discussed, stands in as a ghostly figure of Rachel's dead brother George, and Rachel in this moment stands in as a replacement target for the label "ma" that she directed toward her own mother in act 2. The opening of act 2, then, is haunted by the shadow of George calling Mrs. Loving "ma dear" more than a decade earlier, before he was lynched with his father. The intricate kinship ties that exceed biological relation are also in this moment complexly navigating the hauntological contours of living in the wake of lynching.

The play also demonstrates the kinship between Tom and John as they help each other survive in their day-to-day experiences of anti-Blackness. Grimké's play thus both looks fully in the face the fact of Black social and literal death *and* vehemently clings to the possibility that life happens under the sign of social death, not because of hope for a better future, but because of the queer kinship networks that are forged between its Black characters as ways of insisting toward a Black future. Jimmy may be destined for a life full of anti-Black violence, both micro and macro, but he is alive in the play's *here and now,* and although Rachel will not bring her own biological children into the world, she will do her best to get Jimmy to some kind of *then and there,* even if there is indeed no protection. And because of the underlying logic of substitution expressed through chiasmus, repetition ("ma dear"), address (to self or other), and spectrality (Jimmy as George), the play develops a poetics of breath whereby Mr. Loving's extinguished breath is the air on which Rachel aspirates Jimmy and his friends into the future, even as Mr. Loving and his son can never be resurrected.

Rachel figures the slash in *im/possible futures* in the kinship networks that its Black characters build to inhabit a future designed to destroy them to ensure its own existence. When we stay with the text through its eruptions of melodramatic affect, we see that through chiasmatic poetics, repetition and revision, contrasting modes of monologue, and ghostly figuration, *Rachel* is doing more than diagnosing the impossibilities imposed on Black life by the law of white supremacy. Its poetics of breath manifest in those rhetorical techniques that figure impossibility to forge possibilities in a world lived otherwise in the here and now of quotidian violence. The play therefore occupies the terrain of impossibility imposed by law's grammar of futurity secured through expendability precisely as the terrain on which possibility secured without reproduction is forged.

It is important not to romanticize Rachel's ethics of care or the queer kinship networks that she, following Manu's directions, builds and sustains. Like Sharpe, I believe that any analysis of the ways in which anti-Blackness is resisted must simultaneously attend to the overwhelming force of anti-Blackness that makes such resistance imperative from the start. This way, neither defeatism nor triumphalism emerges from such analyses. This is why I have carried Eric Garner's last words with me as I have written this final chapter about breathing. With Sharpe's and Wilderson's meditations on breath in mind, and with Muñoz's utopianism and Erica Garner's dissatisfaction with waiting for a future to come, I am drawn to the radical imagining of resurrection, of putting breath back into the body, and to the radical practice of refusal, of refusing to birth bodies while nourishing others on their journey to breathe.

Ultimately, this final poetics of justice—a poetics of breath—that closes *Abolition Time* is probably the least definable. Like air, it escapes my grasp even as I am assured of its movement. This is, in essence, where and how we are left in abolition time. In the face of the solid, powerful grammar of the law that prescribes linear, retributive modes of justice, it is not just new or different grammars that are necessary but rather poetics that refuse to refuse law's grammar. Poetics of justice do more than critique or negate or undo law's grammar. They may do all of that. But they also exceed it. They move just out of grasp, requiring our fullest, closest attention to pick up on their movements, would we but sit in the discomfort of our uncertainty and vulnerability in the face of the task to think precisely the matrix of possibilities deemed impossible by our available, hegemonic grammars.

We cannot undo the past that we live in as our present. We cannot turn away from the future we are enacting with every choice we make in our now. We cannot be paralyzed by the overwhelming weight of a present stretching in all directions or the uncertainty lurking behind every decision underpinned by undecidability. The condition of possibility for ethics is risk. So in abolition time, when justice cannot be an event but must be a practice, when we may have to inhabit the very structures that have been causing us harm, when in beholding each other we open ourselves up to the vulnerability of being held, justice can never be an answer. Justice is a set of questions to which we perpetually return.

One question is, Who is responsible?

Another is, Can we read?[77]

Coda

Impossibility may very well be our only possibility.
—Morgan Bassichis, Alexander Lee, and Dean Spade,
"Building an Abolitionist Trans and Queer Movement
with Everything We've Got"

Maybe the best political poems are blockades, strikes,
protests, mutual aid, cities on fire. Maybe direct action
is a poetic form.

—Kemi Alabi, Twitter

Angelina Weld Grimké's Rachel is under no illusion that the World
that she and the residents of her apartment complex inhabit is a
World built on the ubiquitous possibility of their destruction. She
knows that at any minute and around any corner, the violence of
white supremacy can appear to extinguish her life or the life of
any Black person. But like Denver in *Beloved,* the initial figure of
im/possible futurity with which *Abolition Time* opened, Rachel
knows it, and steps out of the ~~yard~~marriage. She knowingly steps
out of the false security of heteronormative marriage as part of a
Strong-Loving family, knowingly opts out of re-producing Black
life through her body, and, like Denver, seeks community through
which to insist Black being into the wake. In *Beloved,* Denver never
hears a counterargument to Baby Suggs's declaration that there is
no defense against white people. Protection is impossible. With no
way to deny that impossibility, Denver leaves 124 and makes a life
for her mother and herself possible, precisely by venturing into

the World that it is impossible to escape. In impossibility, Denver and Rachel make, in concert with others, possibility. This search for possibility in the midst of—*not* outside of or in opposition to or alongside or fugitive from but *in the midst of*—impossibility has been my persistent journey throughout *Abolition Time*. How do we, and how does literature help us, think the im/possible?

As M. NourbeSe Philip argues in *Zong!*, grammar is an "ordering mechanism, the mechanism of force," and "that ordering that is the impulse of empire."[1] Throughout *Abolition Time*, I have taken her lead in articulating *grammars of law* as the ordering force of juridical conceptions of time and ethics that result in conceptions of justice that are linear, punitive, and ultimately carceral. Working in opposition to and in excess of the ordering impulse of empire manifest in law's grammar are *poetics of justice*: accumulation, perforation, witnessing, and breath. These poetics disarticulate linear, periodized juridical temporalities of justice wherein retribution after a discernable, singular moment of harm enacted against an individuated agent of harm counts as the law's only vision of justice. The new temporality opened by these poetics, an excessive present in which past, present, and future crash together, is the abolition time of our now.

The individual chapters of this book have outlined four examples of a general category of literary effects I have called poetics of justice: accumulation, perforation, witnessing, and breath. In a way, each chapter can stand as just that—an example from a list of poetics. Poetics of accumulation utilize repetition and revision not only to change meanings but to gather potential meanings together. Poetics of perforation utilize the language of dominant grammars of law in ways that gesture toward those possible meanings and new questions that are just beyond the normative terms of those grammars. Poetics of witnessing do not merely represent scenes of recognition but rather dramatize, through narrative focalization and shifting point of view, the failure of knowledge itself as a figure of witnessing as catalyst for ethical action that requires an uncertain, risky decision beyond the moment of witnessing itself. Poetics of breath move along the line of the slash in *im/possibility* by utilizing realist representations of insurmountable violence alongside complex layerings of ambiguous or excessive subjects through, in the examples I have chosen in this book, queer (as in antinormative) character relationships. But in addition to being separate examples of literary manipulations of language, the chapters are woven together through, first, the combined effects of those literary manipulations and, second, a fundamental displacement of one particular grammar of law.

Beginning with J. M. W. Turner's painting appearing at the end of Claudia Rankine's *Citizen*, continuing through Philip's poetic engagement with law's archive in *Zong!* and with Fred D'Aguiar's fabulation of a slave rebellion in *Feeding the Ghosts*, and returning to Turner's painting as it is dissolved into David Dabydeen's poetic insistence of life in the Middle Passage's abyss in "Turner," *Abolition Time* grounds its four chapters in the history and afterlife of the 1781 *Zong* Massacre. Accumulation gathers referents for the murdered objects of white supremacist violence and the murdering subjects of whiteness itself across temporal borders, rupturing law's grammars of "event-time" so that we can return to the massacre *as* massacre, even though the law itself only ever recognized the killing in grammars of property, not of murder. With the language of murder made available again by accumulation, perforation inhabits the law's grammars of killing and property together to anagrammatically retrieve the irretrievable subjects jettisoned from both the *Zong* and the discourse of Humanity. In retrieving the irretrievable, the impossibility of recovery or repair is laid bare, and thus the recognition inherent to the law's grammar of witnessing is reconfigured as nothing more than capture and therefore a failure of a different kind of justice whose poetics begin to gain form in a witnessing that is beyond the law. Witnessing as the failure of emancipation opens to witnessing as the potential for abolition because perforation has inhabited the law's grammars of murder, property, and (remembering *partus sequitur ventrem*) gendered inheritance, thus making available to thought horizons of ethics unbound from the event-time ruptured by accumulation. In the dynamic indeterminism of this rupture, breath emerges as the possibility for life that exists in the impossibility of resurrection. The grammar of murder-denied at work in the *Zong* Massacre reemerges as the grammar of murder-denied, emphasized by law's grammar of recognition-as-witnessing, in the killing of Eric Garner, who told his witnesses that he could not breathe.

As we witness the archive of Garner's (Eric's and Erica's and Margaret's) extinguished breath, we are powerless to do the justice that that particular violence demands, and we are inadequate to do justice for the 133 human beings thrown overboard the *Zong*. But this journey through accumulation, perforation, witnessing, and breath is a journey that, by refusing to escape the terrain of impossibility, by inhabiting the grammars of law's ordering force, and by manipulating that force even in the moments it cannot be resisted, does the work of making another kind of justice thinkable—not justice as response to a harm that has ended, but justice as unceasing, reverberating, uncertain, critically utopian, and risky decision-making. Justice as perpetual nonarrival, and nonarrival as precisely the possibility of abolition as that which never arrives because it is always in practice, never a settled answer but always a set of questions in motion. The losses of the *Zong* Massacre cannot be recovered. Eric Garner cannot be given back his breath. But blank spaces in the list of future targets of white supremacy's violence can be held as blank, as we behold each other's vulnerability and choose to do what is necessary, even though we cannot know in advance what that is, to keep those spaces in the ledger blank.

In all of this, the most fundamental grammar of law that the four chapters of *Abolition Time* work to disarticulate is the grammar of individuation. If the hegemonic grammars of law within what I have been capitalizing throughout this book as the World have been set in place by the violent processes of chattel slavery and (settler) colonialism, we can trace how these twin processes are both set in motion by and reify a logic of private property as necessary for their consolidation in the governing order of sociality.[2] The logic of private property, in turn, is structured by a grammar of individuation. In other words, the very fabric of our current World's thinkability is the assumption of an absolutely discrete unitary self as the basic unit of subjectivity. From this assumption, it follows that questions of justice (where the ethical becomes the juridical) are shaped by grammars of individuation that produce a demarcated terrain of possibility bound by discrete units of individual guilt, innocence, and discernable injury that are filtered through a framework of individual rights and recognition. Against this grammar of individuation that underpins logics of private property and the recognition/rights-based framework for justice within liberalism, the poetics of justice in *Abolition Time* seek a conception of justice that is unbound not from law but from the very underpinning assumptions of individuation that are, arguably, the most fundamental grammars of law. I have not figured out how to write without grammars of individuation, and none of the texts I've read in this book rejects individuation *in total,* but the four poetics I read do at least make possible thinking in excess of this grammar of law—perhaps toward what Alexis Pauline Gumbs calls the "strength of no separation":

> this is what it takes. the strength of no separation. the bravery of flow. the audacity of never saying this is me, this is not you. this is mine, this is not yours. this is now, this was never not before.[3]

On the way to undoing the carceral World—that is, of undoing a World that could even have prisons in the first place—I humbly offer that literature and the poetics of justice we find therein may help us find the "audacity of never saying this is me, this is not you"[4]—of course, though, only if we practice together.

Besides the four specific poetics of justice that I flesh out in this book, there are, of course, many more I have not named or even perceived. *Abolition Time* is not an exhaustive project; it is an invitation. There are undoubtedly other literary traditions in all possible languages whose authors offer further poetics of justice that open readers' imaginations and epistemologies beyond the received grammars of law. There are other histories of atrocity in addition to chattel slavery that demand a language for justice unbound from juridical logics. I look forward to learning about those poetics of justice that I have failed to perceive or imagine here.

I opened this book with a preface situating my project as ultimately insufficient for the task at hand. That is, abolition is the task of simultaneously tearing down entire structures of carceral violence and the systems that enable it (so, the end of global white supremacy and its attendant vectors of queerantagonism, cisheteropatriarchy, and ableism; all forms of imperialism and settler colonialism—including the end of all settler nation-states and the very possibility of borders; and all possible configurations of racial capitalism) and building up systems, structures, and social forms that enable collective care as an organizing force of meeting everyone's needs, keeping everyone safe in right relation. A book of literary criticism cannot do that. But I want to end *Abolition Time* with this short thought on what literary studies *can* do as a small part of this multipronged project of razing and building.

I am left thinking about the slash in the word *im/possible* that I've employed throughout my fourth chapter as a way of making sense of what I think I mean by how poetics of breath work. Rather than the parentheses technique that allows us to read two different words in the space of one word—*(im)possibility*—which operates within an additive logic of "both/and," the slash, for me, denotes something else. Rather than saying "it is both impossible and possible," when I write "im/possibility," I am trying to represent that possibility and impossibility are constituted by each other—that, as Morgan Bassichis, Alexander Lee, and Dean Spade articulate, it is precisely in that which is impossible where we find the possibility of abolition. And in the other direction, impossibility itself coalesces around the possible. This is the tension produced by and that produces the pairing of grammars of law and poetics of justice. To put it clearly, grammars of law demarcate the terms of possibility, defining for us what is even able to be thought of as possible in the first place. When we think in the grammars that have been established by the forces that hold our World together, entire forms of thinking and doing are rendered impossible. The grammar that Philip finds in *Gregson v. Gilbert* tells her that it is impossible to put air back into the lungs of those Africans jettisoned from the *Zong*. But in excess of law's grammar are poetics of justice. These poetics are not bound by law's grammar and thus can make the impossible thinkable as the ordering force of grammar falls away.

Of course, these are not purely distinct concepts, as I hope is clarified by even a quick reading of my arguments in this book. So I am not painting a picture of two diametrically opposed forces, one "bad" (law's grammar) and one "good" (poetics of justice). Accumulation deploys the grammar of periodization to rupture it; perforation inhabits law's logic in order to escape elsewhere without ever leaving; witnessing follows the map drawn by law's demand for a paradigm of recognition; and breath starts in the abyss of emptied lungs before finding other ways to breathe. Instead of an oppositional binary, then, grammars of law and poetics of justice figure, as a dynamic pairing, the slash in *im/possibility*. Close attention to the contours of law's grammar reveals the borders of possibility that define what is impossible, and disciplined tracing of poetics of justice unpacks the necessary possibility within that impossibility. Through sustained attention to this dynamic between grammars and poetics that is trained and deployed in literary studies, we can make the impossible thinkable.

As a literary scholar, I risk metaphorizing too much. So, in summer 2022, when I read the poet Kemi Alabi's tweet "Maybe the best political poems are blockades, strikes, protests, mutual aid, cities on fire. Maybe direct action is a poetic form," I was so grateful for the concise concrete distillation of what I had been obscuring under metaphors. Alabi's examples—blockades, protests, mutual aid, and cities on fire—are, themselves, what I think Bassichis, Lee, and Spade mean in their provocative articulations of finding possibility in the impossible. The grammar of the law that demarcates participation in politics through a division between legal and illegal activities deems certain forms of justice—such as refusing an eviction—impossible. One cannot simply remain in a house after failing to pay rent during a pandemic. That's impossible. But, in Alabi's words, "maybe direct action is a poetic form."

I think it is. I think once we put down the books, poetics of justice look like setting up autonomous zones free of police; striking in solidarity with fellow workers, tenants, and community members; circulating resources outside of logics of private property so whoever needs something has it without owing anyone thanks under a logic of (moral) debt; or burning a police precinct.

These forms of action constitute the impossible demarcated by grammars of law, and they are, in their impossibility, the very possibility for justice that instantiates the future in our now. Abolition Time is the recognition that the impossible future is possible because it is necessary. And its necessity is constituted by its very impossibility. That's the paradox of the slash: we need to think the *im/possible.* And as we do, that slash can shift position, from bisection to strikethrough. Doing abolitionist close reading may not do the work that the political poetry of direct action will do, but it can, perhaps, allow us to think the ~~im~~possible toward . . .

Acknowledgments

It seems obvious to say so, but I could not have written this book without the support, guidance, tutelage, and nourishment of so many people. At the same time, it seems equally obvious to me that this book is a product of both generous institutional support and privileged access to resources as well as an array of conditions aligned against the work of producing scholarship in the humanities. I want to acknowledge both of these dimensions of the context and conditions of possibility for the work that manifests in this book.

This book has developed across many iterations of writing and thinking as I have journeyed across a number of geographical and institutional locations since graduate school, and I am thankful that Marquis Bey has been with me in spirit and mind, if not in place, along each turn in the road. Our intellectual kinship has pushed my thinking in directions I am certain I would not have gone otherwise; Marquis's presence is quite literally a condition of possibility for this book. I also would not be finishing this project without the encouraging friendship and thoughtful mentorship of Brigitte Fielder, Xine Yao, and Danielle Fuentes Morgan. I continue to look up to all three of them as models for how to be a generous and rigorous mentor, colleague, and friend while navigating this racket called academia. I thank them for their multivalent support over the years, without which I surely would have never finished this book—and perhaps not even graduate school. I want to resist the language of debt, so instead of saying that I owe each of them, I will say that I aspire to be for others what each has been to me.

Of course, I am grateful for the labor and professional care of Leah Pennywark, who has ushered this project from our initial conversations about how to envision transforming my dissertation into a book through the peer review and publication stages with the University of Minnesota Press. I am also grateful for Anne Carter's efforts to make sure the project came together in the final stages, and I am honored by the rigorous and encouraging feedback offered by the anonymous readers who agreed to review the manuscript. And I am thankful to Rebecca Colesworthy, Elizabeth Ault, Michael Dango, and Simon Stern for feedback on post-dissertation but prebook iterations of different sections of writing that evolved into *Abolition Time*.

Although this book differs greatly from the dissertation I wrote while a graduate student at Cornell, it would not exist, and I would not be the writer I am today, without the guidance of my dissertation advisers. Margo Crawford, Grant Farred, Dagmawi Woubshet, and Shirley Samuels generously allowed me to fail many times over to find the words to say what I wanted to say, only to always help me find the tools to begin again each time so I could complete this project's first full iteration. In addition to my formal mentors, other faculty at Cornell indelibly shaped my thinking. I am enormously grateful to Sara Warner, Elisha Cohn, Olúfẹ́mi Táíwò, and Mary Pat Brady. And I am thankful for C. Riley Snorton's guidance in not only helping me find language through which to articulate relationships between race, law, time, and queerness but also modeling an ideal of rigorous scholarly pedagogy.

Before I even applied to graduate school or knew what a dissertation was, Beth A. McCoy mentored my younger, more ignorant undergraduate mind toward a conception of literary and cultural studies as sites to do the most exciting and, to me at the time and in many cases still, most urgent intellectual work on questions about which I care deeply. I thank Beth for her mentorship; she continues to inspire me as a writer, teacher, and person. I will never forget her words from my first semester of college, a time when I was trying to re-figure out who exactly I was in the world: "Just because a goal is impossible to achieve, that does not excuse one from the responsibility of trying to achieve it." I didn't know it, but this started my journey of trying to think impossibility.

A number of more senior scholars have taken the time to support me on the journey that has produced this book in the years since it was a dissertation. I am deeply appreciative to Kathryn Walkiewicz, Christina Sharpe, Robin Bernstein, Koritha Mitchell, Jonathan Senchyne, LaToya Eaves, Sarah Haley, Kimberly Juanita Brown, Colleen Boggs, S. M. Rodriguez, Kevin Quashie, Herman Beavers, Matthew Seybold, Annie McClanahan, Anna Mae Duane, Caleb Smith, Jordan Alexander Stein, Martha Schoolman, J. Logan Smilges, Maria Lima, Donald Pease, Ryan Sharp, and Dylan Rodriguez for sharing their time in different ways that have helped me not only to write this book but to understand what it means to craft a career as an academic while remaining critical of the institutions in which we all move.

I have also had the opportunity to share space dedicated to questions of abolition both within and beyond the academy. I am thankful to Nancy Quintanilla for co-organizing with me the 2022 "Abolition Studies" Quarry Farm Symposium at Elmira College's Center for Mark Twain Studies and to the participants for enriching my thinking well beyond the weekend: Alex Alston, M. Cecilia Azar, Thomas Ditcher, Christopher Paul Harris, remus jackson, Cait N. Parker, LaVelle Ridley, Margarita Lila Rosa, Kia Turner, Michelle Velasquez-Potts, Darion Wallace, and Harry Washington Jr. And beyond the academy, I am grateful to my Decarcerate Tompkins County comrades—Tali, Paula, Phoebe, Edwin, Cruz, Keeli, Erin, Joey, Sarah, Laura, Aurora, Zillah, Shari, Lily, Elan, and everyone else—who, through organizing work, put into practice a future of the here and now. Finally, my thinking and writing in these pages have been deeply nurtured by the opportunities I have had to work with the Cornell Prison Education Program and the Penn State Restorative Justice Initiative. Thanks to Robert Scott, Jessica Brewer, Efraín Marimón, Divine Lipscomb, Irvin Moore, and all of the students with and from whom I've learned so much.

Particular individuals at each institutional stop on my career journey since graduate school have sustained this project and my research and writing more broadly. At Longwood, Mary Carroll-Hackett was truly a big sister to me from the moment I arrived, and I was blessed to have shared space with her in my two years at the university. I am thankful that Kat Tracy and Sean Barry made a point to make me feel like a full member of the department despite my contingent status, and I deeply appreciate the intentionally proactive ways that David Magill supported my pedagogical growth, research, and career trajectory as department chair. Revising a dissertation into a book while teaching four courses per semester as a contingent academic means adding the unpaid part-time job of applying for jobs to one's official full-time job, then stealing time in between all of that for writing and research. These conditions of the increasingly neoliberal academy, which actively relies more and more each year on precarious labor to function, are quite simply not conducive to completing rigorous research, and although my colleagues could not dismantle the conditions of precarious labor under which I worked while at Longwood, I am sincerely grateful that they helped me find moments of genuine thriving.

After my nonrenewable contract expired at Longwood, I was lucky enough to be hired into a full-time, still non–tenure track teaching position at Auburn University. However, while employed by Auburn as an instructor, I never taught a single class there. During summer 2020, as the Covid-19 pandemic was beginning and the Movement for Black Lives was catalyzing a renewed, vigorous spirit of police and prison abolition, some Auburn alumni and right-wing politicians took exception to my social media activity because of my furious critique of the white supremacy baked into American policing. During that summer and into the academic year, I received hundreds of emails and direct social media messages threatening me with violence and hate speech, and the university was fielding calls and petitions for me to be fired. During this time, I was grateful for the unequivocal support of my colleagues in the College of Arts and Sciences, most particularly Emily Friedman and Austin McCoy for their offers of personal solidarity. I mention this here for two reasons. First, I draw attention to another of the detrimental conditions of doing academic work in fields focused on questions of social justice: speaking out as an independent member of society while drawing on one's expertise potentially draws backlash, censorship, or even termination. In my case, I was lucky not to have been fired—which I am convinced is because of the support I received from my colleagues and from scholars from numerous other institutions—instead, I was reassigned from a teaching role to a research role. This means that although I am still healing from the trauma of the anti-Semitism, queerantagonism, and threats of violence from total strangers that flooded my inboxes for eight months, these reactionaries bought me a year of paid research time to work on the manuscript that would become this book. I still resent that, in a way, these reactionaries "won" by getting me removed from the classroom, but at the same time, I was granted time to write. There's something here I can't yet articulate about how I was at that time thinking through the paradox of im/possibility at the heart of *Abolition Time* while writing in that context.

After Auburn, I was offered a year as a research fellow at the Humanities Institute at Penn State University. I am thankful for the professional community I developed with my cofellows Belén Noroña, Rebekah McCallum, and Merle Eisenberg and for the feedback we were able to exchange on our works in progress. It was also a dream to be able to work with the Restorative Justice Initiative while I was there, even though that was not my official affiliation.

After Penn State, I now find myself on the tenure track at New Mexico Highlands University, where I am lucky to have found supportive colleagues. Peter Buchanan's proactive welcoming immediately eased my transition from the East Coast to New Mexico and gave me permission to be myself in all ways, and Amanda May consistently helps me to show up as my full and best self every day. I have learned so much about teaching from Donna Woodford-Gormley, Ben Villarreal, and Veronica Black. And Juan Gallegos, Eric Romero, and Brandon Kempner continue to teach me more about the New Mexico region, which is so new to me. I have lucked into another supportive department chair in Lauren Fath, whose steadfast advocacy I appreciate almost beyond words. And finally, I could not be luckier to have started this job at the same time as

Rebecca L. Schneider, whose friendship has been invaluably nourishing and who has been a sincerely generous and supportive colleague in offering feedback on research, exchanging pedagogical questions and insights, and navigating the terrain of the tenure track without losing sight of the intellectual and ethical integrity that exceeds the parameters of an employment contract.

I am tremendously lucky that my path through academia has crossed with folks who have touched my life in so many different ways, be it through mutual struggle; the creation of safe and comforting spaces to figure out who we are; reading and/or writing together; or sharing the beauty of laughing, cooking, crying, or silence. I cannot be more thankful that M. Aziz, Richard Daily, and I happened to be at Penn State at the same time, in totally different capacities, and I could say the same of the fortune of being at Futures of American Studies at the same time as Aly Corey. These three individuals continue to ground me in the world and all of its messiness when I most need to be grounded, even if intermittently, and even if from afar, and even if unintentionally. Thanks to Julia Bernier for her continuing friendship as we push each other to finish our respective books without being consumed by our projects. And thanks to so many others, without whom I would not have grown as a writer or a person: Diego Millan, Lara Fresko Madra, Lucien Baskin, Neelofer Qadir, Julia Dauer, Sean Gordon, Kristen Angierski, Anna Waymack, Lette Bragg, Verdie Culbreath, Anna McCormick, Jane Glaubman, Mee-Ju Ro, Amber Harding, Esmeralda Arrizón-Palomera, Ji Hyun Lee, Nolan Bennet, Alex Black, Emily Rials, Kaylin O'Dell, Brianna Thompson, Gabriella Friedman, Joshua Bastian Cole-Kurtz, Katherine Thorsteinson, Nathaniel Stetson, Breanne Kisselstein, Yumi Pak, Tyrone Palmer, Cera Smith, Kyessa Moore, Susan Quesal, Nirmala Vasigaren, Mina Nikolopoulou, RJ Boutelle, Lanre Akinsiku, Alex Chertok, Vincent Hiscock, Pablo García Piñar, Evan Bruno, Stephen Kim, Madeline Reynolds, Noah Loyd, Becky Lu, Jessica Rodriguez, Philippa Chun, Maggie O'Leary, and Alec Pollak.

My academic journey is inseparable from my martial arts journey. To my long lineage of martial arts family I am especially indebted, for without my martial arts practice and those who sustain it, I would have been nowhere near able to finish this project. My deepest gratitude goes to my instructors: Olen and Mary Lane, Nick Owczarek, Robert Hursey, and Richard Fescina. Osu!

There are still others whose love and friendship have nourished my soul-hunger over the years I have been pouring myself into this writing. No matter how frequently or rarely we pass into or out of each other's shifting currents, I contain bottomless appreciation for Eli, Michael-Birch, Todd, Mario, Jade, Leanne, Alanna, Logan, Ariel, Mike, Maeghan, and Jacqueline.

Finally, words fail to help me adequately thank those who have seen and held the darkest parts of me and given them back when I was ready. Michael, you will always have my unwavering gratitude. Rah, you are my hero. Thank you for your bravery and your radical honesty, and for your generous patience. Jamie, thank you for helping me learn how to think beyond words, to slow down, and to greet vulnerability with gentleness. And thank you all for the greatest gift you could give—for challenging me relentlessly to show up in full, honest presence.

The last words of thanks are for my furry companions. Pilate, Mo, and Smoky Quartz have been the best research assistants I could have ever asked for.

To those whose names I have forgotten to write, I offer my humble apologies. I am not who I am today and this project is not what it is today without the influence of countless individuals. I can only hope that I have done justice to the processes and relations and histories that have produced me.

Notes

1. Joy James, "Introduction: Democracy and Captivity," in *The New Abolitionists: (Neo)Slave Narratives and Contemporary Prison Writing* (Albany: SUNY Press, 2005), xxiii. I should note that not every abolitionist's historical analysis of prisons and slavery is exactly the same. Ruth Wilson Gilmore, for example, famously argues *against* the position that the prison–industrial complex, or PIC, is a continuation of slavery early in *Golden Gulag: Prisons, Surplus, Crisis, and Opposition in Globalizing California* (Berkeley: University of California Press, 2007), while scholars like James and Dennis Childs explicitly draw such connections. Related, I use the term PIC throughout my work to refer to the larger network of industries and institutions that feed and are fed by the prison system as a larger network existing within racial capitalism. In doing so, I am aligned with most abolitionists in understanding that "abolishing prisons" is far more expansive than only getting rid of literal jails and prisons themselves but instead is a project aimed at carceral and policing institutions that are embedded in the furthest corners of society.

2. I also have in mind Kyla Wazana Tompkins's reflection on the "state of the field" in the shadow of the Covid-19 pandemic. See Tompkins, "The Shush," *PMLA* 136, no. 3 (2021): 420.

3. As my repeated invocation of the date suggests, I am thinking primarily in this preface with Wynter's essay "1492: A New World View" found in *Race, Discourse, and the Origin of the Americas: A New World View,* ed. Vera Lawrence Hyatt and Rex Nettleford, 5–57 (Washington, D.C.: Smithsonian Institution Press, 1995). Separate from my citation

of Wynter, I also note here that my thinking draws extensively on scholarship in Black feminist and queer theory that delineates how forces of oppression along axes of gender, sex, sexuality, and disability are inseparable from the forces of white supremacy and historical processes of global capitalism and settler colonialism; so as *Abolition Time* unfolds, I will continue to pare down my naming of the objects of critique to individual phrases, most often the nonsynonyms *white supremacy, settler colonialism,* and *racial capitalism,* because every time I use those phrases, I am also, automatically, invoking cisheteropatriarchy, ableism, and xenophobia as intrinsic to those systems.

4. Toni Morrison, quoted in Paul Gilroy, "Living Memory: A Meeting with Toni Morrison," in *Small Acts: Thoughts on the Politics of Black Culture* (London: Serpent's Tail, 1993), 178.

5. During graduate school, I spent two years working with a coalition called Decarcerate Tompkins County. DTC, as we called ourselves for short, was a diverse coalition of community members of varying racial, educational, and class backgrounds and with varying social identities and political ideologies. That experience, along with my experience teaching in the Cornell Prison Education Program and, later, working with Penn State's Restorative Justice Initiative; my time working with mutual aid groups in Virginia; and my time doing the work of labor organizing, has been just as foundational to my intellectual development as was any seminar I've taken or book I've read. On "deference politics," see a number of interviews with Táíwò, including Astra Taylor's conversation with him in *Lux* magazine and his discussion with Jared Ware and Joshua Briond on the *Millennials Are Killing Capitalism* podcast, as well as Táíwò's book *Elite Capture: How the Powerful Took Over Identity Politics (and Everything Else)* (Chicago: Haymarket Books, 2022).

INTRODUCTION

1. Tina M. Campt, *Listening to Images* (Durham, N.C.: Duke University Press, 2017), 17.

2. Saidiya V. Hartman, *Scenes of Subjection: Terror, Slavery, and Self-Making in Nineteenth-Century America* (New York: Oxford University Press, 1997), 116.

3. Toni Morrison, *Beloved* (1987; repr., New York: Vintage, 2004), 248.

4. Rinaldo Walcott, *The Long Emancipation: Moving toward Black Freedom* (Durham, N.C.: Duke University Press, 2021), 3, 105.

5. Toni Morrison, "Unspeakable Things Unspoken: The Afro-American Presence in American Literature," in *The Black Feminist Reader,* edited by Joy James and T. Denean Sharpley-Whiting (Hoboken, N.J.: Blackwell, 2000), 196. (Morrison's essay was first published in 1989.)

6. Christina Sharpe, *Ordinary Notes* (New York: Farrar, Straus, and Giroux, 2023), 147.

7. When reflecting on this class discussion—from a section of "Neo-Slave Narratives" that I taught at Longwood University, a predominantly white institution in Virginia—I find myself regreting my choice to ask this question. In the moment, it was a response to, as I write, a white woman's claim to authority to know how to interpret the text better than anyone else because she was a mother, and I wanted to rhetorically empty that identity of "mother" of the authority this student (and some of her peers) had claimed it granted over the text. But in doing so, I was not thinking about the possibilities that students in the class may have been victims of trafficking or other forms of violence that could have been triggered by my question. I write this footnote here to acknowledge that when I discuss teaching, I am not operating under any delusion that I have the *right* answers, because I think the improvisational nature of teaching necessitates that our choices always come with risk and will never be perfectly unharmful to our students. This doesn't excuse the potential for harm but only names it as a condition of possibility for pedagogy. My thinking in this footnote is elaborated by my thinking about ethics and risk in chapter 3.

8. In transtemporal abolitionist thought, Mumia Abu-Jamal's *Have Black Lives Ever Mattered?* (San Francisco: City Lights Open Media, 2017) and Harriet Jacobs's *Incidents in the Life of a Slave Girl* (Boston, 1865) both explicitly theorize justice as existing beyond or even against the law. In both "Force of Law: The 'Mystical Foundations of Authority,'" *Cardozo Law Review* 11, no. 5-6 (1990): 920–1045, which of course is a reading of Walter Benjamin's "Critique of Violence" (1921), and *Specters of Marx: The State of the Debt, the Work of Mourning, and the New International,* trans. Peggy Kamuf (Oxfordshire: Routledge, 1994), Jacques Derrida posits that justice cannot be reduced to the

law, which itself is defined by violence. James Baldwin, too, makes a strong distinction between the law and justice in *No Name in the Street* (New York: Dial Press, 1972). Readers can surely think of a multitude of other thinkers who have drawn similar distinctions. Benjamin's writings have been released as collections a number of times. A new book-length critical edition of the essay was recently published as *Toward the Critique of Violence: A Critical Edition*, edited by Peter Fenves and Julia Ng (Stanford, Calif.: Stanford University Press, 2021).

9. Derrida, *Specters of Marx*.

10. https://incite-national.org/incite-critical-resistance-statement/.

11. Christina Sharpe, *In the Wake: On Blackness and Being* (Durham, N.C.: Duke University Press, 2016), 9, 62.

12. José Esteban Muñoz, *Cruising Utopia: The Then and There of Queer Futurity* (New York: NYU Press, 2009), 1; Kara Keeling, *Queer Times, Black Futures* (New York: NYU Press, 2019), 17. On "critical fabulation," see esp. Saidiya V. Hartman, "Venus in Two Acts," *Small Axe* 12, no. 2 (2008): 1–14. On "anagrammatical blackness," see Sharpe, *In the Wake*, 75–87.

13. Karla FC Holloway, *Legal Fictions: Constituting Race, Composing Literature* (Durham, N.C.: Duke University Press, 2014).

14. Daylanne K. English, *Each Hour Redeem: Time and Justice in African American Literature* (Minneapolis: University of Minnesota Press, 2013), 24.

15. Dennis Childs, *Slaves of the State: Black Incarceration from the Chain Gang to the Penitentiary* (Minneapolis: University of Minnesota Press, 2015), 10; Patrick Eliot Alexander, *From Slave Ship to Supermax: Mass Incarceration, Prisoner Abuse, and the Neo-Slave Novel* (Philadelphia: Temple University Press, 2017), 4.

16. C. Riley Snorton, *Black on Both Sides: A Racial History of Trans Identity* (Minneapolis: University of Minnesota Press, 2017), esp. part I, "Blacken"; Sarah Clarke Kaplan, *The Black Reproductive: Unfree Labor and Insurgent Motherhood* (Minneapolis: University of Minnesota Press, 2021), esp. chap. 2, "Love and Violence/Maternity and Death"; Marquis Bey, *Black Trans Feminism* (Durham, N.C.: Duke University Press, 2022), esp. chap. 2, "Fugitivity, Un/Gendered"; Patrice D. Douglass, "Black Feminist Theory for the Dead and Dying," *Theory and Event* 21, no. 1 (2018): 106–23; Sarah Haley, *No Mercy Here: Gender,*

Punishment, and the Making of Jim Crow Modernity (Chapel Hill: University of North Carolina Press, 2016), esp. chap. 2, "Convict Leasing, (Re)Production, and Gendered Racial Terror."

17. Jennifer L. Morgan's *Laboring Women: Gender and Reproduction in the Making of New World Slavery* (Philadelphia: University of Pennsylvania Press, 2004) is widely recognized as a foundational touchstone for the study of Black reproduction during Atlantic slavery, but it is her more recent article *"Partus sequitur ventrem*: Law, Race, and Reproduction in Colonial Slavery," *Small Axe* 22, no. 1 (55) (2018): 1–17, that is most influential on my own intellectual development on these questions. Alys Eve Weinbaum, *The Afterlife of Reproductive Slavery: Biocapitalism and Black Feminism's Philosophy of History* (Durham, N.C.: Duke University Press, 2019), esp. chap. 3, "Violent Insurgency, or 'Power to the Ice Pick'"; Brigitte Nicole Fielder, *Relative Races: Genealogies of Interracial Kinship in Nineteenth-Century America* (Durham, N.C.: Duke University Press, 2020), esp. part II, "Reproduction: Genealogies of (Re)Racialization."

18. Snorton, *Black on Both Sides*, 183.

19. See Keeling, *Queer Times, Black Futures*, esp. 32–36, for Keeling's sketching of this temporal configuration.

20. Eric A. Stanley, "Fugitive Flesh: Gender Self-Determination, Queer Abolition, and Trans Resistance," in *Captive Genders: Trans Embodiment and the Prison Industrial Complex*, 2nd ed., edited by Eric A. Stanley and Nat Smith (Chico, Calif.: AK Press, 2015), 14.

21. Alexander Weheliye, *Habeas Viscus: Racializing Assemblages, Biopolitics, and Black Feminist Theories of the Human* (Durham, N.C.: Duke University Press, 2014), 78, 72.

22. Derrick Bell, *Faces at the Bottom of the Well: The Permanence of Racism* (New York: Basic Books, 1992); Mari Matsuda, "Looking to the Bottom: Critical Legal Studies and Reparations," *Harvard Civil Rights–Civil Liberties Law Review* 22 (1987): 323–99.

23. Anthony Reed, *Freedom Time: The Poetics and Politics of Black Experimental Writing* (Baltimore: Johns Hopkins University Press, 2014), 22.

24. John Roberts, opinion of the Court, Shelby County v. Holder, 570 U.S. 529 (2013).

25. Ruth Bader Ginsburg, dissenting, *Shelby County v. Holder,* 570 U.S. 529.

26. Derrida, "Force of Law," 925.

27. Roberts, *Shelby County v. Holder*, 570 U.S. 529.

28. Roberts.

29. Sara Ahmed, *On Being Included: Racism and Diversity in Institutional Life* (Durham, N.C.: Duke University Press, 2012), 179.

30. Roberts, *Shelby County v. Holder*, 570 U.S. 529.

31. Renisa Mawani, "Law's Archive," *Annual Review of Law and Social Science* 8 (2012): 354.

32. Ginsburg, *Shelby County v. Holder*, 570 U.S. 529.

33. Ginsburg.

34. Denise Ferreira da Silva identifies this as "the liberal grammar [that] efficiently translates demands for racial justice back into the logic that renders any mechanism deployed to bring it about . . . into something *extraordinary*." Ferreira da Silva, "Extraordinary Times: A Preface," *Cultural Dynamics* 26, no. 1 (2014): 5.

35. Jacques Derrida, *The Gift of Death*, in *"The Gift of Death" and "Literature in Secret,"* trans. David Wills (Chicago: University of Chicago Press, 2008), 27.

36. Mariame Kaba, *We Do This 'til We Free Us: Abolitionist Organizing and Transforming Justice* (Chicago: Haymarket Books, 2021), 167.

37. Mariame Kaba and John Duda, "Towards the Horizon of Abolition: A Conversation with Mariame Kaba," Next System Project, November 2017, https://thenextsystem.org/learn/stories/towards-horizon-abolition-conversation-mariame-kaba.

38. Avery Gordon, *Ghostly Matters: Haunting and the Sociological Imagination*, 2nd ed. (Minneapolis: University of Minnesota Press, 2008), 166.

39. Saidiya V. Hartman, "The Time of Slavery," *South Atlantic Quarterly* 101, no. 4 (2002): 763.

40. Walter Benn Michaels, *The Shape of the Signifier: 1967 to the End of History* (Princeton, N.J.: Princeton University Press, 2004), 132.

41. Stephen Best, "On Failing to Make the Past Present," *Modern Language Quarterly* 73, no. 3 (2013): 459.

42. Best, 460.

43. Douglas A. Jones Jr., "The Fruit of Abolition: Discontinuity and Difference in Terrance Hayes's 'The Avocado,'" in *The Psychic Hold of Slavery: Legacies in American Expressive Culture* (New Brunswick, N.J.: Rutgers University Press, 2016), 41–42.

44. Best, "On Failing to Make the Past Present," 460, my emphasis.

45. Morrison, *Beloved*, 275.

46. Keeling, *Queer Times, Black Futures*, 204. I read *Beloved* as an apocalyptic text in "Living after, and before, the End of the World: Toni Morrison's *Beloved* and N.K. Jemisin's *Broken Earth*," *Women's Studies* 52, no. 2 (2023): 173–91.

47. Morrison, *Beloved*, 244.

48. Morrison, 243.

49. Morrison, 244.

50. Fred Moten, *In the Break: The Aesthetics of the Black Radical Tradition* (Minneapolis: University of Minnesota Press, 2003), 210.

51. Aida Levy-Hussen, *How to Read African American Literature: Post–Civil Rights Fiction and the Task of Interpretation* (New York: NYU Press, 2016), 133.

52. Morrison, *Beloved*, 248.

ONE. ACCUMULATION

1. Claudia Rankine, *Citizen: An American Lyric* (Minneapolis, Minn.: Graywolf Press, 2014), 159. In a 2014 interview with Lauren Berlant, Rankine offers a sentence of explanation beyond this statement I've excerpted from *Citizen*'s final textual page: "The book ends with Turner's Slave Ship, because it seemed funny that those trips across the Atlantic would have us disgorging still." "Claudia Rankine by Lauren Berlant," *Bomb Magazine*, October 2014, https://bombmagazine.org/articles/claudia-rankine/.

2. Joseph Roach, *Cities of the Dead: Circum-Atlantic Performance* (New York: Columbia University Press, 1996), 9.

3. I have intentionally packed this sentence with a number of references. Kara Keeling demonstrates how "quotidian violence" (17) holds together "the spatiotemporal disaster we call modernity" (204) in *Queer Times, Black Futures*. My thinking on "the Human," which influences my constant capitalization of the word when referring to the conceptual figure of the Human as distinct from the biological species, is most strongly influenced by Sylvia Wynter, as my language makes reference to her foundational essay "Unsettling the Coloniality of Being/Power/Truth/Freedom: Towards the Human, after Man, Its Overrepresentation—an Argument," *CR: The New Centennial Review* 3, no. 3 (2003): 257–337. Wynter's work influences both Dylan

Rodríguez and Eric A. Stanley, whom I invoke in the last clause of the sentence. On "civilization as a genocidal project of White Being," see Rodríguez, *White Reconstruction: Domestic Warfare and the Logics of Genocide* (New York: Fordham University Press, 2020), and on "atmospheres of violence," a phrase borrowed from Frantz Fanon's *Wretched of the Earth*, see Stanley's *Atmospheres of Violence: Structuring Antagonisms and the Trans/Queer Ungovernable* (Durham, N.C.: Duke University Press, 2021).

4. Ian Baucom, *Specters of the Atlantic: Finance Capital, Slavery, and the Philosophy of History* (Durham, N.C.: Duke University Press, 2005), 331.

5. Sharpe, *In the Wake*, 116.

6. Anthony Reed, "The Erotics of Mourning in Recent Experimental Black Poetry," *The Black Scholar* 47, no. 1 (2017): 28.

7. Rankine, *Citizen*, 116.

8. Hartman, "Time of Slavery," 759; Muñoz, *Cruising Utopia*, 91. My phrasing also draws on Frank B. Wilderson III's argument, in *Red, White, and Black: Cinema and the Structures of U.S. Antagonisms* (Durham, N.C.: Duke University Press, 2010), that "the imaginary of the state and civil society is parasitic on the Middle Passage. Put another way, No slave, no world" (11).

9. Catherine Zuromskis argues that this does a kind of injustice to Hammons's work, and I do not wish to dispute that. See Zuromskis, "Complicating Images," as part of "Reconsidering Claudia Rankine's *Citizen: An American Lyric*: A Roundtable," *Los Angeles Review of Books*, January 2016, https://lareviewofbooks.org/article/reconsidering -claudia-rankines-citizen-an-american-lyric-a-symposium-part-i/. Subsequent citations will include the author's individual name and title followed by "*LARB* Roundtable 2016."

10. Sharpe, *In the Wake*, 12.

11. Rankine, *Citizen*, 30.

12. Rankine, 25.

13. Evie Shockley, "Race, Reception, and Claudia Rankine's 'American Lyric,'" *LARB* Roundtable 2016.

14. Emphasis added.

15. Liat Ben-Moshe, *Decarcerating Disability: Deinstitutionalization and Prison Abolition* (Minneapolis: University of Minnesota Press, 2020), 26. For more on Blackness and "insanity," see Therí Alyce Pickens's

Black Madness :: Mad Blackness (Durham, N.C.: Duke University Press, 2019) and La Marr Jurelle Bruce's *How to Go Mad without Losing Your Mind: Madness and Black Radical Creativity* (Durham, N.C.: Duke University Press, 2021).

16. Rankine, *Citizen*, 26.

17. James Walvin, *The Zong: A Massacre, the Law, and the End of Slavery* (New Haven, Conn.: Yale University Press, 2011). See pages 202–5 as well as all of chapter 1, "A Painting and a Slave Ship," for more on the influences of the *Zong* Massacre on Turner's painting and on his ideological relationship to Clarkson.

18. Sharpe, *In the Wake*, 36.

19. Sharpe, 38.

20. Hartman, *Scenes of Subjection*, 116.

21. Jared Sexton, "People-of-Color Blindness: Notes on the Afterlife of Slavery," *Social Text* 28, no. 2 (2010): 36.

22. Stephanie Smallwood, *Saltwater Slavery: A Middle Passage from Africa to American Diaspora* (Cambridge, Mass.: Harvard University Press, 2007), 82.

23. Katherine McKittrick, "Mathematics Black Life," *Black Scholar* 44, no. 2 (2014): 19. Jennifer L. Morgan builds on the work of McKittrick, along with Hartman's formulation of "political arithmetic" in her paradigmatic definition of "the afterlife of slavery" and Smallwood's critique of quantitative data in slavery's archive, in *Reckoning with Slavery: Gender, Kinship, and Capitalism in the Early Black Atlantic* (Durham, N.C.: Duke University Press, 2021). For more on Blackness and mathematics, see Calvin Warren, "The Catastrophe: Black Feminist Poethics, (Anti)form, and Mathematical Nihilism," *Qui Parle* 28, no. 2 (2019): 353–72.

24. Here I have in mind both classic and recent work on histories of slavery and capitalism. See Edward Baptist's *The Half Has Never Been Told: Slavery and the Making of American Capitalism* (New York: Basic Books, 2015); Daina Ramey Berry's *The Price for Their Pound of Flesh: The Value of the Enslaved, from Womb to Grave, in the Building of a Nation* (Boston: Beacon Press, 2017); Stephanie E. Jones-Rogers's *They Were Her Property: White Women as Slave Owners in the American South* (New Haven, Conn.: Yale University Press, 2020); Sven Beckert and Seth Rockman, eds., *Slavery's Capitalism: A New History of American Economic*

Development (Philadelphia: University of Pennsylvania Press, 2018); Eric Williams's *Capitalism and Slavery,* 3rd ed. (Chapel Hill: University of North Carolina Press, 2021); Angela Y. Davis's *Women, Race, and Class* (New York: Vintage Books, 1983); Cedric Robinson's *Black Marxism: The Making of the Black Radical Tradition* (Chapel Hill: University of North Carolina Press, 1983); and, of course, W. E. B. Du Bois's *Black Reconstruction in America* (Oxford: Oxford University Press, 2007). This is not an exhaustive list of work on capitalism and slavery, and it is not a list of homogenous arguments, as many of these thinkers build on, depart from, and critique each other. I am also thinking about more recent work on slavery, settler colonialism, and ecology that draws connections between the history of racial capitalism and ongoing catastrophes of climate change in the fields of Indigenous studies, Black studies, and the environmental humanities, including ongoing debates around the term *plantationocene.*

25. For one example of such a reading of *Citizen,* see Joel Alden Schlosser's "A Poetics of American Citizenship: Blackness, Injury, and Claudia Rankine's *Citizen," Law, Culture, and the Humanities* 16, no. 3 (2016): 432–53.

26. See Jennifer C. James, "Black Incarceration: Before and beyond the Afterlives of Slavery," in "Abolition's Afterlives" cluster, *American Literary History* (2021), https://doi.org/10.1093/alh/ajab006, for an invigorating analysis of the limits of framing incarceration as an "afterlife of slavery." For Gilmore's critique, see *Golden Gulag,* 17–25, esp. 21. See Joy James's introduction to *New Abolitionists* as well as Childs's *Slaves of the State,* 16, and Sharpe's *In the Wake,* 75, for framings of a slavery/PIC continuity that is not based on labor.

27. Wilson discusses his research in conversation with Gilmore in "Study and Struggle Conversation #3: Abolition Must Be Red" on the Haymarket Books YouTube channel, November 2021, https://www.youtube.com/watch?v=E2OWObx5J9A.

28. Angela Davis, *Are Prisons Obsolete?* (New York: Seven Stories Press, 2003), 16. For more on the differences between prison labor and enslaved labor, see "Some Reflections on Prison Labor: Ruth Wilson Gilmore with James Kilgore," *Brooklyn Rail,* June 2019, https://brooklynrail.org/2019/06/field-notes/Some-Reflections-on-Prison-Labor.

29. Walcott, *Long Emancipation*, 43. See also Walcott, "The Black Aquatic: Water, Art, and Black Movement," unpublished manuscript.

30. Walcott, "Black Aquatic," 2.

31. Rankine, *Citizen*, 73.

32. Kamran Javadizadeh, "The Atlantic Ocean Breaking on Our Heads: Claudia Rankine, Robert Lowell, and the Whiteness of the Lyric Subject," *PMLA* 134, no. 3 (2019): 487.

33. Gilmore, *Golden Gulag*, 28.

34. Morrison develops her conceptualization of "Africanist presence" in *Playing in the Dark: Whiteness and the Literary Imagination* (New York: Vintage Books, 1992).

35. Rankine, *Citizen*, 82–86.

36. Rankine, 85; Baucom, *Specters of the Atlantic*, 330.

37. Rankine, *Citizen*, 109.

38. Walter Benjamin, "Critique of Violence," in *Reflections: Essays, Aphorisms, Autobiographical Writings*, ed. Peter Demetz, 277–300 (New York: Mariner, 2019).

39. Derrida, "Force of Law."

40. Smallwood, *Reckoning with Slavery*, 207.

41. Compare, e.g., Smallwood's chapter "Life and Death in the Diaspora," *Saltwater Slavery*, 182–207, and Walcott's chapters "The Atlantic Region and 1492," *Long Emancipation*, 27–32, and "Problem of the Human, or the Void of Relationality," *Long Emancipation*, 55–58. In Hartman, see esp. "The Burdened Individuality of Freedom," *Scenes of Subjection*, 115–24. And in Sharpe, *In the Wake*, see p. 21 for "the semiotics of the slave ship" as well as chapter 2, "The Ship," for an expanded theorization of these semiotics through the *Zong* as it is figured by Turner's painting and through contemporary refugee crises as coterminous with the Middle Passage.

42. Rankine, *Citizen*, 14, my italics.

43. Shockley, "Race, Reception, and Claudia Rankine's 'American Lyric.'"

44. Nikki Skillman, "Lyric Reading Revisited: Passion, Address, and Form in *Citizen*," *American Literary History* 31, no. 3 (2019): 445.

45. Michelle M. Wright takes to task what she sees as the dominant paradigm of Black studies—a Middle Passage epistemology that privileges Atlantic slavery as the thing that inaugurates Blackness on the world stage—before proceeding to model a linear progress narrative

from slavery through the post–civil rights era. See her *Physics of Blackness: Beyond the Middle Passage Epistemology* (Minneapolis: University of Minnesota Press, 2015). I concede that my literary archive in this book leans Americanist even as it seeks an Atlantic frame, but I would emphasize that the temporality I am discussing is anything but linear. I also echo Walcott's aquatic thinking in *Long Emancipation,* esp. chapter 7, "The Atlantic Region and 1492," in which he writes, "To insist on the world-changing impact of the ongoing colonization of the Americas and transatlantic slavery as central to Black diaspora studies is neither to argue for exceptionalism nor to produce a singular grand narrative of modernity's birth" (27).

46. Haley, *No Mercy Here,* 6.

47. Tyrone Palmer, "'What Feels More Than Feeling?': Theorizing the Unthinkability of Black Affect," *Critical Ethnic Studies* 3, no. 2 (2017): 45; Rankine, *Citizen,* 36.

48. Rodríguez, *White Reconstruction,* 7–8.

49. Rankine, *Citizen,* 91.

50. Palmer's reading of *Citizen* is generative for my thinking, but I should note that his argument differs from mine here. For Palmer, my invocation of "Black subjects" in the terrain of *Citizen* would be mistaken because "the racialized, nameless 'you' of the text marks blackness as a state of perennial objecthood." Palmer, "'What Feels More Than Feeling?,'" 49.

51. Rankine, *Citizen,* 54.

52. Rankine, 43.

53. Rankine, 94.

54. Skillman, "Lyric Reading Revisited," 439.

55. Critiques of hate crime legislation abound. For a consolidated introduction, see part III, "Prisons Will Not Protect You," in Ryan Conrad, ed., *Against Equality: Queer Revolution Not Mere Inclusion* (Chico, Calif.: AK Press, 2014).

56. Stanley, *Atmospheres of Violence,* 71.

57. Mumia Abu-Jamal, "Trayvon Is One, They Are Many," in *Have Black Lives Ever Mattered?* (San Francisco: City Lights Books, 2017), 103.

58. Childs, *Slaves of the State,* 28. On "the nonevent of emancipation," see Hartman, *Scenes of Subjection,* 116.

59. Suzan-Lori Parks, "Possession," in *"The America Play" and Other Works* (New York: Theater Communications Group, 1995), 5. All Parks citations are from this volume.

60. Parks, "From Elements of Style," 10.

61. Parks, *Imperceptible Mutabilities in the Third Kingdom*, 28.

62. Parks, "From Elements of Style," 11.

63. Parks, *Imperceptible Mutabilities*, 29.

64. Parks, "From Elements of Style," 9.

65. Parks, 8.

66. Parks, *Imperceptible Mutabilities*, 25.

67. Parks, 25–26.

68. Parks, 37.

69. Parks, 39.

70. Parks, 40.

71. Parks, "From Elements of Style," 11.

72. Childs, *Slaves of the State*, 34–35.

73. Rodríguez, *White Reconstruction*, 205.

74. Sharpe, *In the Wake*, 16.

75. Parks, *Imperceptible Mutabilities*, 61.

76. Parks, "From Elements of Style," 17.

77. Parks, *Imperceptible Mutabilities*, 38–39.

78. William Wells Brown, *The Escape; or, A Leap for Freedom* (Boston, 1858), 51.

79. Walcott, "Black Aquatic," 1.

80. Hartman, "Venus in Two Acts," 11.

81. Sharpe, *In the Wake*, 75, 100–101.

82. Muñoz, *Cruising Utopia*, 37.

83. Grant Farred, "*Citizen*, a Lyric Event," *Diacritics* 45, no. 4 (2017): 108–9.

84. Shermaine M. Jones, "'I Can't Breathe!': Affective Asphyxia in Claudia Rankine's *Citizen: An American Lyric*," *South: A Scholarly Journal* 50, no. 1 (2017): 43; Sarah Nance, "Memorial Time: Claudia Rankine, C. D. Wright, and the Temporal Space of Remembering," *Arizona Quarterly* 76, no. 2 (2020): 38.

TWO. PERFORATION

1. Sharpe, *In the Wake*, 76.

2. Sharpe, 77.

3. Grant Farred, *In Motion, at Rest: The Event of the Athletic Body* (Minneapolis: University of Minnesota Press, 2014), 11.

4. The comparison between Jacobs and Douglass has become old fare in early African American literary scholarship. See Stephen Matterson's chapter "Shaped by Readers: The Slave Narratives of Frederick Douglass and Harriet Jacobs," in *Soft Canons: American Women Writers and Masculine Tradition*, 82–98 (Iowa City: University of Iowa Press, 1999), and Kimberly Drake's essay "Rewriting the American Self: Race, Gender, and Identity in the Autobiographies of Frederick Douglass and Harriet Jacobs," *MELUS* 22, no. 4 (1997): 91–108, for just two examples whose bibliographies open up more representative scholarship on this comparison. More generally, Jacobs's book has become one of the most canonical texts in African American literary studies, and like anyone who writes on her text today, I build on the work of a number of critics who have rightly focused our scholarly attention on Jacobs. An incomplete list of these scholars would include, in addition to those whom I cite elsewhere, Farah Jasmine Griffin, Francis Smith Foster, Valerie Smith, Hazel Carby, P. Gabrielle Foreman, and Jean Fagan Yellin.

5. Harriet Jacobs, *Incidents in the Life of a Slave Girl* (1861; repr., Mineola, N.Y.: Dover, 2001), 97.

6. Campt offers powerful reflection on the overlaps, divergences, and tensions between *acts* and *practices* in *Listening to Images*, esp. 32: "The quotidian practice of refusal I am describing is defined less by opposition or 'resistance,' and more by a refusal of the very premises that have reduced the lived experience of blackness to pathology and irreconcilability in the logic of white supremacy. Like the concept of fugitivity, practicing refusal highlights the tense relations between *acts* of flight and escape, and creative *practices of refusal*—nimble and strategic practices that undermine the categories of the dominant."

7. See Campt, 96, and Stephen Dillon, *Fugitive Life: The Queer Politics of the Prison State* (Durham, N.C.: Duke University Press, 2017), 21, 124.

8. For Miranda Green-Barteet, the garret places Linda "in a position of power over Flint" in a way that "is startlingly similar to Jeremy

Bentham's Panopticon." See Green-Barteet, "'The Loophole of Retreat': Interstitial Spaces in Harriet Jacobs's *Incidents in the Life of a Slave Girl,*" *South Central Review* 30, no. 2 (2013): 63. Less declaratively, Sarah Jane Cervenak writes that "Jacobs uses the tight space to enact other kinds of free terrain" in her theorization of wandering as philosophical performance of freedom. See Cervenak, *Wandering: Philosophical Performances of Racial and Sexual Freedom* (Durham, N.C.: Duke University Press, 2014), 71. Holloway, recognizing that "the attic 'loophole of retreat' is only a sanctuary of her mind," nonetheless argues that "its site as domestic refuge where the property of [Brent's] body becomes her own only through this torturous imprisonment underscores the complex and differential effects of a claim to property." See Holloway, *Legal Fictions,* 37.

9. Hartman, *Scenes of Subjection,* 104, my emphasis.

10. Georgia Kreiger, "Playing Dead: Harriet Jacobs's Survival Strategy in *Incidents in the Life of a Slave Girl,*" *African American Review* 42, no. 3–4 (2008): 619.

11. Recent work in surveillance studies richly engages critical questions unfolding from these paradoxes of resistance, (in/non)/visibility, domination, agency, and vulnerability. See Simone Browne's *Dark Matters: On the Surveillance of Blackness* (Durham, N.C.: Duke University Press, 2015) and Mia Fischer's *Terrorizing Gender: Transgender Visibility and the Surveillance Practices of the U.S. Security State* (Lincoln: University of Nebraska Press, 2019) for just two examples. Kelly Ross reads *Incidents in the Life of a Slave Girl,* specifically, through surveillance studies frameworks in "Watching from Below: Racialized Surveillance and Vulnerable Sousveillance," PMLA 35, no. 2 (2020): 299–314.

12. Keeling, *Queer Times, Black Futures,* 32–48.

13. Hartman, *Scenes of Subjection,* 116. On the distinction between emancipation and abolition, see Walcott, *Long Emancipation,* 36. My articulation of "what might have been and was not but yet must be" is a riff on Keeling's "futures past" as well as Campt's "grammar of black feminist futurity" (17).

14. In employing a series of italicized elaborations of how I am using the term *perforation* throughout this chapter, I am intending to extend the first chapter's attention to "poetics of accumulation" through

my own writing. I leave it to the reader to determine if I have done so successfully.

15. Snorton, *Black on Both Sides*, 69, my emphasis.

16. Weheliye, *Habeas Viscus*, 2.

17. See Colin Dayan's *The Law Is a White Dog: How Legal Rituals Make and Unmake Persons* (Princeton, N.J.: Princeton University Press, 2013) for more on how the law "unmakes persons."

18. Walcott, *Long Emancipation*, 106.

19. Sutton E. Griggs, *Imperium in Imperio* (1899; repr., New York: Modern Library, 2003), 124.

20. Griggs, 124.

21. Baldwin, *No Name in the Street*, 455, my emphasis.

22. Farred, *In Motion, at Rest*, 27.

23. Griggs, *Imperium in Imperio*, 32.

24. Griggs, 33–34.

25. See W. E. B. Du Bois, *Black Reconstruction in America*, esp. the chapters "The Black Worker" and "The General Strike."

26. Griggs, *Imperium in Imperio*, 34–35.

27. Griggs, 36.

28. Griggs, 177, my emphasis.

29. My reading of Trout's structural role as narrator departs from Nicole A. Waligora-Davis's. In *Sanctuary: African Americans and Empire* (New York: Oxford University Press, 2007), Davis writes, "By anticipating the failure of the plan for black secession, the text refuses black violence, shifting attention back to the question of black citizenship" (23). I share Davis's trenchant critique of the juridically imposed "state of exception" in which African Americans are inscribed by anti-Black violence in the United States, and Davis does not herself argue that liberal recognition of juridical rights will redress this order of things. But I disagree that Trout's narration "shifts" the attention of the novel. Reading against what Davis identifies as Griggs's authorial intent described as "an ideology of peace," and instead continuing to lean into the layers of the "perhaps" outlined in my elaboration of poetics of accumulation, I see *Imperium in Imperio* as articulating both a call for Black citizenship and a threat of forthcoming Black violence.

30. For more on Child's editorial decisions, see Albert Tricomi, "Harriet Jacobs's Autobiography and the Voice of Lydia Maria Child," *ESQ* 53, no. 3 (2007): esp. 227–31. For more on the general relationship between Jacobs's writing and Child's editing, see Bruce Mills, "Lydia Maria Child and the Endings to Harriet Jacobs's *Incidents in the Life of a Slave Girl*," *American Literature* 64, no. 2 (1992): esp. 263–65; Alice A. Deck, "Whose Book Is This? Authorial versus Editorial Control of Harriet Brent Jacobs's *Incidents in the Life of a Slave Girl: Written by Herself*," *Women's Studies International Forum* 10, no. 1 (1987): esp. 38–39; and, of course, Jean Fagan Yellin's *Harriet Jacobs: A Life* (London: Civitas Books, 2005), as well as Yellin's introduction to the Harvard University Press edition of *Incidents*.

31. See Lovalerie King's *Race, Theft, and Ethics: Property Matters in African American Literature* (Baton Rouge: Louisiana State University Press, 2007) on the ways in which ethics and law come into conflict across the principles of property and labor under conditions of chattel slavery.

32. Jacobs, *Incidents*, 41.

33. Insofar as Mr. Litch is "the embodiment of the power to murder," he is the sovereign of the biopolitical framework of the plantation, the one who decides life and death. It is beyond the scope of my work here to give a theory of biopolitics, but I would suggest that there is more to say about how perforation emphasizes the multidirectionality of power in biopolitical regimes in ways that resonate with Weheliye's engagements with Black feminist theory and European biopolitical theory in *Habeas Viscus*.

34. I am also thinking, here, with Fred Moten and Stephen Dillon. First Moten: "I think I probably [see blackness as a kind of pathogen], or at least hope that it is, insofar as I bear the hope that blackness bears or is the potential to end the world." Moten, "Blackness and Nothingness (Mysticism in the Flesh)," *South Atlantic Quarterly* 112, no. 4 (2013): 739. And Dillon: "For millions of people the political violence occurring across the country and around the world [in the 1960s and 1970s] was the sign of new possibilities and new worlds. If many imagined the end of the world as it was, Nixon was afraid of their success. But he was not concerned with the fate of *the* world, but

'your world,' your way of life—what Frank Wilderson calls 'white life.' Nixon declared that for the white subject, life was under threat, and the law would realign the racial order of things." Dillon, *Fugitive Life*, 37.

35. Jacobs, *Incidents*, 46.

36. Of course, race is a social construct, and so biologically there is no such thing as "black blood" or "white blood." I use this term here to borrow the language of the well-known "one drop rule," even as I recognize the scientific racism in which this terminology traffics.

37. Brigitte Fielder, *Relative Races: Genealogies of Interracial Kinship in Nineteenth-Century America* (Durham, N.C.: Duke University Press, 2020), 39.

38. Fielder, 207.

39. Angela Davis, Gina Dent, Erica Meiners, and Beth Richie, *Abolition. Feminism. Now.* (Chicago: Haymarket Books, 2022). Other key texts on abolition feminism, anticarceral feminism, and queer abolitionist praxis that influence my reading here as well as my thinking throughout *Abolition Time* include *Color of Violence: The INCITE! Anthology*, ed. INCITE! Women, Gender Non-conforming, and Trans People of Color Against Violence (Durham, N.C.: Duke University Press, 2006); Stanley and Smith, *Captive Genders*; Gilmore, *Golden Gulag*; Beth Richie, *Arrested Justice: Black Women, Justice, and America's Prison Nation* (New York: NYU Press, 2012); Emily Thuma, *All Our Trials: Prisons, Policing, and the Feminist Fight to End Violence* (Champaign: University of Illinois Press, 2019); and Davis, *Are Prisons Obsolete?*

40. Hartman, *Scenes of Subjection*, 115–24.

41. In addition to *Scenes of Subjection,* a myriad of texts I have in mind critique, on different threads and toward different conclusions, what we might call "inclusion as remedy" politics: Rodríguez's *White Reconstruction*; Denise Ferreira Da Silva's *Toward a Global Idea of Race* (Minneapolis: University of Minnesota Press, 2007); Jodi Melamed's *Represent and Destroy: Rationalizing Violence in the New Racial Capitalism* (Minneapolis: University of Minnesota Press, 2011); Conrad's edited volume *Against Equality*; Wilderson's *Red, White, and Black*; Glen Sean Coulthard's *Red Skin, White Masks: Rejecting the Colonial Politics of Recognition* (Minneapolis: University of Minnesota Press, 2014); and Eve Tuck and K. Wayne Yang's "Decolonization Is Not a

Metaphor," *Decolonization: Indigeneity, Education, and Society* 1, no. 1 (2012): 1–40.

42. I focus on my students' responses to the text as an example of an umbrella of readings of *Incidents* against which to posit my argument in this chapter, not to disparage them, but because it is in conversation with my students, who are also my teachers, that I have most clearly rethought my own readings of the text. I also sketch my students' readings of the text as a foil for my argument because of just how widely written about *Incidents* is as a canonical work of American literature. That is, although certainly dozens of readings of the text in published scholarship fit the text within a (perhaps more nuanced) version of the "inclusion as remedy" framework of liberal feminist humanism, also dozens of readings refuse that framework. There is no single "common" reading of such a widely read text to consolidate into a recognizable position in order to posit a brand-new interpretation, as is the common practice for scholarship in literary criticism. Eschewing the impulse (enforced through the structured precarity of academic labor and pressures to publish according to preexisting assumptions about what makes good argumentation) to assert my interpretation's originality against a consolidated body of scholarship, I instead here unearth how my thinking has been shaped with and against patterns that have emerged in my classrooms as I work with students.

43. Patrice D. Douglass, "Assata Is Here: (Dis)Locating Gender in Black Studies," *Souls* 22, no. 1 (2020): 95.

44. Bey, *Black Trans Feminism*, 70.

45. My reading of Spillers's concept of *ungendering* has been deeply instructed by the scholarship of C. Riley Snorton, Alexander Weheliye, Stephanie Smallwood, Zakkiyah I. Jackson, Patrice D. Douglass, Samantha Pinto, and Oyèrónkẹ́ Oyěwùmí. In addition, my thinking on racial capitalism and reproduction is fundamentally informed by the work of Jennifer L. Morgan, Alys Eve Weinbaum, and Sarah Clarke Kaplan.

46. Hortense J. Spillers, "Mama's Baby, Papa's Maybe: An American Grammar Book," in *Black, White, and in Color* (Chicago: University of Chicago Press, 2003), 222; Aliyyah Abdul-Rahman, *Against the Closet: Black Political Longing and the Erotics of Race* (Durham, N.C.: Duke

University Press, 2006), 41. I borrow the phrase "monstrous intimacy" from Sharpe.

47. Haley, *No Mercy Here: Gender,* 86.

48. Angela Davis, "Reflections on the Black Woman's Role in the Community of Slaves," *Black Scholar* 12, no. 6 (1981): 7, 8, 12–15.

49. Spillers, "Mama's Baby," 206, 215.

50. Hortense J. Spillers, "Interstices: A Small Drama of Words," in *Black, White, and in Color,* 155.

51. Hartman, *Scenes of Subjection,* 102, 100.

52. Jennifer L. Morgan, *Reckoning with Slavery: Gender, Kinship, and Capitalism in the Early Black Atlantic* (Durham, N.C.: Duke University Press, 2021), 162.

53. Bey, *Black Trans Feminism,* 25; Snorton, *Black on Both Sides,* 74.

54. Snorton offers a more fleshed-out account of what I am getting at in my refusal of these two more simplified interpretations of "ungendering" in *Black on Both Sides* when he engages Frank Wilderson both to hold up what Wilderson offers as valuable insight and to critique Wilderson's analysis of gender. Snorton writes, "In posing gender as contingent to blackness, Wilderson's argument becomes incapable of perceiving un/gendering as a mode of violence that makes black fungibility palpable, which is to say that his assertion rests on a refusal of the ways gender is itself a racial arrangement that expresses the transubstantiation of things" (83).

55. Dorothy Roberts, *Killing the Black Body: Race, Reproduction, and the Meaning of Liberty* (New York: Vintage Books, 1997), 33; Sharpe, *In the Wake,* 13.

56. Jacobs, *Incidents,* 66.

57. I am not at all insinuating that no other cultures or peoples anywhere on the globe recognized some kinds of gender systems that had some kind of role or identity approximate to what we in the United States call today "women" before the inauguration of Atlantic slavery. Thus my shorthand of "Western, modern woman" is still not precise enough. Thinking with Spillers, as well as, more recently, Zakiyyah Iman Jackson, on the point that the Black woman is the portal between human and nonhuman being, along with Sylvia Wynter on Western Man as only one possible *genre* of the Human, and Oyèrónkẹ́ Oyěwùmí's field-shifting work in *The Invention of Women: Making an*

African Sense of Western Gender Discourses (Minneapolis: University of Minnesota Press, 1997), I am both holding open the possibility of other ways of doing gender and insisting that gender and race were historically being meaningfully coproduced through anti-Black violence in the Middle Passage and the genocidal violence of colonial conquest and dispossession in the Americas, Africa, Australia, and Asia.

58. Jacobs, *Incidents*, 46, my italics.

59. Another question I've been thinking about: if gender can be "possessed," how can we think that alongside Cheryl Harris on "whiteness as property"? Harris, "Whiteness as Property," *Harvard Law Review* 106, no. 8 (1993): 1707–91.

60. Spillers, "Mama's Baby," 206.

61. Michel Foucault, *The Order of Things: An Archeology of the Human Sciences* (1970; repr., New York: Vintage Books, 1994), 311.

62. "Security Does Not Mean Safety: #1," *Dreaming Freedom, Practicing Abolition* (blog), July 19, 2019, https://abolitioniststudy.wordpress.com /2019/07/19/security-does-not-mean-safety-1/.

63. Kaba and Duda, "Towards the Horizon of Abolition."

64. Jacobs, *Incidents*, 26.

65. Jacobs, 16.

66. Imani Perry, "Occupying the Universal, Embodying the Subject: African American Jurisprudence," *Law and Literature* 17, no. 1 (2005): 99, 100.

67. Spillers, "Mama's Baby," 207, my emphasis.

68. Jacobs, *Incidents*, 42, 46. Mrs. Flint and Mrs. Wade cannot be read as exceptional in their violence, as Jones-Rogers's *They Were Her Property* demonstrates.

69. Sharpe, *In the Wake*, 22.

70. Spillers, "Mama's Baby," 228–29.

71. On "counterinsurgency," see esp. chapters 1 and 2 of Rodríguez's *White Reconstruction*. My capitalization of "Gender" in "colonial Western Gender" is a nod to Bey's conceptualization of "genders that might have arisen but for Gender" (25) in *Black Trans Feminism.*

72. Walvin, *Zong*, 112. See chapter 8, "A Matter of Necessity," for a thorough and concise account of the insurance trials following the massacre, including discussion of the evidentiary ambiguities at play in the formal historical archive.

73. Walvin, 1–2.

74. Patricia Saunders, "Defending the Dead, Confronting the Archive: A Conversation with M. NourbeSe Philip," *Small Axe* 12, no. 2 (2008): 70.

75. M. NourbeSe Philip and Setaey Adamu Boateng, *Zong!* (Middletown, Conn.: Wesleyan University Press, 2008), 200.

76. Renisa Mawani, "Law's Archive," *Annual Review of Law and Social Sciences* 8 (2012): 340.

77. Mawani, 350.

78. Derrida, "Force of Law," 925.

79. Mawani, "Law's Archive," 357.

80. Patricia Saunders, "Trying Tongues, E-raced Identities, and the Possibilities of Be/longing: Conversations with M. NourbeSe Philip," *Journal of West Indian Literature* 14 (2005): 218.

81. On situating *Zong!* in relation to the form of the lyric, see Reed, *Freedom Time*; Sarah Dowling, "Persons and Voices: Sounding Impossible Bodies in M. NourbeSe Philip's *Zong!*," *Canadian Literature* 210/211 (2011): 43–58; and Daniel Benjamin, "On Ecstatic-Aesthetic Universality—in *Zong!*," *Small Axe* 23, no. 1 (2019): 17–34. On *Zong!* as fugue, see Anne Quéma, "M. NourbeSe Philip's *Zong!*: Metaphors, Laws, and Fugues of Justice," *Journal of Law and Society* 43, no. 1 (2016): 58–104. On *Zong!* as ecopoetics, see Diana Leong, "The Salt Bones: *Zong!* and an Ecology of Thirst," ISLE: *Interdisciplinary Studies in Literature and Environment* 23, no. 4 (2016): 798–820, and Lisa Fink, "'Sing the Bones Home': Material Memory and the Project of Freedom in M. NourbeSe Philip's *Zong!*," *Humanities* 9, no. 22 (2020): 1–16. On *Zong!* as (anti-) elegy, see Almas Khan, "Poetic Justice: Slavery, Law, and the (Anti-) Elegiac Form in M. NourbeSe Philip's *Zong!*," *Cambridge Journal of Postcolonial Literary Inquiry* 2, no. 1 (2015): 5–32. On *Zong!* as counter-archive, see Nicole Gervasio, "The Ruth in (T)ruth: Redactive Reading and Feminist Provocations to History in M. NourbeSe Philip's *Zong!*," *differences: A Journal of Feminist Cultural Studies* 30, no. 2 (2019): 1–29. For an academic analysis of *Zong!* in performance, see Sasha Ann Panaram, "Afrosporic Intimacies: Breath, Song, and Wind in M. NourbeSe Philip's *Zong!*," *Black Scholar* 49, no. 3 (2019): 21–35.

82. Reed, *Freedom Time*, 57.

83. Philip and Boateng, *Zong!*, 211.

84. Philip and Boateng, 193.

85. Sharpe, *In the Wake*, 69.

86. Saunders, "Defending the Dead," 72.

87. Philip and Boateng, *Zong!*, 197.

88. Dowling, "Persons and Voices," 50.

89. Quéma, "M. NourbeSe Philip's *Zong!*," 88.

90. Panaram, "Afrosporic Intimacies," 22.

91. Dowling, "Persons and Voices," 52.

92. Gervasio, "Ruth in (T)ruth," 21, my emphasis.

93. Philip and Boateng, *Zong!*, 198, 199, 205.

AN INTERLUDE ON METHOD, OR ABOLITION IS NOT A METAPHOR

1. Sylvia Wynter, "'No Humans Involved': An Open Letter to My Colleagues," *Forum NHI: Knowledge for the 21st Century* 1, no. 1 (1994): 42–73; Bell, *Faces at the Bottom of the Well*; Rodríguez, *White Reconstruction*.

2. On "antagonism," see Wilderson's *Red, White, and Black*. On "law as the purview of the human," see Jared Sexton's essay "Racial Profiling and the Societies of Control," in *Warfare in the American Homeland: Policing and Prison in a Penal Democracy*, ed. Joy James, 197–218 (Durham, N.C.: Duke University Press, 2007), and Patrice D. Douglass's essay "On (Being) Fear: *Utah v. Strieff* and the Ontology of Affect," *Journal of Visual Culture* 17, no. 3 (2018): 332–42.

3. Toni Morrison, *Song of Solomon* (New York: Vintage Books, 1977), 82.

4. Saidiya V. Hartman, "Instinct and Injury: Bodily Integrity, Natural Affinities, and the Constitution of Equality," in *Scenes of Subjection*, 164–206.

5. For a reading of *Dred Scott v. Sanford* as a case of "unrecognizability before the law," among other analytical threads, see chapter 5, "Law: Property," in Weheliye's *Habeas Viscus*, esp. 79–83.

6. Derrida, "Force of Law."

7. Joy James, "The Womb of Western Theory: Trauma, Time Theft, and the Captive Maternal," in *Carceral Notebooks*, vol. 12, *Challenging the Punitive Society*, ed. Perry Zurn and Andrew Dilts, 255–96 (New York: Publishing Data Management, 2016).

8. Erica Garner, "Exclusive: Blavity Publishes Erica Garner's Final Essay on Her Relentless Fight for Justice," untitled essay, *Blavity*, January 23,

2018, https://blavity.com/exclusive-blavity-publishes-erica-garners
-final-essay-on-her-relentless-fight-for-justice.

9. officialERICA GARNER (@es_snipes), "When you report this you remember she was human: mother, daughter, sister, aunt," Twitter,
December 30, 2017, 9:41 A.M., https://twitter.com/es_snipes/status
/947115409550999558.

10. Sharpe, *In the Wake*, 110.

11. Ruth Wilson Gilmore, "Public Enemies and Private Intellectuals:
Apartheid USA," *Race and Class* 35, no. 1 (1993): 70.

THREE. WITNESSING

1. See the respective introductions to Hartman's *Scenes of Subjection*
and Moten's *In the Break* for a generative debate on questions of ethical reading practices that inform my work both in this chapter and
throughout *Abolition Time*.

2. Hartman, *Scenes of Subjection*, 19–25, 35, 62, 115–24, 130–40, 147, 175–83;
Weheliye, *Habeas Viscus*, 74–88; Dean Spade, *Normal Life: Adminis-
trative Violence, Critical Trans Politics, and the Limits of Law* (Durham,
N.C.: Duke University Press, 2015), 38–49; Coulthard, *Red Skin, White
Masks*, 25–50; Lisa Lowe, *The Intimacies of Four Continents* (Durham,
N.C.: Duke University Press, 2015), 7, 16, 43–72.

3. Levy-Hussen, *How to Read African American Literature*, 133.

4. Michel-Rolph Trouillot, *Silencing the Past: Power and the Production of
History*, 20th anniv. ed. (Boston: Beacon Press, 2015).

5. Katherine McKittrick, "(Zong) Bad Made Measure," in *"Dear Science"
and Other Stories* (Durham, N.C.: Duke University Press, 2020), 148.

6. Saidiya V. Hartman, *Lose Your Mother: A Journey along the Atlantic Slave
Route* (New York: Farrar, Straus, and Giroux, 2007), 170.

7. Stephen Best, *None Like Us: Blackness, Belonging, Aesthetic Life*
(Durham, N.C.: Duke University Press, 2018), 64. My parenthetical
comment responds to Best's compound: "Why must our relationship
to the past be ethical in the first place—and is it possible to have a
relation to the past that is not predicated on ethics?" I grapple more
explicitly with Best's argument in my essay "The Restored Literary
Behaviors of Neo-Slave Narratives," *Callaloo* 40, no. 4 (2017): 57–77,
which is a much earlier iteration of an argument built around readings of *A Mercy* and *Feeding the Ghosts*.

8. Hartman, "Venus in Two Acts," 12.

9. Hartman, 11.

10. Hartman, 12.

11. Reed, *Freedom Time*, 57.

12. Hartman, "Venus in Two Acts," 12.

13. Philip and Boateng, *Zong!*, 196.

14. McKittrick, "(Zong) Bad Made Measure," 146.

15. Philip and Boateng, *Zong!*, 197.

16. Philip, 200.

17. Hartman, "Venus in Two Acts," 8.

18. Fred D'Aguiar, *Feeding the Ghosts* (New York: Ecco, 1997). In this sense, I read *Zong!* and *Feeding the Ghosts* as "histories of the present" as defined by Lowe in *Intimacies of Four Continents*, 136.

19. D'Aguiar, *Feeding the Ghosts*, 126–27.

20. D'Aguiar, 5.

21. Responsibility as response-ability as the *ability to respond* is by now a ubiquitous formulation across numerous philosophical traditions of ethics. I draw here on Jacques Derrida's *The Gift of Death* (Chicago: University of Chicago Press, 1995), John D. Caputo's *Against Ethics: Contributions to a Poetics of Obligation with Constant Reference to Deconstruction* (Bloomington: Indiana University Press, 1993), and Kelly Oliver's *Witnessing: Beyond Recognition* (Minneapolis: University of Minnesota Press, 2001) as the trifecta of philosophical texts most directly influencing my use of the language of response-ability. Notably, Morrison's *Song of Solomon* is also foundational for me here in its description of the character Pilate Dead: "Without ever leaving the ground, she could fly" (336).

22. Best, *None Like Us*, 15.

23. Hartman, *Scenes of Subjection*, 19.

24. Philip and Boateng, *Zong!*, 204.

25. Weheliye, *Habeas Viscus*, 75.

26. This critique of inclusion as method of continuing domination by absorbing dispossessed subjects into the machinations of Empire is familiar at this point, and my thinking here is influenced by a number of scholars in addition to Weheliye and, of course, Hartman. See Ferreira Da Silva's *Toward a Global Idea of Race*, Rodríguez's *White Reconstruction*, Melamed's *Represent and Destroy*, Walcott's *Long Emancipation*, and Spade's *Normal Life*.

27. D'Aguiar, *Feeding the Ghosts*, 36.

28. D'Aguiar offers his own critique of literatures of slavery in an essay titled "The Last Essay about Slavery" in *Age of Anxiety*, ed. Sarah Dunant and Roy Porter, 125–47 (London: Virago Press, 1996).

29. My placing of "feeling right" in quotation marks calls back to Harriet Beecher Stowe's *Uncle Tom's Cabin* and to the prodigious amount of scholarship from the mid-twentieth century to today on sentimentality in American literature. The "feeling" versus "action" (non/)binary has been thoroughly analyzed by a still-growing body of scholarship focused on nineteenth-century literary studies, feminist literary criticism, and, more recently, affect theory. To point to just three touchstones from different eras, see Ann Douglas's *The Feminization of American Culture* (New York: Avon, 1977), Shirley Samuels's edited collection *The Culture of Sentiment: Race, Gender, and Sentimentality in Nineteenth-Century America* (New York: Oxford University Press, 1992), and Xine Yao's *Disaffected: The Cultural Politics of Unfeeling in Nineteenth-Century America* (Durham, N.C.: Duke University Press, 2021). It is not my goal to enter into the enormity of these ongoing debates here in my chapter, nor do I see *Abolition Time* more broadly as invested in theorizing literary sentimentality. Rather, I am focused on the way that I see the poetics of *Feeding the Ghosts*, specifically, as pointedly emphasizing the gap between the feeling produced by recognition (or empathy) and the action necessary to intervene in violence.

30. D'Aguiar, *Feeding the Ghosts*, 67.

31. D'Aguiar, 173.

32. Levy-Hussen, *How to Read African American Literature*, 20.

33. Toni Morrison, *A Mercy* (New York: Vintage, 2008), 25.

34. Morrison, 26.

35. Morrison, 30–31.

36. Morrison, 27.

37. Morrison, 191.

38. Morrison, 191.

39. Significantly, rape is ubiquitous on the pages of *A Mercy*, and yet D'Ortega is the only person who commits this form of violence to get properly named. I would not argue that *A Mercy* is simply a rewriting of *Incidents in the Life of a Slave Girl*, but the analogs abound, from Florens crouching and creeping along the corners of Jacob's

second house as a refiguring of Linda's cramped garret to the ubiquity of sexual violence to D'Ortega's parallels with Dr. Flint. Rather than fully extrapolate this comparison, I note it here and hope that my reading of Harriet Jacobs's text in chapter 2 gathers to my reading of Morrison's novel here to make possible further analysis beyond the bounded pages of my own book. (This is again my modest attempt to practice a poetics of accumulation alongside *Abolition Time*'s own self-perforation that I described in the interlude. To what degree it takes effect I cannot know in advance.)

40. Harris, "Whiteness as Property," 1714.

41. Morrison, *A Mercy*, 32.

42. Morrison, 41.

43. By thinking with Jacques Derrida on hauntology and Ian Baucom on accumulation, I write about *A Mercy* as a historicization of slavery-as-capitalism in "Slavery's Ghosts and the Haunted Housing Crisis: On Narrative Economy and Circum-Atlantic Memory in Toni Morrison's *A Mercy*," MELUS 41, no. 4 (2016): 116–39.

44. My reading of Jacob's sneer calls back to my reading of "In Memory of James Craig Anderson" in my analysis of Claudia Rankine's *Citizen*. Again, *Abolition Time* returns to a critique of law's grammar of individuation.

45. The quoted phrase is taken from my undergraduate notebooks as something I recall McCoy saying in the classroom. McCoy also critically meditates on the distancing force of scorn in her published scholarship. See Beth A. McCoy, "Trying Toni Morrison Again," *College English* 68, no. 1 (2005): 43–57.

46. I owe Grant Farred for the phrasing "stew in the discomfiture," a phrase I use with a weight I cannot sufficiently explain in words.

47. Morrison, *A Mercy*, 3.

48. D'Aguiar, *Feeding the Ghosts*, 229.

49. Octavia Butler, *Kindred* (Boston: Beacon Press, 1979), 101.

50. Philip and Boateng, *Zong!*, 198.

51. Caputo, *Against Ethics*, 63.

52. Morrison, *A Mercy*, 133.

53. See Beth A. McCoy, "Race and the (Para)Textual Condition," PMLA 121, no. 1 (2006): 156–69.

54. Morrison, *A Mercy*, 135.

55. Morrison, 187–88.
56. Goldberg, "Restored Literary Behaviors," 69.
57. D'Aguiar, *Feeding the Ghosts*, 229, my italics.
58. D'Aguiar, *Feeding the Ghosts*, 229–30.
59. Reed, *Freedom Time*, 53.
60. Derrida, *Gift of Death*, 27.
61. D'Aguiar, Feeding the Ghosts, 230.
62. Caputo, *Against Ethics*, 174.
63. D'Aguiar, *Feeding the Ghosts*, 229–30.
64. Philip and Boateng, *Zong!*, 198, 199, 205.
65. Sharpe, *In the Wake*, 100–101.

FOUR. BREATH

1. Muñoz, *Cruising Utopia*, 91.
2. Wilderson, *Red, White, and Black*, 338.
3. Sharpe, *In the Wake*, 109–11.
4. See the Combahee River Collective's 1977 "A Black Feminist State-ment," in *The Black Feminist Reader*, ed. Joy James and T. Denean Sharpley-Whiting, 261–70 (Hoboken, N.J.: Blackwell, 2010): "if Black women were free, it would mean that everyone else would have to be free since our freedom would necessitate the destruction of all the systems of oppression" (267). Relatedly, Walcott writes in *Long Emancipation*, "Furthermore, Black freedom is not just a freedom for Black subjects; it is a freedom that inaugurates an entirely new human experience for everyone" (5).
5. Cathy Cohen, "The Radical Potential of Queer? Twenty Years Later," GLQ 25, no. 1 (2019): 142.
6. Jeffrey Q. McQune, "The Queerness of Blackness," QED: *A Journal of LGBTQ Worldmaking* 2, no. 2 (2015): 173, 174.
7. Stanley, *Atmospheres of Violence*, 78.
8. Snorton, *Black on Both Sides*, 175.
9. Patrice D. Douglass, "Black Feminist Theory for the Dead and Dying." *Theory & Event* 21, no. 1 (2018): 114.
10. Haley, *No Mercy Here*, 86.
11. In *Wayward Lives, Beautiful Experiments: Intimate Histories of Social Upheaval* (New York: W. W. Norton, 2019), Saidiya V. Hartman writes, "Maybe if they could find their way beyond this language of being a man and being a woman, this grammar of the human that regarded

them both as monsters and deviants, and break free of a scheme never fashioned for them but imposed indifferently and cruelly, they might find their way to another kind of love and support, one capable of withstanding the daily assault of a world set against them" (274).

12. Sharpe, *In the Wake*, 113.
13. Stephanie Pocock Boeninger, "'I Have Become the Sea's Craft': Authorial Subjectivity in Derek Walcott's *Omeros* and David Dabydeen's 'Turner,'" *Contemporary Literature* 52, no. 3 (2011): 481.
14. Bey, *Black Trans Feminism*, 25.
15. David Dabydeen, *Turner* (Leeds, U.K.: Peepal Tree Press, 2002), 42.
16. For a compelling reading of "absent presence" in "Turner," see Hillary Gravendyk, "Intertextual Absences: 'Turner' and Turner," *The Comparatist* 35 (2011): 161–69.
17. Dabydeen, *Turner*, 7.
18. Édouard Glissant, *Poetics of Relation*, trans. Betsy Wing (Ann Arbor: University of Michigan Press, 1997).
19. Baucom, *Specters of the Atlantic*, 330.
20. Dabydeen, *Turner*, 8.
21. Stef Craps, "Learning to Live with Ghosts: Postcolonial Haunting and Mid-Mourning in David Dabydeen's 'Turner' and Fred D'Aguiar's *Feeding the Ghosts*," *Callaloo* 33, no. 2 (2010): 471.
22. Dabydeen, *Turner*, 7, my italics.
23. Douglass, "Black Feminist Theory," 116.
24. See Douglass, 108; Abdur-Rahman, *Against the Closet*, 40; Hartman, *Scenes of Subjection*, 99–101; Spillers, "Mama's Baby," 207, 222–23; Kaplan, *Black Reproductive*, 17; and Samantha Pinto, "Black Feminist Literacies: Ungendering, Flesh, and Post-Spillers Epistemologies of Embodied and Emotional Justice," *Journal of Black Sexualities and Relationships* 4, no. 1 (2017): 27.
25. Dabydeen, *Turner*, 22–23.
26. Smallwood, *Saltwater Slavery*; Morgan, *Laboring Women*. Additionally, see McKittrick, "Mathematics Black Life."
27. Spillers, "Mama's Baby," 218.
28. I am more concisely rehearsing here a genealogy of Black feminist scholarship on "ungendering" and sexual violence that I engage at greater length in chapter 2.
29. Kaplan, *Black Reproductive*.
30. Dabydeen, *Turner*, 40.

31. Veronica J. Austen, "Self-Consumption and Compromised Rebirth in Dabydeen's 'Turner,'" *Cambridge Journal of Postcolonial Literary Inquiry* 3, no. 2 (2016): 227–39.

32. Oyěwùmí, *Invention of Women*, 124.

33. Dabydeen, *Turner*, 34.

34. Austen, "Self-Consumption," 234.

35. There is a critique to be made of my entire argument that I am too quick to define "mothering" as "nourishing children into the future," since numerous members of any community within many cultures do this nourishing work without being called "mothers." I cannot dismiss this criticism. What I hope my argument does is demonstrate the contingency and uncertainty of the word *mother*, since I *do* believe that for any definition we posit, we could find exceptions or examples that the definition would fail to account for yet we would think ought to be included.

36. Austen, 235. In a footnote, Austen cites words to build a reading of section xxiv in which Turner figuratively "impregnates" the children, resulting in "an impregnation from which nothing productive will come" (236).

37. Dabydeen, *Turner*, 36.

38. Dabydeen, 9.

39. Dabydeen, 21.

40. Dabydeen, 21

41. Dabydeen, 41.

42. Austen, "Self-Consumption," 238.

43. Austen, 239.

44. Soyica Diggs Colbert, "Drama in the Harlem Renaissance," in *The Cambridge Companion to African American Theater*, ed. Harvey Young, 85–102 (Cambridge: Cambridge University Press, 2012). See Koritha Mitchell, *Living with Lynching: African American Lynching Plays, Performance, and Citizenship 1890–1930* (Champaign: University of Illinois Press, 2012), especially the first two chapters. *Rachel* has received renewed critical attention in the twenty-first century after a long period of scholarly neglect, and I would point to Mitchell's scholarship, along with the work of Jacqueline Goldsby, as the most significant driving force around critical attention to the play and its author. See Goldsby, *A Spectacular Secret: Lynching in American Life and Literature*

(Chicago: University of Chicago Press, 2006). For a reading of *Rachel* that insists that "reading Rachel as anti-lynching confines the characters' lives to being defined in consequence of and as response to anti-Blackness" (5), see Kya Cunningham, "The Death of Social Death: Im/possibility of Black Maternity in Angelina Weld Grimké's *Rachel*," *SubStance* 51, no. 2 (2022): 3–20. Though I believe Cunningham's understanding of a narrow definition of "anti-lynching" misreads Mitchell's expansive fleshing out not only of the literary genre of "anti-lynching plays" but of Black life itself, because Mitchell never in her scholarship (in *Living with Lynching* or elsewhere) reduces any aspect of Black culture to mere response to white racism, I still think it is productive to read Cunningham's analysis of the play in dialogue with the field-shaping work of Mitchell and Goldsby. K. Allison Hammer offers a queer reading of *Rachel* through Julia Kristeva's concept of *abjection* in her article "'Blood at the Root': Cultural Abjection and Thwarted Desire in the Lynching Plays and Poetry of Angelina Weld Grimké," *Frontiers: A Journal of Women's Studies* 42, no. 1 (2021): 27–57. Cunningham's article explicitly reads the play in conversation with a certain distillation of Afro-pessimism.

45. Sharpe, *In the Wake*, 11. On "heavy-handed name," Robin Bernstein writes incisively about Grimké's naming conventions in her essay contextualizing *Rachel* as a response to the cultural figure of "Topsy" as imagined by George Aiken's theatrical rendition of *Uncle Tom's Cabin*. See Bernstein, "'Never Born': Angelina Weld Grimké's *Rachel* as Ironic Response to Topsy," *Journal of American Drama and Theatre* 19, no. 2 (2007): 61–75.

46. Sharpe, *In the Wake*, 78.

47. Angelina Weld Grimké, *Rachel* (Boston: Cornhill, 1920), 12. The play was originally written and produced in 1916 but was published in book form in 1920. My references are to the 1920 book.

48. Grimké, 13.

49. Morrison, *A Mercy*, 195. To this point, existing scholarship on *Rachel* has thoroughly contextualized the play as a response not only to the specific form of anti-Black violence enacted by lynching but to a long history of anti-Black violence and racism that includes other works of theater and literature. My chapter, therefore, will not repeat a tendency in *Rachel* scholarship of outlining at length the nature of

lynching as a form of terroristic violence with a racial-sexual libidinal economy, though I will by necessity address lynching throughout this section. Ultimately, I will emphasize formal readings of the play's language and staging rather than offering a new theorization or analysis of lynching itself. For more on the racial-sexual libidinal economies of lynching, see Goldsby and Mitchell as well as Harvey Young's *Embodying Black Experience: Stillness, Critical Memory, and the Black Body* (Ann Arbor: University of Michigan Press, 2010). For an analysis of the sexual economy of lynching as it is engaged by Black feminist theory, see Hazel Carby, "'On the Threshold of Woman's Era': Lynching, Empire, and Sexuality in Black Feminist Theory," *Critical Inquiry* 12 (1985): 262–77. Ida B. Wells's writings on lynching are also indispensable for contextualizing *Rachel* and for analytically understanding lynching's racial, sexual, gendered, and economic dimensions. See Wells-Barnett, *On Lynchings* (Mineola, N.Y.: Dover, 2014). And for analysis of lynching as a rupture of the distinction between legal and extralegal violence, see Bryan Wagner, *Disturbing the Peace: Black Culture and the Police Power after Slavery* (Cambridge, Mass.: Harvard University Press, 2009), and Ken Gonzales-Day, *Lynching in the American West, 1850–1935* (Durham, N.C.: Duke University Press, 2006).

50. Grimké, *Rachel*, 23. Historical scholarship on lynching has overwhelmingly demonstrated that the mob violence it names was more often enacted by such white folks "in good standing," often in broad daylight and without the infamous facial coverings of the Ku Klux Klan. Every time I teach about lynching, I make a point of having students understand that it was not an exceptional form of violence enacted by a pathologized extreme minority of white people but a quotidian terror enacted by "average," middle-class citizens. Though I do not show lynching photographs in my classes, I describe the phenomenon with reference to Goldsby's and Young's scholarship to illustrate the point.

51. For more on the significance of the middle-class status of the Loving family and the dramatic portrayal of domestic space, see Bernstein, "'Never Born,'" 64–69; Mitchell, *Living with Lynching*, 53–59, 62–64, 71–76; Hammer, "Blood at the Root," 28; Cunningham, "Death of Social

Death," 7–9; and Anne Mai Yee Jansen, "Under Lynching's Shadow: Grimké's Call for Domestic Reconfiguration in *Rachel*," *African American Review* 47, no. 2–3 (2014): 391–402.

52. In thinking about Jimmy as substitute, I am thinking with Joseph Roach's *Cities of the Dead*, esp. chapter 2.

53. *Rachel* was performed by the Quintessence Theatre Group in Philadelphia, Pennsylvania, in 2020. I will also note that each time I have taught the play, my students, without my urging, have connected the play to anti-Black police brutality against Black children during our class discussions.

54. My use of the verb *gathers* here comes out of Farred's theorization of "the event" in *In Motion, At Rest*: "in its dispersion, the event gathers that which does not appear properly, if at all, to belong to it: those historical moments, the event into the event (if we can, for a moment, conceive of the Civil Rights Act symptomatically, as the event of justice)" (46).

55. Grimké, *Rachel*, 28.

56. Sharpe, *In the Wake*, 74.

57. Angelina Weld Grimké, "*Rachel*, the Play of the Month: The Reason and Synopsis by the Author," *Competitor* 1 (1920): 51–52.

58. For a more nuanced rendering of this thread of argument, see Perry, "Occupying the Universal."

59. Lee Edelman, *No Future: Queer Theory and the Death Drive* (Durham, N.C.: Duke University Press, 2004), 11.

60. Mitchell and Bernstein both helpfully unpack the "race suicide" response to *Rachel*, and Cunningham helpfully contextualizes it within growing eugenics discourse in the early twentieth century.

61. Muñoz, *Cruising Utopia*, 94.

62. Grimké, *Rachel*, 63.

63. For a rich archive of Grimké's unpublished writing that sheds light on her personal queerness, see *Selected Works of Angelina Weld Grimké*, ed. Carolivia Herron, Schomburg Library of Nineteenth-Century Black Women Writers (Oxford: Oxford University Press, 1991).

64. Hammer, "Blood at the Root," 32.

65. Hammer, 40.

66. Sharpe, *In the Wake*, 16.

67. James Bliss, "Hope against Hope: Queer Negativity, Black Feminist Theorizing, and Reproduction without Futurity," *Mosaic* 48, no. 1 (2015): 86.

68. Frank B. Wilderson III and Saidiya V. Hartman, "The Position of the Unthought," *Qui Parle* 13, no. 2 (2003): 183–201; Wynter, "Unsettling the Coloniality of Being/Power/Truth/Freedom."

69. Grimké, *Rachel*, 42, my emphasis. I use underlining and italics as contrasting forms of emphasis to visually signal the chiasmus I proceed to unpack.

70. Keeling, *Queer Times, Black Futures*, 67.

71. Jared Sexton, "The Social Life of Social Death: On Afro-Pessimism and Black Optimism," *InTensions* 5 (2011): 6.

72. Grimké, *Rachel*, 63.

73. My hope is that my emphasis on a tension produced by shifting narrative modes of internalization and externalization recalls the poetics of witnessing that I address in chapter 3.

74. Grimké, *Rachel*, 96.

75. Grimké, 96.

76. Patricia Hill Collins, *Black Feminist Thought* (Philadelphia: Routledge, 2000), 187–215.

77. Morrison, *A Mercy*, 3.

CODA

1. Philip and Boateng, *Zong!*, 192–93, 205.

2. For a more expanded analysis of the logic of private property than I engage in this short Coda, see Rinaldo Walcott, *On Property* (Windsor, ON: Biblioasis, 2021).

3. Alexis Pauline Gumbs, *M Archive: After the End of the World* (Durham, N.C.: Duke University Press, 2018), 107.

4. Although the idea expressed by this phrasing is long established in abolitionist activism beyond the attribution of any proper noun, the particular linguistic phrasing of abolition as a world that could even have prisons, for me, comes from Fred Moten and Stefano Harney, *The Undercommons: Fugitive Planning and Black Study* (New York: Minor Compositions, 2013), 42.

Index

ableism, viii, 3, 46, 212, 224n3

abolition, 97, 125–26, 212, 256n4; and accumulation, 65; and anti-Blackness, 24; and *Beloved*, 2; and British law, 47; and Civil War, 85; and emancipation, 7, 209, 237n13; and ethics, 41; feminism, 95–96, 99, 240n39; and "future," 15, 85, 172; and gender, 97; and Harriet Jacobs, 107; and justice, 22, 210; and law, 6; and poetics, 133; prison, 51, 131; time, 1, 7–8, 14, 29, 36, 76, 79–80, 85, 174–75, 187, 205–6, 208, 214; total, 85, 100, 128; and United States, 73, 77; and violence, 10, 55; and whiteness, 55; and white supremacy, 35; work, 8, 16, 34–35, 83

abolitionists, 35, 77, 85, 126, 132, 155, 240n39; and accumulation, 53, 56; and activism, 10, 133, 256n4; and ethics, 15, 41, 175; and feminism, 97, 105–6; and justice, 7–8, 26, 29; and Mariama Kaba, 22–23; and literary studies, 12, 15–16, 18, 33, 79, 119, 126, 131, 133; and novels, 32; and politics, 95; and reading practice, 44, 53, 56, 64, 80, 111, 119, 125, 175, 214; thought, 6, 50–51, 97, 103, 174, 225n8; white, 77; and whiteness, 55; and world building, 2, 41

accountability, xiii, 8, 33

accumulation, 49, 57, 70, 128, 209–10, 213; capital, 132; capitalist, 52; and injustice, 46; and justice, 208; of narrative, 46; poetics of, 33, 41–43, 45, 52–56, 58, 61–65, 67–68, 100, 125, 174, 177, 208, 237n14, 238n29, 249n39; property, 99; and reading practice, 44; and release, 45; tidalectical, 52; and time, 46; wealth, 160; work of, 43

Africa, 49, 158, 160, 185

African Americanist scholarship, 25, 178, 236n4, 253n49; and lynching, 254n50

Africans, 48, 82, 91, 108, 129, 139, 144–46, 150–53, 157–58, 169, 180, 212 afterlife of slavery, 10, 14, 28, 98, 180, 195, 231n23, 232n26; and anti-Blackness, 11, 13; and Beloved, 32; and criminalization, 23; and futurity, 13; and incarceration, 23; and justice, 6, 164; and law, 125; and prisons, 50; and settler colonialism, 59; and temporality, 9, 40, 181; and white supremacy, 11

A Mercy, 34, 140–41, 151, 156, 158, 162–66, 177, 193, 246n7, 248n39, 249n43

anagramatical Blackness, 10, 78, 87

anti-Blackness, 11, 13, 24, 31, 60, 73, 84, 87, 179, 200–201, 203–5, 253n44; and surveillance, 85

art forms, 4

Atlantic (framework), 57, 73

Atlantic Ocean, 48–49, 52–57, 62, 66, 102, 114, 146–47

Beloved, 4, 8, 15, 23, 25–28, 30, 148; and abolition, 2, 7, 32; as antislavery novel, 24, 29, 32; and Denver, 207; and emancipation, 2; and ethics, 5–6; and justice, 5; and law, 17, 24; and narrator, 6, 32; and sexual economy, 158; and slave interiority, 27; and slavery, 31–32, 158; and temporality, 2, 24

Black Atlantic, 6, 25, 40, 83

Black bodies, 47, 86, 98, 102, 127–28, 173, 175, 179; and law, 94; and lynching, 60; and Middle Passage, 79; and slavery, 49, 94, 102

Black Codes, 92

Black feminism, 15, 21, 101, 178, 199; and futurity, 2, 14, 237n13; and scholarship, 97, 99, 251n28; and theory, 13, 35, 95, 97, 99, 224n3, 239n33, 254n49

Black literature, 12, 83

Black Lives Matter movement, 43, 218

Blackness, 94, 97–102, 105, 127, 166, 173, 176, 178–79, 195, 233n45, 234n50, 236n6; and gender, 182, 198, 242n54; and political ontology, 181; as racial positions, 54, 58

Black people, 66, 71, 90, 179, 183; and Aspiration, 199, 202; and breath, 118, 177; and children, 93–94, 176, 193–97, 201–2, 255n53; and citizenship, 50, 129, 238n29; and death, 178; and emancipation, 77; and experience, 5, 10–11, 62, 79, 199–200, 205, 207; and family, 176, 184; and flesh, 102, 106; and freedom, 89, 175, 250n4; and futurity, 133, 177, 198–99, 202–4; and gender, 97–98, 178, 182, 198; and historical fiction, 139; and kinship, 188; and lynching, 194, 253n44; and men, 88–89, 104–5, 166; and Middle Passage, 75, 101; mixed-race, 94; and modernity, 59; and motherhood, 195, 202–3; and murder, 172; and newspapers, 193; and parenthood, 99; and performance, 84; and plays, 76; and political

thought, 91; and queerness,
192; and racism, 57-58, 196; and
radical tradition, 6, 133, 173; as
readers, 5; and reproduction,
227n17; and self-emancipation,
91; and sociality, 176; and state
violence, 128; and subjectivity,
99; and violence, 31, 92, 126, 194,
204, 238n29, 243n57, 253n49;
and Serena Williams, 47-49, 55;
and women, 59-61, 96, 98-100,
103, 105, 118, 184, 192, 242n57; as
writers, 4, 43, 139
black reproductive, 184
Black River, 107
Black subjects, 12, 58, 60, 90, 98,
101, 176, 178-79, 199, 234n50,
250n4
Brent, Linda, 33, 82-83, 85-86, 93

capitalism, 161; and accumulation,
52; finance, 82; gendered, x;
global, 224n3; modern, 49, 51;
racial, viii, 3, 18, 63, 125, 131,
203, 212, 223n1, 224n3, 232n24,
241n45; and slavery, 249n43
carcerality, 23, 65, 85, 211, 223n1;
and anti-Blackness, 13; and
carceral formation, 50; and
carceral gendering, 58-59;
and carceral life, 12, 208; and
carceral logic, 46, 50, 73, 75,
120; and carceral model, 65, 72;
and carceral technology, 79,
106; and cisheteropatriarchy,
125; and confinement, 82; and
necro-carceral inhabitation, 82;

and power, 59; and slavery, 85;
and violence, 212
carceral studies, 11; and epistemology, 35, 72
Chinese immigrants, 44
cisheteropatriarchy, viii, 3, 18, 63,
125, 212, 224n3
Citizen: An American Lyric, 33, 39-43,
47-48, 50-60, 62-65, 79, 81, 95,
128, 169, 175, 177, 179, 209
citizens, 23, 54, 88, 104, 126, 129, 197,
254n50
citizenship, 50, 54, 57, 83, 88, 177,
238n29
Civil Rights Act (1964), 20
Civil War, 57, 77-78, 85, 87-91
class, 178, 193, 224n5, 254nn50-51
class discussions, 4-5, 78, 148, 170,
225n7, 255n53
collective care, 212
collectivity, 54
colonial conquest, 49, 164, 243n57
colonial epistemology, 69
colonial nation-state, 172, 186
colonial practices, 4
colonial space, 16
colonial violence, 188
colonial Western Gender, 96-97,
106, 177, 186, 243n71
colonization, 3, 70, 178, 234n45
critical fabulation, 10, 34, 78, 142,
144-45, 153, 166, 168, 177, 192, 209,
226n12
critical prison studies, 12
critical race theory, 21, 127
cultural competence, 4
cultural criticism, 25, 139

cultural difference, 127
cultural formation, 183, 187
cultural memory, 29, 150
cultural production, 59, 137, 144
culture, 15, 127–28, 132, 186, 253n44

D'Aguiar, Fred, 140–41, 145, 149, 153, 155–56, 159, 170, 248n28. See also *Feeding the Ghosts*
Davis, Angela, viii, 7, 51, 95, 98, 238n29
Department of Justice (DOJ), 19, 129
domination, 22, 81, 84, 161, 237n11, 247n26; hierarchical, 3; political, 86; racial, 187; racial-sexual, 184; structures of, 85; and violence, 183
Douglass, Frederick, 84, 236n4
Douglass, Patrice, 13, 97, 178, 182, 195
Dred Scott v. Sanford, 128

economic extraction, 8
economic formation, 13
enslaved people, 2, 92–93, 102, 108, 120, 156, 167, 169; and abolition- ists, 77; and *Beloved*, 32; and capitalism, 49; and children, 5, 101; and disposability, 73; and escapes, 76; experiences of, 139, 141–43, 149, 157–58, 162; human- ity of, 154; and labor, 73; and law, 109, 117, 183; in literature, 77, 79, 157–58, 165; and men, 96, 101, 104; and Middle Passage, 51, 75, 79; and motherhood, 96; murder of, 92–94, 129, 140, 180–81; pain of, 153–54, 157–58; and plantation,

76; and quarters, 146; and queer utopian memory, 79; rape of, 93, 97, 99, 158, 184; status of, 83, 102; and subjectivity, 147, 184; and torture, 92, 102, 158, 162; and transatlantic journey, 71; treatment of, 113, 181–84; and Underground Railroad, 146; and vulnerability, 86; and women, 57, 98, 100–101; and *Zong* Massacre, 48, 55, 66. See also slavery
enslavers, 76–77, 82, 84, 91–92, 99–101, 182. See also slavery
Escape, The; or, A Leap for Freedom, 76–80
ethics, 2, 8, 27, 61, 143–44, 161, 166–67, 203, 208–9, 246n7, 247n21; and abolition, 15, 41, 80, 175; and *Beloved*, 5, 24; of care, 205; and historiography, 25; and justice, 22, 148; and law, 11, 15–16, 239n31; logic of, 7; modes of, 133, 137, 159, 161–62, 174; and novels, 29, 34, 36, 141; of reading, 155, 163; as risk, 206, 225n7; and rule-making, 6; and slavery, 11
event-time, 10, 125, 174, 209
excessive present, 23, 40–42, 46–48, 63–65, 67, 70, 79, 191; and abolition, 32, 208; and the dead, 80; and ethics, 33, 76, 174; and justice, 125; and Middle Passage, 10; and slavery, 11, 102; and temporality, 22; and "whirlpool," 190
expression, 1, 71, 148

familial structure, 101, 176

Feeding the Ghosts, 34, 146, 157, 164, 168–69, 177, 209, 246n7; and empathy, 155; and focalization, 156, 160; and narrator, 162–63; and neo-slave narrative, 147; poetics of, 158, 248n29; reading of, 149; and risk, 166; and suffering, 151; and *Zong* Massacre, 140–41, 145

feminism: abolition, 95, 99, 105–6, 240n39; anticarceral, 240n39; and critique, 7; and humanism, 241n42; liberal, 241n42; and literary criticism, 248n29

flesh, 1, 14, 109, 117, 185, 190; Black, 94, 102, 106, 177; and body, 15, 102; as commodity, 157, 160–61; and death, 108; and ethics, 15; female, 97; and flesh-body distinction, 97, 101–2; and gender, 103, 105–6; and *Incidents*, 97; and law, 87, 109; and liberation, 106; and ungendering, 87, 105; and violation, 86, 174

forms of life, 13–14

freedom, 26, 73, 95, 110, 237n8; Black, 89, 90–91, 175, 250n4; deferring, 14; democratic, 90; forms of, 26, 82, 84; and fugitivity, 87; imaginations of, 191; individual, 146; juridical, 85; and justice, 174; pursuit of, 76–79, 88; and slavery, 1, 48, 84, 89

Fugitive Slave Law (1850), 78, 90, 129

Garner, Eric, 27, 34, 126–29, 131, 133, 137–38, 141, 149, 164, 174, 205, 210

Garner, Erica, 126, 129–30, 133, 141, 164

Garner, Margaret, 131

gender, 7, 14, 101, 145, 176, 178–79, 184, 189–90, 224n3, 242n57; and anti-Blackness, 13, 179; binary, 131; Black, 97–99, 106, 182, 198; and Blackness, 98, 181, 242n54; colonial, 96–97, 177, 186; difference, 99; equality, 106; and flesh, 103; and gender-sex binary, 17; grammar of, 97, 99–100, 192; and intersectionality, 96; language of, 35; and law, 103–7; liberation, 8; normative, 35; and possession, 101; production, 100; and race, 96, 100, 106, 178; and reproduction, 13, 35; and violence, 106–7; Western, 106, 177, 187; white, 58, 60, 105; and white supremacy, 182; and women, 59, 186

genocide, 41, 48, 65, 230n3; Indigenous, x; logics of, 127; and violence, 199, 243n57

genre, ix, 35, 64, 125, 138, 147, 153, 194, 198, 253n44

genres of being, 13–15, 242n57

Ginsburg, Ruth Bader, 18–19, 21–22

grammars of law, 1, 24, 64, 80, 100, 109, 154–55, 162, 164, 174, 209, 249n44; and abolition, 7, 14; and *Beloved*, 29; and carceral logic, 75; and death, 170; definition of, 2, 15; and ethics, 175; and flesh,

87, 102; force of, 177; functions of, 177; and gender, 13, 99, 103–7; and hegemony, 210; and individuation, 61–63, 166, 211; and justice, 214; and language, 17, 208; and literature, 6, 36; and order, 125; and ordering force, 3, 56, 83, 116, 208; and *partus sequitur ventrem*, 99, 101; and the past, 170; and perforation, 120, 172; and periodizing force, 20; and plantations, 94; and poetics of justice, 3, 7–8, 16, 34, 82, 85, 110, 119, 145, 205, 208, 212–13; and sexuality, 13; and teleology, 14; and violence, 120; and women, 103; and worlding, 18. *See also* law

Gregson v. Gilbert, 34, 47, 108, 110–11, 114, 116–18, 144, 146, 150, 212

Griggs, Sutton E., 83, 87–91, 107, 238n29

Grimké, Angelina Weld, 35, 176, 192–93, 195, 197–98, 200, 204, 207

Haley, Sarah, 13, 58–59, 97, 179

Hartman, Sadiya V., 10, 144; and "afterlife of slavery," 9; and black feminist futurity, 2; and Blackness, 178, 198; and Civil War, 85; and gender, 101, 250n11; and Fred Moten, 137; and the past, 40; and race, 195, 199; and slavery, 40, 48, 84, 98, 140; and subjection, 138, 199; and "The Time of Slavery," 24; and "Venus in Two Acts," 141; and violence, 195. See also *Scenes of Subjection*

hate crimes, 62–64, 234n55

heteronormativity, 176, 183–84, 192, 196, 207

hierarchical structures, viii, 3, 18, 69

historical analysis, 25, 223n1

historical archive, 25, 27–28, 141, 144, 183, 243n72

historical fiction, 2, 29, 31, 139–40

historical production, 100, 142

historical progress, 18

historical selves, 57–60

human being, 59–60, 102, 153–54, 157–58

identity, 4, 25, 33, 65, 75, 86, 177–79, 186, 225n7

Imperceptible Mutabilities in the Third Kingdom (1989), 33, 41, 65–67, 70, 74–76, 79, 177

imperialism, 74, 212

Imperium in Imperio, 83, 87–92, 238n29

incarceration, 8, 12, 20, 23, 50–51, 56, 65, 73, 98, 103, 232n26

Incidents in the Life of a Slave Girl, 33, 82–83, 85–86, 92–93, 95–97, 99–101, 103–5, 107, 154, 177, 241n42, 248n39

Indigenous genocide, x

Indigenous peoples, xii, 44, 75, 156, 172

Indigenous studies, 232n24

individuation, 73, 163, 169, 179, 210–11; and law's grammar, 61–63, 162, 166, 249n44; logic of, 32–33, 162; and whiteness, 65

inhabitation, 33, 82, 96, 107, 110–11, 114, 116, 120, 125, 145
injustice, 4, 20, 45–46, 64, 127, 139, 151, 153, 158, 161–62, 164, 230n9
intersectionality, 96

Jacobs, Harriet, 82–83, 169, 237n8; and abolition, 107; and abolitionist feminism, 106; and Frederick Douglass, 236n4; and enslavement, 83, 86; and female flesh, 105; and gender, 103; and law, 97, 93, 107; and legal emancipation, 83; and plantations, 87, 95; and protection, 104; and resistance, 85; and sexual economy, 158; and slavery, 92, 158; and surveillance, 120; and ungendering, 100, 105; and white supremacy, 88; and white women, 96, 105; and womanhood, 96–97; and writing, 92, 104. See also *Incidents in the Life of a Slave Girl*
Jim Crow, 19–21
justice, 1, 30, 65, 107, 116, 139, 141, 150, 152, 206, 209–10, 214; and abolition, 7–8, 24, 26, 29; and *Beloved*, 5; and death, 149, 171; definition of, 11; and ethics, 148; and Eric Garner, 133, 137, 149; and Erica Garner, 129–31, 133; grammar of, 166, 177; and hauntology, 180; and law, 9, 22, 33–35, 56, 145, 150, 154, 173–74, 200, 226n8; and memory, 149; model of, 33; poetics of, 2–3,

6–7, 15–18, 29, 34–35, 56, 61–63, 82–83, 85, 106, 110, 119–20, 125, 145, 155–56, 170, 172, 174, 176–77, 205, 208, 211–13; practices of, 41; racial, 228n34; retributive, 94; and slavery, 164; theories of, 225n8; and time, 12, 14, 31, 83, 111; universal, 104; and violence, 126

kinship, 181, 183, 188–89, 191, 203–4
knowledge, 18, 22, 71, 120, 164, 169; and ethics, 166; gendered, 59; historical, 142; and ignorance, 166; limits of, 168, 208; literary, 142; and *The Naturalist*, 69; ordered, 23; and plantation law, 94; and reading, 163; and slavery, 139, 165; unspoken, 92

labor, 57, 89, 183, 232n26, 239n31, 241n42; action, 35–36, 224n5; agricultural, 50; extraction of, 50, 51, 73; slave, 49; unpaid, 49. *See also* prison labor
law, 57, 70, 89–90, 111, 150, 202, 240n34; and abolition, 22; and archive, 82–83, 108–11, 113–14, 116–17, 119, 129, 131, 143, 147; and Black people, 90, 127–28, 176, 178, 200, 205, 245n5; and bodies, 72, 102, 127–28; British, 47; and citizenship, 88, 129; and colonialism, 172; and discrimination, 88; and emancipation, 83; and enforceability, 19, 95; and enslavement, 83; and ethics, vii, 239n31; and exclusion, 54;

force of, 10, 22, 33, 56, 71, 86, 118, 151; and gender, 17, 59, 104, 105–7; and individuation, 61, 63, 166; and juridical events, 68; and justice, 9, 11, 34, 173–74, 200, 226n8; language of, 171; and legal studies, 12; and legal writing, 19; and literature, 12; and miscegenation, 94; and order, 46, 83, 106, 125; and ordering force, 64, 82, 84; and *partus sequitur ventrem*, 103–4; and personhood, 14, 98; of the plantation, 93–94; and property, 79; and protection, 106, 166; and punishment, 126; and race, 58; reach of, 133; and rights, 138; as rules, xi, 6; and slavery, 13, 92, 96, 114, 183; and social structure, 92; structure of, 42, 55, 128; and subjects, 34, 90; and temporality, 56; and theorization, 15; and violence, 15, 34, 45, 87, 94, 102, 108, 110, 113, 120, 128, 130, 174, 203, 254n49; and vulnerability, 86, 93

lawsuits, 149
literacy, 141, 163, 168
literature scholarship, 12, 50, 118, 120, 253n44; and *Beloved*, 25–27, 31

Martin, Trayvon, 43, 60, 196
memory, 6, 129, 138, 143, 149, 155, 182–83, 185, 190–91; and anti-Black history, 44; framework, 40; language of, 33; studies, 23, 174; time, 31
Mexicans, 44

Middle Passage, 10, 32–33, 54, 57, 66, 79, 144, 182, 230n8, 233n41, 233n45; and Atlantic Ocean, 55–56; and Blackness, 58; and Black subjects, 101, 176; and carceral logic, 75; and carceral models, 72; and commodification, 49; ghosts of, 48; histories of, 51; and oceans, 51; as ongoing disaster, 41, 56, 65, 75, 78, 147; and race, 60; representations of, 67, 110; and slavery, 42, 65, 141; and Third Kingdom, 67, 72, 73; and violence, 56, 58, 63, 75, 143, 243n57; and Western modernity, 48
Mintah, 146–49, 151–52, 154–55, 163–64
Missouri Compromise, 90
modernity, 29, 41, 58–59, 63, 72–73, 75, 102, 229n3; Western, 40, 48, 60, 70, 108, 199
moral imaginations, 41, 137, 153
moral progress, 149
moral protest, 153
moral reasoning, 157, 159–60
moral responsibility, 168
Morrison, Toni, 2, 159, 162; and Africanist presence, 3, 55, 233n34; and *A Mercy*, 24, 140, 151, 156, 177; and antislavery, 24; and *Beloved*, 8, 23, 25, 27, 148; and diversity, 4; and focalization, 159; and novels, 6, 27–29, 141, 164, 249n39; and slavery, x; and *Song of Solomon*, 127, 247n21
motherhood, 179, 187, 189, 192–95; Black, 96, 202–3; and ungendering, 176, 186

mothering, 35, 130, 133, 175–76, 181, 185–86, 188, 190–92, 199, 201, 252n35

narrational structure, 91
necro-carceral inhabitation, 82
neo-slave narratives, 5, 139, 156, 165, 225n7; and ethics, 151; and Florens, 167–68; and Mintah, 147–48; and temporality, 138; witnessing of, 133

parallel structure, 200
partus sequitur ventrem, 13, 34, 93–95, 99, 101, 103–4, 106, 120, 145, 192, 209
patriarchy, 97, 106, 186
people of color, xii, 44
perforation, 88–89, 92, 161, 175, 210, 237n14, 239n33, 249n39; and Atlantic Ocean, 114; and freedom, 84; and inhabitation, 107; and justice, 83, 125, 208; and law, 85–86, 93–94, 107, 110–11, 116, 209, 213; logic of, 87; poetics of, 33–34, 83, 95–96, 106–7, 110–11, 116, 120, 145, 174, 177; and subjection, 87
Philip, M. NourbeSe, 82–83, 108–11, 116, 118–20, 132, 142–44, 147–50, 165, 169. See also *Zong!*
plantations, 12, 33, 76, 87, 92–95, 157, 239n33
poetry, 142, 144, 170, 180, 183, 198; and accumulation, 43, 65; of David Dabydeen, 35, 176, 179–82, 184–91, 193; lyric, 42, 44; narrative, 191; of M. NourbeSe

Philip, 33–34, 82, 109–11, 113–18, 143, 147, 149, 170–71; political, 207, 213–14; prose, 45; of Claudia Rankine, 39, 42, 45–46, 49, 52–58, 61–62, 64; scene, 60
police, 16, 41, 43, 77, 126–29, 131, 137, 175, 194, 213–14, 255n53
political economy, 132
post–civil rights era, 31, 234n45
power structures, 18, 50, 56, 69, 103
prison abolition, 23, 50–51, 95
prison house, 10
prison industrial complex, 7, 50, 126
prison labor, 51, 73, 232n28
prisons, viii, ix, xi, 16, 50, 72, 106, 131, 172, 195, 211, 223n1, 256n4
prison sentences, 7
prison slavery, 50–51
punishment, 8, 56, 98, 126, 162, 164

queer futurity, 14, 173, 176, 187, 192, 202
queer kinship, 176, 189–90, 204–5
queer politics, 198, 240n39
queer relations, 35, 209
queer studies, 11, 13–14, 101, 178, 197–98, 253n44
queer subjects, 177–78
queer temporality, 181
queer theory, 21, 95, 97, 184, 196, 199, 224n3
queer utopian memory, 79

race, 58, 99, 240n36, 243n57; Anglo-Saxon, 90; and freedom, 88; and gender, 96–97, 106, 178; mixed, 94, 156; production of, 98; and queer subjects, 178–79;

regime of, 60; suicide, 192, 195, 198, 255n60

Rachel (1916), 35, 176–77, 192–99, 201–5, 207–8, 252–53n44–45, 254n49, 255n53

racial positions, 54, 58

racial-sexual domination, 184

racial-sexual libidinal economy, 254n49

racial-sexual order, 11

racial-sexual terror, 13

racial-sexual violence, 99, 103, 178, 195

racism, 46, 48–49, 53, 58, 128–29, 162, 196; and anti-Black violence, 253n49; and anxieties, 94; and attacks, 35; and Blackness, 181; and discrimination, 19–20; experiences of, 194, 199; and extrajudicial killings, 88; and law, 126; and Middle Passage, 48; and permanence, 15, 79, 127; and poetry, 58, 64; and prison-industrial complex, 126; and Claudia Rankine, 40, 46, 48, 64; scientific, 240n36; victims of, 54; and violence, 42, 44, 48, 55, 64, 184; white, 253n44

Rankine, Claudia, 48, 50, 53, 61–62, 79–80, 102, 175, 229n1; and accumulation, 41–42, 44–45, 54–58, 62, 65, 68, 128; and Blackness, 54; and *Citizen: An American Lyric*, 33, 39–42, 51, 57, 63, 81, 169, 177, 209; and George Holliday, 43; and justice, 63; and poetics, 46, 55; and poetry, 49, 52–54, 57, 59;

and racism, 40; and seascapes, 51, 73; and slavery, 48, 51; and Serena Williams, 45, 47, 58

rape, 93, 97, 101, 118, 158–59, 184–85, 248n39

reading, 32, 46, 58–59, 133, 149, 153, 168, 171–72, 238n29, 240n39, 241n42; abolitionist, ix, 53, 64, 80, 111, 119, 125, 175, 214; close, viii, 2, 9, 15–16, 35, 64, 76, 111, 119–20, 125, 131–32, 164, 174–75, 214; collective, 9; ethical, x, 119, 155, 165, 246n1; groups, 9; and law, 128; methodology, xi, 10, 15, 29, 105, 141–42; and neo-slave narratives, 139–40, 151; of novels, 5, 29, 31, 36, 50–51, 138, 152, 155, 162–63, 249n39; of poetry, 114, 186, 191; practices, 3–4, 12, 17, 43–44, 54, 56–57, 85, 95–96, 99, 103, 110, 120, 139, 143–44, 170, 246n1; queer, 197, 253n44; and unmeaning, 118

recognition, 34, 50, 79, 84, 97, 138, 151–53, 158–61, 167, 169, 177, 208–9, 213–14; critique of, 150; cross-generational, 75; discourse of, 162; and diversity, 4; and empathy, 248n29; failure of, 140–41, 166; and gender, 103; grammar of, 156–57, 168; and law, 150; and law's grammar, 85, 210; logic of, 155; and rights, 211, 238n29; and slavery, 155; and womanhood, 96

repetition, 30, 46, 162, 187, 194, 204–5, 208; and *Citizen: An*

American Lyric, 42, 64; and *Imperceptible Mutabilities in the Third Kingdom*, 41, 66–67, 70; as literary strategy, 70; and Middle Passage, 75; and novels, 33, 152; in poetry, 113, 118; and Claudia Rankine, 68; and temporality, 33, 35; and J. M. W. Turner, 53

reproduction, 13, 73, 99, 203, 205, 241n45; biological, 98, 184; Black, 227n17; economies of, 179; and futurity, 187; and gender, 179; heterosexual, 198; interracial, 94; language of, 35; property, 101; and slavery, 95; violence's, 63

responsibility, 21–22, 33, 148, 168, 170, 194, 203, 217, 247n21

rights, 107; and African Americans, 91; civil, 19, 95, 129–30, 138; human, 150; individual, 211; juridical, 238n29; and justice, 155; legal, 138; and police, 89; property, 103, 105–6; and recognition, 155, 177, 211; and rights-based framework, 96; voting, 18

Roberts, John, 18–22

Scenes of Subjection, 2, 9, 48, 57, 81, 84, 137

Sethe, 5–6, 30–32

settler colonialism, viii, 3, 18, 59, 63, 125, 131, 139, 176, 210, 212, 224n3, 232n24

Sharpe, Christina, 4, 48, 78, 93, 99, 106, 192, 195, 199; and anagrammatic poetics, 83; and

anti-Blackness, 31, 205; and aspiration, 175, 179; and Black subjection, 44; and critical fabulation, 10; and language, 68, 116, 140; and slavery, 40; and slave ships, 57, 72, 171; and wake, 9–11, 14, 40, 73, 131

Shelby County, Alabama v. Eric Holder, 18, 21

"Site of Memory, The," 27

slave insurance, 49

slave interiority, 27

slave narratives, 91, 147, 154–55

slave patrollers, 129

slave plantations, 12

slave revolts, 91–92, 209

Slavers Throwing Overboard the Dead and Dying — Typhon Coming on (The Slave Ship), 38–41, 47–49, 58, 63, 65, 73, 81, 180–81, 191, 229n1

slavery, 5–6, 24, 70, 84, 89, 102, 108, 131, 145, 160, 165, 195, 242n57; and abolition, 20, 92, 105, 125; atrocities of, 30; and *Beloved*, 25; and capitalism, 49, 231n24, 249n43; chattel, 11, 50, 65, 98, 138–41, 158, 210–11, 239n31; economy of, 101; and emancipation, 78, 96, 127; experience of, 97, 100, 148–49, 161, 179–80, 183, 227n17; and gender, 97–98; and law, 13, 92, 114; and legal archive, 83; and literature, 26, 30, 48–49, 138, 140, 155, 162–64, 248n28; loss of, 31; and Middle Passage, 48–50, 57, 65, 233n45;

modern, 50; and modernity, 102; and necropolitics, 95; and neo-slavery, 12; in painting, 73; prison, 50–51, 223n1; process of, 3; resistance to, 84; and sexual violence, 158, 184; and slave ships, 73; time of, 42; violence of, 106, 151, 154, 162, 176, 179, 184. *See also* afterlife of slavery

slave ships, 6, 12, 32, 48, 66, 149, 171; and beholding, 78; and Blackness, 195; experiences in, 181; and killings, 108, 113, 153, 159, 191; and rape, 159; and semiotics, 57, 72, 106, 233n41; and Third Kingdom, 73; and *Zong*, 107

Snorton, C. Riley, 13–14, 86–87, 97–98, 102, 178, 198, 242n54

social control, 12

social data, 4

social death, 14, 102, 141, 199, 204

social exclusion, 54

social order, 56, 196

social structures, 63, 92, 101

South Carolina, 146

spectrality, 194, 204

Spillers, Hortense, 14, 97–98, 101, 105, 172, 178, 184, 195, 198, 242n57

Stanley, Eric A., ix, 7, 63, 178, 196, 230n3

structure, 29, 33, 64–65, 70, 91, 113–14, 118, 156

subjection, 42, 44, 87, 97, 159, 162; Black, 44, 73, 82, 201; legal, 1; and violence, 138

subjectivity, 60–61, 64, 87, 97, 147, 169, 181, 210; Black, 99; trans, 190

temporality, 7–8, 11, 29, 33, 40, 67–68, 70, 125, 174, 191, 208, 234n45; antilinear, 69, 74; bounded, 56–57; and ethics, 24; and excessive present, 10, 22; and justice, 83; linear, 6, 138; narrative, 156; periodized, 2; queer, 181; theorizations of, 9; and violence, 107

temporal structure, 6, 24, 31, 33, 42, 56, 66, 83, 227n19

transatlantic slave trade, x, 48–49, 53, 66, 108, 140–41, 157, 159–60, 180, 191, 227n17, 233–34n45, 242n57

transatlantic voyages, 48, 71, 229n1

trans-exclusionary athletics, 60

trans people, 172

trans studies, 14, 178

trans subjectivity, 190

trans theory, 97

trauma, 33, 118, 156–57, 167, 183

"Turner" (poem), 35, 176–77, 179–88, 192, 195, 209

Turner, J. M. W., 38–41, 66, 73, 81, 180–82, 191, 209, 229n1; and massacres, 50, 57, 231n17, 233n41; and seascapes, 47–50, 53–55, 57–59, 61–63, 79; and slavery, 49–50, 57

Turner, Nat, 91

Underground Railroad, 76, 146

ungendering, 13, 59, 86–87, 97–101, 103, 105, 175, 179, 181–82, 186, 203, 241n45, 242n54, 251n28

unlivability, 83, 120

(un)natural disaster, 40, 55–56

violence, 10, 48, 59, 68, 77, 152, 157, 167, 169, 180, 190, 203, 248n29; and abolitionism, 26; anti-Black, 126, 179, 194, 199, 204, 238n29, 243n57, 253n49; atmospheres of, 230n3; and Black bodies, 79, 128; and Blackness, 99, 178, 192, 201, 242n54; Black revolutionary, 92; and civil society, 128; and colonialism, 65, 176, 188; and Angela Davis, 98; and domination, 22, 84; double logic of, 109–10; and ethics, 22; extra/legal, 45; and flesh, 102; gender, 7, 106–7; genocidal, 65; and hate crime legislation, 63; and hierarchy, 18; and incarceration, 79, 212; and inhabitation, 107; and Harriet Jacobs, 83–84, 92, 94, 104; and justice, 226n8; of the law, 3, 15, 34, 41, 56, 63, 82–84, 87, 94, 102, 104, 108–11, 113–14, 118–20, 125, 130–31, 174; material, 102, 105, 182; and Middle Passage, 58, 75, 143; military, 74; mob, 254n50; and modernity, 106; political, 150–51, 239n34; racial, 42, 44, 48, 55, 64, 107, 181, 183, 185; racial-sexual, 99, 103, 178, 184, 195, 254n49; and resistance, 84; quotidian, 10, 40, 79, 205, 229n3; and safety, 104; and settler colonialism, 63; sexual, 76, 94, 98, 104–6, 118, 162, 177, 182–84, 185, 187, 249n39, 251n28; and slavery, x, 65, 106, 139–40, 159, 162, 184, 191; state, 42, 56, 128, 137, 172; technologies of, 42, 105; and temporality, 107; threats of, xii, 8, 79; and Western modernity, 40; and whiteness, 31, 54–55, 94; and white supremacy, 44, 193, 195, 207, 209–10

Voting Rights Act (VRA, 1965), 18–21

vulnerability, 54, 73, 85–86, 92, 97, 99, 101, 110, 118, 167–68, 170, 174, 205–6, 210, 237n11

Walcott, Rinaldo, 2, 51–52, 250n4

Weheliye, Alexander, 14–15, 86–87, 102, 138, 150–51, 155, 162, 239n33, 247n26

well-being, 104

White Being, 41, 59

White Man's Burden, 69

whiteness, xii–xiii, 63, 94, 97; and anti-Blackness, 60, 62; logic of, 65; and Robert Lowell, 54; and patriarchy, 97; and privilege, 54; as racial positions, 54, 58; and violence, 55, 209

white people, 151, 154, 170, 195–97, 199–200, 254n50; as abolitionists, 77; as agricultural laborers, 49–50; and bodies, 102; defense against, 30–31, 207; and discourse, 54; as enslavers, 92–93; and femininity, 58; and gender, 58, 60; and hate crimes, 62; as indentured servants, 156; and men, 76–77, 94, 118; and parenthood, 93; and privilege, 55; and property, 76, 161; and racism, 53, 253n44; and religion, 166; and self, 57; as shipowners, 48; and slavery, 127; as subjects, 60, 102, 240n34; and J. M. W. Turner, 58; and violence, 94, 209–10; and women, 5, 59–60, 94, 96–97, 100–101, 103–6, 192, 225n7; as writers, 43

white supremacy, 18, 212, 218, 224n3, 236n6; and abolition, 35; and anti-Blackness, 11, 88; and Blackness, 176, 182, 195, 197; and capitalism, x; and free subjects, 93; and futurity, 184; and heteronormativity, 183; law of, 93, 205; limits of, 104; and queerness, 199; and racial capitalism, 3; and violence, 44, 193, 207, 209; and worlding, 18

Williams, Serena, 45–49, 53, 55, 58–60, 128

Zong! (2008), 33, 141, 153–54, 179–80, 208, 210, 212; and abolitionist close reading, 125; and confusion, 149, 171; construction of, 113–14, 116; and critical fabulation, 142; and critical readings, 119; and empty space, 116; and ethics, 144; and Feeding the Ghosts, 151–52, 168; and Gregson v. Gilbert, 108, 110, 117, 132, 150; and irrationality, 143; and justice, 120; and law, 83, 108–9, 209; and murder, 129, 145–46; and ordering mechanism, 116; and reader interpolation, 34; reading of, 114, 116, 171, 177; and rememory, 140; and scholarship, 118; and semiotics, 233n41; and slavery, 129, 140, 144; and subjection, 82; teaching of, 170–71; and temporality, 111; and unmeaning, 118; and violence, 107, 169

Zong Massacre (1781), 55, 58, 79, 83, 131, 191, 210; afterlife of, 209; and A Mercy, 141; and Feeding the Ghosts, 140, 145; and finance capitalism, 81–82; and insurance claims, 48; and law, 128; and law's archive, 108, 113, 175; and literature, 155, 165; as mass murder, 127; and Middle Passage, 147; and slavery, 165; and Specters of the Atlantic, 82; and J. M. W. Turner, 54, 63, 66, 180–81; and violence, 48, 169

JESS A. GOLDBERG is assistant professor of English at New Mexico Highlands University.